THE BLACK FAMILY
DINNER
QUILT
COOKBOOK

HEALTH CONSCIOUS RECIPES & FOOD MEMORIES

Dorothy I. Height, President, &
The National Council of Negro Women, Inc.

A FIRESIDE BOOK
Published by Simon & Schuster

NEW YORK   LONDON   TORONTO   SYDNEY   TOKYO   SINGAPORE

FIRESIDE
Rockefeller Center
1230 Avenue of the Americas
New York, New York 10020

First Fireside Edition   1994
Published by arrangement with The Wimmer Companies, Inc.

FIRESIDE and colophon are registered trademarks of Simon & Schuster Inc.

Manufactured in the United States of America

10 9 8 7 6 5 4 3 2 1

Library of Congress Cataloging-in-Publication Data
The Black family dinner quilt cookbook : health conscious recipes &
food memories / Dorothy I. Height & the National Council of Negro Women, Inc.
    p.   cm.
  Originally published: Memphis, Tenn. : Tradery House, © 1993.
  "A fireside book."
  Includes index.
  1. Afro-American cookery.   I. Height, Dorothy I. (Dorothy Irene), 1912–
II. National Council of Negro Women.
TX715.B548   1994
641.59'296073—dc20   94-2758
                                            CIP

ISBN: 0-671-79630-5

TABLE OF CONTENTS

ABOUT THE TITLE

The dinner quilt is a time-honored African-American tradition. At holiday meals, a quilt would be used as a table covering. At each place would be a piece of paper with the name of a relative or a great character in African-American history, and each person would be responsible for speaking about that person, carrying forward the oral history of the family.

ABOUT THE COVER QUILTS

FRONT COVER—*TAR BEACH 2* The cover quilt, *Tar Beach 2* (65" x 65"), is the work of the renowned African-American artist Faith Ringgold. It is a silkscreen version of an original handpainted quilt inspired by happy childhood memories of summer evenings spent on cool rooftops in New York City. *Tar Beach* is one of five works from Ringgold's Women on a Bridge series, in which she sets women against bridges in New York and San Francisco. The geometric patterns created by spaces between the bridge girders are seen as quilts suspended in the air. The quilt reflects the artist's belief in magic, as Cassie Louise Lightfoot, the heroine and narrator, flies over buildings and the George Washington Bridge. Flying is an African-American folktale theme—in many of these tales Africans flew to freedom. Copyright © 1990 by The Fabric Workshop, Philadelphia, Pennsylvania.

DEDICATION

They were women then
My mama's generation
Husky of voice—Stout of
Step
With fists as well as
Hands
How they battered down
Doors
and ironed
Starched white
Shirts
How they led
Armies
Headragged Generals
Across mined
Fields
Booby-trapped
Kitchens
To discover books
Desks
A place for us
How they knew what we
Must know
Without knowing a page
Of it
Themselves.[1]

Alice Walker

In the beginning, there were the women. Small, soft women, delicate in their beauty and resolute in their hearts. Women with the energy reserved for forces of nature. Large, rough hewn women, daughters of other women who had survived slavery, which is the worst trial that Western Civilization had to offer. These women made food for the girl child and shared their skill and recipes. For them, to feed was to nurture and to nurture was to love.

Some of the women who walked before her were women of color. Skin in shades of the rural Pennsylvania autumns she knew as a child. Umber, gold, hazy browns, dark earthy tones shot with flashes of red. Women who seen together made a patchwork quilt of shapes and sizes and colors.

Other women who made it possible for her to become what she is were women of European ancestry. Immigrant women new to this country, clinging to the traditions of their native lands. Women who made their own chewy breads, their own spicy sausages. Foreign women fed the child with food and with stories of what it meant for them to become "real" Americans. These women showed her their own

particular strengths....they too were outsiders...but for their children they had different dreams.

Finally, there were the patrician women, the American aristocrats by virtue of their birth or their own accomplishments. These women saw in Dorothy Irene Height an intensity of purpose that has not dimmed throughout her eighty years of life. They sustained in her the wonder and faith they longed to find within themselves.

Dorothy Height was not born into a world that gave women their due. She came of age in a time when women were expected to remain in their preordained roles. Yet she did not. It was for her to lead.

On her behalf, women who wielded such power as was available to them opened doors and made a way for her. They fed her spirit with their own enthusiasm. Women of strength and vision were key in the development of Dorothy Height. She has never forgotten the part that women have played in her life.

Throughout her life, she has surrounded herself with capable women. She has developed programs that support and nurture the leadership abilities of women....she has been an advocate for women and their organizations around the world. For her, the concerns of women have always had a high priority. She has befriended and guided women and given them courage to achieve.

She has never lost sight of the fact that generations of women lived, worked and overcame obstacles in America so that she could be who she was destined to be. Their struggles made it possible for her to become a world leader, an activist, a defender of human rights and a beacon for other women to follow.

These women are bound to each other and to Dorothy Irene Height like squares in a patchwork quilt. Throughout the book are the silk and satin names of the famous..the sturdy calico names of friends..and the ordinary polished cotton names of women known only to a few. It is to these women and to women all over the world that **The Black Family Dinner Quilt Cookbook** is dedicated.

INTRODUCTION

A downtown Washington, D.C. office building on a hot Sunday afternoon in midsummer seems an unlikely place for a cookbook to begin. In fact, that is where **The Black Family Dinner Quilt Cookbook** had its birth. Four women gathered to talk that day over Louisiana Crunch Cake and Shortbread Cookies. A more dissimilar group of women would be hard to imagine. The foursome was made up of these: a mature African-American educator and elected school board member, a mother of three who had just turned forty and decided that her true vocation was to write, a white, Southern publisher with a mission to create books that strengthen the sense of community through the meal, and Dr. Height herself.

Originally, the subject we had planned to discuss was the vision Dr. Dorothy Height had for a center to serve as a meeting place, archives and clearing house for all that had to do with African-American women. But Dr. Height, in her own inimitable way, directed the conversation first to her mentor and guiding example, Dr. Mary McLeod Bethune, founder of the National Council of Negro Women, Inc. The rest of us, who never had the privilege of meeting Mrs. Bethune, sat spellbound as Dr. Height shared stories of meals and experiences in which Mrs. Bethune played a central role. The stories, so personal and fascinating, captured our imaginations.

We realized, as the conversation progressed, that it was Mrs. Bethune's legacy embodied in Dr. Height's vision that animated us all. It was that powerful legacy which led us to seek a way to capture the reality and the energy of two of the twentieth century's most remarkable women. The stories, the experiences and the memories formed a colorful quilt that wrapped us all in an exquisite warmth that had nothing to do with the sweltering summer day outside. We sipped cold diet soda that day, instead of the genteel cups of hot tea that Dr. Height told us Mrs. Bethune so favored.

Dr. Height told us how she learned from Mrs. Bethune that more business could be done and more decisions made over a dinner table than over a dozen conference tables. Our experience that afternoon supported the theory. We left the office building in the early evening to gather again at a neighborhood restaurant where we were encouraged to sample a dish unfamiliar to several of us...Jamaican Jerk Chicken. We continued to talk, asking Dr. Height to tell us more about Mrs. Bethune and about herself. Dr. Height smiled warmly and began to reminisce. It was as if yesterday and today were meeting again, and Dr. Height was revisiting a place in time left only hours ago instead of over 50 years past.

Here is what Dr. Height told us that day:

"I first met Mrs. Bethune because Cecilia Cabanis Saunders at the YWCA gave me a weekend assignment. My task was to escort Eleanor Roosevelt into a meeting Mrs. Bethune was hosting at the Harlem Y. There were three entrances to the building in those days...each door was labeled...there was Administration, Residences and Service. You can't imagine, but the First Lady could get into her roadster and drive from Washington, DC, park on a Harlem street, go into a meeting, stay for an hour or two, get back into her roadster and drive herself on to Hyde Park. There was no Secret Service with her, no advance team, no fanfare. She just came alone. Of course I was excited and eager to do a good job. You can imagine my surprise when a maintenance man came running to get me. Mrs. Roosevelt had come into the center

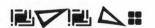

door...the service entrance! I had to run down the hall myself to head her off! I could just see my little job blowing out of the window if I failed! I succeeded in intercepting her and escorting her into the meeting.

She stayed and participated in the meeting. As I escorted her out of the building, Mrs. Bethune pulled my dress and said to me, "What is your name?" I told her and she said, "Well you must come back, we need you." And as you can see, I've been where she needed me ever since.

That was the day I met the two women who outside of my own mother had the most powerful influence on my life."

When we asked Dr. Height what it was about Mrs. Mary Bethune that had such a profound effect, she answered, "Mrs. Bethune was a magnificent human being. She was just thoroughly human in a way few people are. She had such a sense of humor...in fact her sense of humor was as keen as her spirituality was deep. She had a capacity to grasp the big issues, keep them in perspective and understand what was happening to people because of the big issues. Her faith was so real that she would sometimes tell us at the Council that we had to all get down on our knees and pray over something that we couldn't handle by ourselves. Think of that, just telling your staff to pray for a solution...and the solutions always appeared!"

As Dr. Height talked, we realized that the things she admired in Mrs. Bethune were the very qualities we saw and respected in her...humanity, spirituality, vision, wisdom and humor.

We asked her what Mrs. Bethune was like in action. "Oh, she had a sharp sense of the political. Her uncanny ability was to make people act their better selves. She put people into positions where they had to be better than they might ordinarily have been, because she depended on them to be the best.

She understood the federal establishment inside out and she understood organizations perfectly. It was her view that we didn't need another organization, we just needed to harness the ones we had. That's how the National Council of Negro Women, Inc. came into being. Mrs. Bethune knew about the nature of power too. She understood how it is possible to influence what happens to you. I never heard her refer to African-Americans as a powerless people.

She was fond of saying that if I take a finger and touch you, you may not feel it. If I touch you with two fingers, you'll know that you have been tapped. But if I join all my fingers together and make a fist, I can deliver a mighty blow!

I remember once toward the end of her tenure at a meeting in New York, a group of women arrived ready to unseat Mrs. Bethune. They were agitating for change by telling everyone that Mrs. Bethune was old fashioned, an Uncle Tom, not modern enough to lead anymore. They never sat down to talk with her about these concerns though. Mrs. Bethune didn't mince words. She spoke very calmly to them and said something like, "If you see Mary McLeod Bethune's petticoat hanging, don't tell everyone else...tell her. She's the only one who can do anything about it." That pretty much ended the discussion.

Dr. Height continued sharing stories about Mrs. Bethune and Mrs. Roosevelt throughout the meal. It was clear that both women were in fact tremendously powerful factors in the development of Dorothy Irene Height.

The Black Family Dinner Quilt Cookbook is the story, not only of those two powerful influences in the life of Dorothy Irene Height, but also the story of Dr. Height's own powerful influence on the people with whom she has shared meals throughout her long and productive life. Many of those people say that when they sat down and broke bread with Dr. Height, they experienced the power of her energy and her vision, and when the meal was finished they found themselves nourished, not only in body, but in mind and in spirit. Part of her legacy is this restoration of the possibilities which lie dormant in us all.

The lives of Mary McLeod Bethune, Eleanor Roosevelt, Dorothy Height and all the people who have come in contact with Dr. Height form a marvelous fabric that is not seamless, but is quilted together by the threads of shared experiences. The quilt, made up of these lives, is varied and colorful. Pieced together out of scraps...moments of conversation during meals eaten in places high and low to push open a door to the past.

This cookbook captures some of those memories. It also explores quilting as a metaphor for communication, fellowship and the richness of sharing between women of all races. We trust that it will become part of your own legacy for the future.

Brenda Rhodes Cooper
January, 1993

ABOUT THE DEVELOPMENT TEAM

BRENDA RHODES COOPER is the author of a novel, **The Laying on of Hands** and a children's book, **Do They Deliver Pizza to the Zoo**. She lives and cooks with her three children in Washington, D.C.

CAROLYN L. MAZLOOMI is a fiber artist, historian, and founder/coordinator of the Women of Color Quilters Network. Her story quilts, which celebrate the lives of people of color, have been exhibited extensively in the United States, Japan, Europe, and Australia. Mazloomi travels the U.S. lecturing on the history and importance of African-American quilt making. She resides with her husband and three sons in Cincinnati.

FAITH RINGGOLD, internationally known artist and writer of children's books, lives in New York City and La Jolla, California where she is a professor of art at the University of California in San Diego. Ringgold's art is in many private and public collections including The Museum of Modern Art, The Solomon R. Guggenheim Museum, The Studio Museum in Harlem and the Metropolitan Museum of Art. She is the author of the award winning children's book, **Tar Beach**. Her second book, **Aunt Harriet's Underground Railroad In the Sky**, has recently been published.

LONNIE ROBINSON is an up and coming young artist/designer who lives in Memphis, Tennessee. A product of Memphis City Schools, he attended the School of the Art Institute of Chicago. During his studies he was employed by Ogilvy and Mather as a junior art director and by Yoshida Design as a graphic designer. He has coordinated and directed special workshops in art and design for youth in the Memphis City School System. Robinson is currently free-lancing for clients throughout the Mid-South and Midwest.

LAUREN SWANN, MS, RD, is President and Chief Executive Officer of Concept Nutrition, Inc., a Bensalem, Pennsylvania consulting service for nutrition issues in food marketing specializing in marketing communications and regulatory affairs. Prior to establishing her own business, Swann was a project manager responsible for product nutrition at Kraft General Foods, Inc. She also worked as a communications specialist and developed informational publications and educational materials in the Consumer Affairs Department.

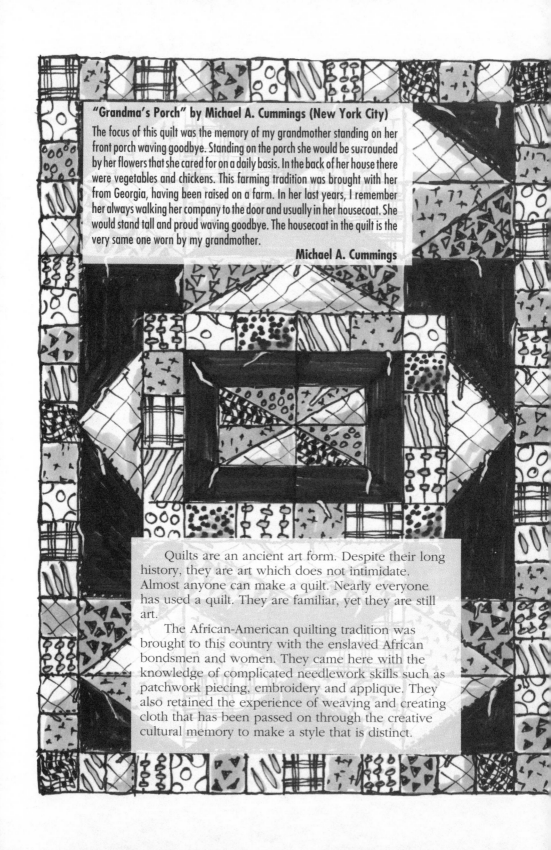

"Grandma's Porch" by Michael A. Cummings (New York City)

The focus of this quilt was the memory of my grandmother standing on her front porch waving goodbye. Standing on the porch she would be surrounded by her flowers that she cared for on a daily basis. In the back of her house there were vegetables and chickens. This farming tradition was brought with her from Georgia, having been raised on a farm. In her last years, I remember her always walking her company to the door and usually in her housecoat. She would stand tall and proud waving goodbye. The housecoat in the quilt is the very same one worn by my grandmother.

Michael A. Cummings

Quilts are an ancient art form. Despite their long history, they are art which does not intimidate. Almost anyone can make a quilt. Nearly everyone has used a quilt. They are familiar, yet they are still art.

The African-American quilting tradition was brought to this country with the enslaved African bondsmen and women. They came here with the knowledge of complicated needlework skills such as patchwork piecing, embroidery and applique. They also retained the experience of weaving and creating cloth that has been passed on through the creative cultural memory to make a style that is distinct.

SOUTHERN HAM & SHRIMP SOUP

2   tablespoons Crisco Shortening
    or Crisco Oil
1   cup chopped onion
½   cup chopped green bell pepper
2   tablespoons minced parsley
1½ quarts water
3   chicken flavor low sodium
    bouillon cubes

1   package (10 ounces) frozen cut
    okra
½   pound raw shrimp, shelled and
    deveined
2   cups cubed lean cooked ham
2   cups hot cooked rice (without
    salt or fat)

1. Heat Crisco Shortening or Crisco Oil in large saucepan on medium heat. Add
    onion and green pepper, sauté 5 minutes. Stir in parsley, water and bouillon
    cubes. Bring to a boil.
2. Add frozen okra to soup. Cook, uncovered, 10 minutes. Stir once.
3. Add shrimp. Cook, uncovered, 2 to 3 minutes or until tender and opaque.
4. Add ham. Heat thoroughly.
5. Ladle over rice in soup bowls.

About 2 Quarts Soup (6 Servings)

270 CALORIES / FAT 9 g (83 CAL or 30% of total calories) / SAT FAT 2 g (6% of total calories) / CARB 27 g /
PROTEIN 19 g / CHOL <5 mg / SODIUM 600 mg

BLACK-EYED PEA SOUP

2   smoked ham hocks, trimmed of
    rind and fat
5   cups water
1½ cups dried black-eyed peas
1   cup chopped onion

½   cup chopped celery
½   teaspoon pepper
⅔   cup evaporated skim milk
1   tablespoon all-purpose flour

1. Clean ham hocks thoroughly. Place water and ham hocks in large Dutch
    oven or kettle. Simmer 45 minutes.
2. Wash and sort peas. Place in large bowl. Cover with warm water. Soak 45
    minutes. Pour water off peas. Add peas, onion, celery and pepper to ham
    hocks. Boil on medium heat 2 hours, or until meat and peas are tender. Stir
    occasionally.
3. Remove ham hocks. Cut meat from bone. Discard bone. Return meat to soup.
4. Combine small amount evaporated milk and flour to make paste. Stir in
    remaining milk gradually. Stir until well blended. Add to soup. Cook and stir
    until mixture comes to a boil and thickens.

8 Servings

235 CALORIES / FAT 7 g (60 CAL or 26% of total calories) / SAT FAT 2 g (9% of total calories) / CARB 24 g /
PROTEIN 20 g / CHOL 15 mg / SODIUM 785 mg

Pound Cake and Lemon Tea with Mary McLeod Bethune

Mary McLeod Bethune was a magnificent human being. She was born of slave parents in 1875, yet she rose to be an advisor to four presidents of the United States. President Franklin Delano Roosevelt appointed her as his special advisor and she served as Advisor on Minority Affairs for the National Youth Administration. It was from her vantage point in the federal government that she came to new understanding of the meaning of collective power. That led her, in 1935, to found an organization of national organization — the National Council of Negro Women, Inc. She is the only African-American woman to have founded a four-year accredited college — Bethune Cookman College in Daytona Beach, Florida. Mrs. Bethune had an uncanny way of going to the heart of the matter. I have a vivid memory of one of countless occasions that illustrates that point. In late 1943, the University of North Carolina asked Mrs. Bethune to write a chapter in a book to be titled

(continued)

MAMA'S CATFISH CHOWDER

2 tablespoons Crisco Shortening or Crisco Oil
1 medium green bell pepper, chopped
1 cup thinly sliced celery, cut on diagonal
¼ cup chopped green onion
⅛ teaspoon instant minced garlic
1 can (28 ounces) whole peeled tomatoes, undrained, cut up
2 cups water
1 teaspoon instant chicken flavor bouillon granules
¼ teaspoon salt
¼ teaspoon dried basil leaves
⅛ teaspoon dried dill weed
3 to 4 drops hot red pepper sauce
1 bay leaf
1 cup frozen whole kernel corn
1 pound fresh catfish, cut into 1-inch chunks
2 cups cooked rice (without salt or fat)
2 slices turkey bacon, cooked, drained and crumbled

1. Heat Crisco Shortening or Crisco Oil in large saucepan on medium heat. Add green pepper, celery, green onion and garlic. Cook and stir until tender. Stir in undrained tomatoes, water, bouillon granules, salt, basil, dill weed, red pepper sauce and bay leaf. Bring to a boil. Reduce heat. Cover. Simmer 15 minutes to blend flavors.
2. Stir in corn. Stir in fish gently. Cook on medium heat 5 minutes, or until fish flakes easily with fork, stirring gently. Remove bay leaf. Stir in rice and bacon.

8 Servings

210 CALORIES / FAT 7 g (61 CAL or 29% of total calories) / SAT FAT 1 g (<5% of total calories) / CARB 25 g / PROTEIN 14 g / CHOL 35 mg / SODIUM 335 mg

GENEVA'S QUICK GUMBO

1 can (14½ ounces) chicken broth
1 can (14½ ounces) tomatoes
3 cups water
1 small bay leaf
1 tablespoon dried thyme leaves
2 tablespoons Butter Flavor Crisco Shortening or Crisco Oil
1 cup chopped onion
¾ cup chopped green bell pepper
1 tablespoon minced parsley
3 tablespoons filé powder (or more according to taste)
1 pound boneless skinless chicken breast (cut in bite-size pieces)
1½ pounds smoked turkey sausage, sliced
½ teaspoon salt
½ teaspoon pepper
½ teaspoon garlic powder
2 cups frozen sliced okra
6 cups cooked rice (without salt or fat)
2 cups frozen baby shrimp, cooked
⅛ teaspoon hot pepper sauce (optional)

1. Combine chicken broth, undrained tomatoes, water, bay leaf, thyme, Butter Flavor Crisco or Crisco Oil, onion, green pepper, parsley, filé powder, chicken, sausage, salt, pepper and garlic powder in stockpot or large Dutch oven. Cook 30 minutes.
2. Add okra. Cook according to time on package (8 to 10 minutes). Add rice and shrimp. Let stand for 5 minutes. Remove bay leaf before serving. (If you prefer, place rice in bowls and pour the gumbo over it.) Season with hot pepper sauce, if desired.

12 Servings

355 CALORIES / FAT 12 g (105 CAL or 30% of total calories) / SAT FAT 3 g (8% of total calories) / CARB 35 g / PROTEIN 26 g / CHOL 95 mg / SODIUM 765 mg

(continued)
"What the Negro Wants." Dr. Rayford Logan at Howard University was the editor. In her characteristic fashion, Mrs. Bethune invited a group to meet with her at her Washington, D.C. home at 9th and Westminster Streets. She often called together members of the "Black Cabinet" — William R. Trent, Department of the Interior; Robert C. Weaver, Special Assistant to the Administrator, U.S. Housing Authority; Ambrose Caliver, Senior Specialist in Negro Education, Department of the Interior; Frank S. Horne, Department of Housing; Lawrence A. Oxley, Field Representative, Department of Labor; James E. C. Evans, Department of Defense; and others.

Arabella Denniston, her secretary, had called each of us to come prepared to advise Mrs. Bethune on what the Negro wants. Mrs. Bethune served pound cake baked at Bethune Cookman College and hot tea. After a few pleasantries, Mrs. Bethune stated the question and asked each person to answer.

Shortly after midnight, when all the carefully thought through statements had been made, Mrs. Bethune

(continued)

COUNTRY PORK SOUP

1   teaspoon Crisco Oil
1   pound trimmed lean boneless pork, cut in ½-inch cubes
½   pound cabbage, shredded
2   medium green bell peppers, chopped
1   medium onion, chopped (about ½ cup)
1   clove garlic, minced
1½   quarts water
2   cans (14½ ounces each) no salt added whole tomatoes, undrained and chopped
1   tablespoon steak sauce
2   teaspoons instant chicken flavor bouillon granules
¼   teaspoon salt
⅛   teaspoon pepper
1   bay leaf
¼   teaspoon red pepper sauce (or to taste)
¾   cup nonfat dairy sour cream alternative

1.   Heat Crisco Oil in large Dutch oven on medium-high heat. Add meat. Brown on all sides. Drain. (Wipe Dutch oven dry with a paper towel.) Return pork to Dutch oven. Add cabbage, green pepper, onion and garlic. Cook on medium heat until vegetables are tender.
2.   Stir in water, undrained tomatoes, steak sauce, bouillon granules, salt, pepper and bay leaf. Bring to a boil. Cover. Reduce heat. Simmer one hour. Remove bay leaf before serving. Stir in hot pepper sauce. Top each serving with one tablespoon "sour cream".

12 Servings

100 CALORIES / FAT 3 g (30 CAL or 30% of total calories) / SAT FAT 1 g (9% of total calories) / CARB 7 g / PROTEIN 10 g / CHOL 25 mg / SODIUM 120 mg

(continued)

leaned back in her chair, and, with a wistful smile, thanked everybody profusely. And then she summarized "I understand what the Negro wants. The Negro wants what everyone else wants!" Respectful laughter filled the room. The clarity was vintage Bethune!

Dorothy I. Height

CRAB GUMBO

2 tablespoons olive oil
2 tablespoons all-purpose flour
1 medium onion, chopped
1 clove garlic, minced
1 can (28 ounces) tomatoes
1 teaspoon sugar
1 teaspoon Worcestershire sauce
Salt
⅛ teaspoon hot pepper sauce

1 bay leaf
1 package (10 ounces) frozen okra, sliced
2 packages (6 ounces) frozen Alaska Snow crab meat, thawed, drained or imitation crab
2⅔ cups cooked rice (without salt or fat)

1. Heat oil in large kettle on medium heat. Add flour, stirring constantly until dark brown, but not burned.
2. Add onion and garlic. Cook until tender, stirring occasionally. Stir in undrained tomatoes gradually. Add sugar, Worcestershire sauce, salt, hot pepper sauce and bay leaf. Stir to break up tomatoes. Bring to a boil. Reduce heat. Cover. Simmer 10 minutes to blend flavors, stirring occasionally.
3. Add okra. Cook 5 minutes or until tender, stirring occasionally.
4. Add crab. Stir gently and heat through. Discard bay leaf. Serve gumbo over rice.

4 servings

415 CALORIES / FAT 9 g (85 CAL or 20% of total calories) / SAT FAT 1 g (<5% of total calories) / CARB 58 g / PROTEIN 25 g / CHOL 85 mg / SODIUM 720 mg

TURKEY VEGETABLE SOUP

1 pound ground turkey
1 can (14½ ounces) no salt added tomatoes
1 can (8 ounces) no salt added tomato sauce
1 cup chopped onion
1 cup diced raw potatoes
1 cup chopped cabbage
1 cup diced green bell pepper
1 package (10 ounces) frozen green beans

1 package (10 ounces) frozen whole kernel corn
1 package (10 ounces) frozen peas
¼ cup thinly sliced fresh carrots
1 bay leaf
½ teaspoon dried basil leaves
¼ teaspoon pepper
¼ teaspoon dried thyme leaves
½ teaspoon garlic powder
6 cups water

1. Brown meat in large skillet on medium heat. Pour off drippings. Add undrained tomatoes, tomato sauce, onion, potatoes, cabbage, green pepper, green beans, corn, peas, carrots, bay leaf, basil, pepper, thyme, garlic and water. Bring to a boil. Reduce heat. Cover. Simmer one hour or until vegetables are tender. Stir occasionally. Remove bay leaf before serving.

8 servings

245 CALORIES / FAT 8 g (74 CAL or 30% of total calories) / SAT FAT 2 g (8% of total calories) / CARB 25 g / PROTEIN 19 g / CHOL 40 mg / SODIUM 265 mg

I Cannot Do My Work Here

It must have been fifty years ago or more when Dorothy came down to Nashville to interview for a job working with all the young people. She arrived by train in the morning and was hungry for some breakfast. Coming from New York City and all, she wasn't used to the way things were in the South back then. We couldn't take her into the train station restaurant where it was against the law for them to serve colored and white in the same place. She had to eat a poor little meal out of a shoe box that we had brought for her knowing the way things were. True enough, there was a little hole in the wall coffee shop but nobody in her right mind would eat or drink anything out of that rat trap. We had fixed a nice little meal with home made bread, fried chicken, boiled eggs and something sweet. We wrapped it up nicely and packed it in a shoe box. That's what a lot of Negroes did when they had to travel in the South and knew they'd want to eat something.

Looking at Dorothy's face just about told the entire story, but she has never been anything but gracious, so even though it

(continued)

MUSTARD GREENS & POTATO SOUP

1	pound red potatoes, peeled and sliced (2 cups)
2	cups water
1	teaspoon instant chicken flavor bouillon granules
1	tablespoon Crisco Oil
1	cup chopped onion
2	cloves garlic, minced
1/8	teaspoon dried thyme leaves
1	package (10 ounces) frozen mustard greens, thawed and drained
1	can (12 ounces) evaporated skim milk
1	teaspoon salt
1/8	teaspoon pepper
1/8	teaspoon hot pepper sauce

1. Combine potatoes, water and bouillon granules in large Dutch oven. Bring to a boil. Cover. Reduce heat. Simmer 15 minutes. Position knife blade in food processor bowl or blender. Add potatoes and cooking liquid. Top with cover. Process until smooth.
2. Heat Crisco Oil in Dutch oven on medium-high heat. Add onion, garlic, and thyme. Sauté 10 minutes, stirring occasionally. Add greens, pureed potato mixture, milk, salt, pepper and hot pepper sauce. Cook until thoroughly heated, stirring frequently. Serve warm.

4 Servings

165 CALORIES / FAT 2 g (15 CAL or 9% of total calories) / SAT FAT <1 g (<5% of total calories) / CARB 29 g / PROTEIN 10 g / CHOL 5 mg / SODIUM 665 mg

SAVORY FALL VEGETABLE SOUP

1   tablespoon Crisco Oil
2   medium onions, thinly sliced
2   cups peeled, chopped rutabaga
2   cups peeled, chopped turnips
1   cup shredded carrot
1   cup shredded cabbage
¼   cup chopped green bell pepper
¼   cup chopped red bell pepper
2   tablespoons minced fresh parsley
2   teaspoons beef flavor bouillon granules
1   bay leaf
¼   teaspoon salt
¼   teaspoon pepper
8¼   cups water, divided
¼   cup all-purpose flour
¼   plus 1 tablespoon grated Parmesan cheese

1. Heat Crisco Oil in Dutch oven on medium high heat.
    Add onion, rutabaga, turnips, carrot, cabbage, green
    pepper, red pepper, parsley, bouillon granules, bay
    leaf, salt and pepper. Sauté until tender. Stir in 8 cups
    water. Bring to a boil. Cover. Reduce heat. Simmer 35
    minutes.
2. Combine flour and remaining ¼ cup water. Stir until
    smooth. Add to vegetable mixture. Cook and stir 10
    minutes. Remove bay leaf before serving. Sprinkle
    each serving with 1½ teaspoons grated Parmesan
    cheese.

10 Servings

65 CALORIES / FAT 2 g (21 CAL or 32% of total calories) / SAT FAT 1 g (8% of total calories) / CARB 10 g / PROTEIN 2 g / CHOL 0 mg / SODIUM 130 mg

(continued)

must have been hard to
do, she ate that little shoe
box meal as if it had been
fancy food served on china
plates. We talked about
how hard it was to do any
kind of meaningful work
when you had to face the
kind of bigotry that
wouldn't even let you eat
in peace. She was
optimistic despite all that,
but as it turned out, she
didn't take the job in
Nashville but went on back
up North to work there.

Anonymous

CREOLE CHICKEN GUMBO

Stock

3½-4	pounds chicken pieces, skinned	1	carrot, cut in thirds
3	quarts water	1	medium onion, quartered
2	ribs celery, with leaves	1	bay leaf

Gumbo

⅓ cup Crisco Shortening or Crisco Oil

½ cup all-purpose flour

1 pound okra, washed and cut in ¼-inch pieces

1 cup chopped onion

¾ cup chopped celery

½ cup chopped green bell pepper

½ cup chopped red bell pepper

½ cup chopped green onions

¼ cup chopped fresh parsley

2 cloves garlic, pressed

1 bay leaf

¾ teaspoon dried thyme leaves

½ teaspoon dried marjoram leaves

½ teaspoon dried basil leaves

1 can (14½ ounces) whole tomatoes

½ pound lean ham, cubed

1 pound smoked turkey sausage, sliced

1 teaspoon Worcestershire sauce

¼ teaspoon salt

¼ teaspoon black pepper

¼ teaspoon cayenne pepper

⅛ teaspoon hot pepper sauce

9 cups hot cooked rice (without salt or fat)

1. For stock, place chicken, water, celery, carrot, onion, and bay leaf in large Dutch oven or kettle. Bring to a boil. Simmer 25 minutes, skimming foam and fat from top. Remove meat from bones and reserve. Return bones to stock. Continue simmering.
2. For gumbo, heat Crisco Shortening or Crisco Oil in large Dutch oven or kettle. Add flour gradually. Cook and stir until medium brown. Add okra, onion, celery, green pepper and red pepper. Cook and stir until okra is crisp-tender. Add green onions, parsley, garlic, bay leaf, thyme, marjoram, basil, undrained tomatoes, ham and chicken meat. Strain stock. Stir slowly into gumbo. Cook sausage. Drain well. Add to gumbo. Simmer 1½ hours, stirring occasionally. Add Worcestershire sauce, salt, pepper, cayenne and hot pepper sauce. Remove bay leaf before serving.
3. To serve, spoon desired amount of rice into individual soup bowls. Ladle gumbo over rice.

18 One Cup Servings

Note: Use 2 packages (10 ounces each) frozen okra if fresh is not available. Make ahead and freeze, if desired.

320 CALORIES / FAT 10 g (90 CAL or 28% of total calories) / SAT FAT 2 g (6% of total calories) / CARB 38 g / PROTEIN 20 g / CHOL 50 mg / SODIUM 480 mg

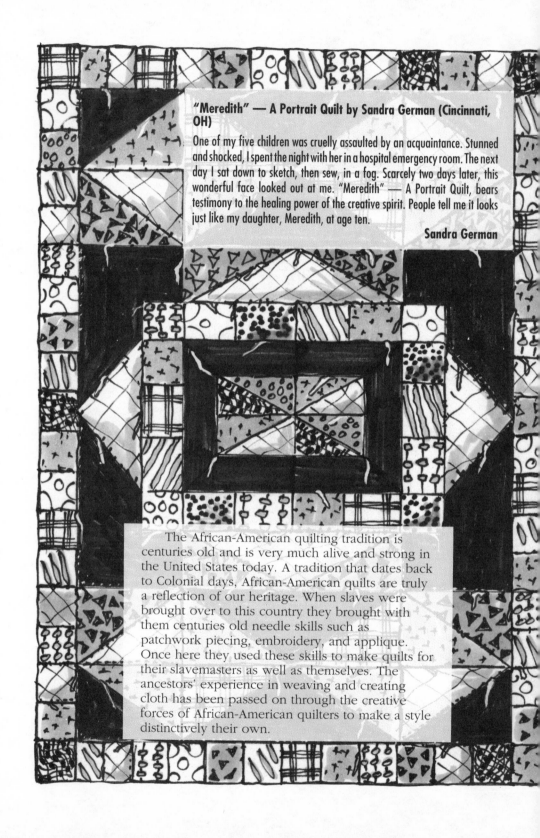

"Meredith" — A Portrait Quilt by Sandra German (Cincinnati, OH)

One of my five children was cruelly assaulted by an acquaintance. Stunned and shocked, I spent the night with her in a hospital emergency room. The next day I sat down to sketch, then sew, in a fog. Scarcely two days later, this wonderful face looked out at me. "Meredith" — A Portrait Quilt, bears testimony to the healing power of the creative spirit. People tell me it looks just like my daughter, Meredith, at age ten.

Sandra German

The African-American quilting tradition is centuries old and is very much alive and strong in the United States today. A tradition that dates back to Colonial days, African-American quilts are truly a reflection of our heritage. When slaves were brought over to this country they brought with them centuries old needle skills such as patchwork piecing, embroidery, and applique. Once here they used these skills to make quilts for their slavemasters as well as themselves. The ancestors' experience in weaving and creating cloth has been passed on through the creative forces of African-American quilters to make a style distinctively their own.

CURRIED BLACK ON BLACK-EYED PEAS & BEAN SALAD

¾   cup dried black beans (2 cups cooked)
¾   cup dried black eyed peas (2 cups cooked)
1   medium onion, diced, divided
½   pound smoked turkey, divided
1½ cups ¼-inch diced green onions
1⅓ cups ¼-inch diced red bell pepper
1¼ cups frozen whole kernel corn
1   cup low calorie Italian Dressing
¼   cup minced cilantro
2   teaspoons curry powder
1   teaspoon crushed red pepper
     Salt
     Pepper
     Scallion flowers
     Tomato wedges

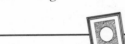

1. To cook beans and peas, place in separate saucepans. Cover with water. Add half onion to each. Bring to a boil. Cover. Remove from heat. Allow to stand one hour.
2. Add additional water to each saucepan, if necessary. Add half smoked turkey to each. Bring to a boil. Reduce heat. Cover. Simmer one hour or until tender, not mushy. Drain excess water. Cut turkey into bite-size pieces. Combine beans, peas and turkey in large glass bowl. Add dressing while beans are hot.
3. Add green onion, red bell pepper, corn, cilantro, curry powder and crushed red pepper. Season with salt and pepper, if desired. Toss to mix thoroughly. Cover. Refrigerate 24 hours.
4. Serve on salad greens, as a side-dish or buffet salad. Garnish with scallion flowers and tomato wedges.

10 Servings

Adaptation from Recipe
Chef William Sharp
Service Master

170 CALORIES / FAT 2 g (21 CAL or 12% of total calories) / SAT FAT 1 g (<5% of total calories) / CARB 25 g / PROTEIN 12 g / CHOL 10 mg / SODIUM 455 mg

I Leave You A Responsibility to Our Young People

Thanksgiving Day has always been a favorite holiday for our family. We all try to get together for the traditional meal, no matter how far flung our numbers may be.

In 1990, my husband and I traveled to our daughter's home for Thanksgiving. We knew that she had invited a dozen friends who were also far from their homes to join with her family to celebrate the big day.

As the other guests began to arrive, we all greeted each other, happy to meet our daughter's friends and anticipating the wonderful meal we knew was forthcoming. She had prepared most of it with our grandchildren, because they all love to cook together, but she had also assigned each guest to bring a dish of his or her own choosing.

When Dr. Height arrived, my enthusiasm knew no bounds. Here she was, a lady that I had heard about, read about and always wanted to meet. And she brought with her two sweet potato pies made, she told me, according to a recipe from Mrs. Mary McLeod Bethune! Dr. Height was as gracious

(continued)

(continued)

and charming as I had expected her to be. I first learned about Dr. Height when she served as president of my sorority and later on as she continued to contribute invaluable service to the black community and the nation, finally as she took up the reins of the National Council of Negro Women.

At dinner, as we dined on turkey, ham, oyster stuffing, dressing, cranberry jelly made by my granddaughter, vegetables washed and prepared by my grandsons, bread pudding, cakes, those sweet potato pies and other delicious foods, Dr. Height kept us enthralled as she gave us accounts of her early days as National President of Delta Sigma Theta Sorority. Her sense of humor is priceless. She gently chided our daughter for her choice of colors on that day. She had worn a pink sweater, black velvet skirt and had topped it off with a bright green apron. Dr. Height immediately said to me, "Soror Rhodes, do you see something amiss here?" She meant that my daughter was wearing the colors that represented another sorority! We were all highly amused at the remark as all of the women in our family,

(continued)

CLASSIC POTATO SALAD

     1   cup nonfat mayonnaise dressing
     2   teaspoons prepared mustard
    1½   teaspoons salt
     ½   teaspoon celery seed
     ⅛   teaspoon pepper
     4   cups diced, peeled, cooked red potatoes
     1   cup diced celery
     ½   cup sliced green onions
     ¼   cup sliced radishes
     2   tablespoons minced fresh parsley or 1 tablespoon
         dried parsley flakes

1. Combine mayonnaise dressing, prepared mustard, salt, celery seed and pepper in small bowl. Stir until well blended.
2. Combine potatoes, celery, onion, radishes and parsley in large bowl. Add dressing. Toss to mix. Cover. Refrigerate several hours.

8 Servings

90 CALORIES / FAT <1 g (2 CAL or <5% of total calories) / SAT FAT <1 g (<5% of total calories) / CARB 23 g / PROTEIN 2 g / CHOL 0 mg / SODIUM 685 mg

CREAMY COLESLAW

     4   cups shredded cabbage
     ⅓   cup shredded carrot
     ¼   cup chopped celery
     1   tablespoon finely chopped green onion
     ⅓   cup nonfat mayonnaise dressing
     2   tablespoons nonfat sour cream alternative
     1   teaspoon sugar
     ¼   teaspoon dry mustard
     ¼   teaspoon salt

1. Combine cabbage, carrot, celery and onion in medium serving bowl.
2. Mix mayonnaise dressing, "sour cream", sugar, dry mustard and salt in small bowl. Add to cabbage mixture. Mix well. Cover. Refrigerate at least 2 hours.

6 servings

30 CALORIES / FAT <1 g (<5 CAL or <5% of total calories) / SAT FAT <1 g (<5% of total calories) / CARB 7 g / PROTEIN 1 g / CHOL 0 mg / SODIUM 215 mg

VEGETABLE HARVEST POTATO SALAD

8   small new potatoes
1   package (9 ounces) frozen cut green beans, cooked,
    rinsed with cold water and drained
1   cucumber, peeled and sliced
¼   cup sliced celery
¼   cup sliced carrot
3   tablespoons sliced ripe olives
⅓   cup red wine vinegar
¼   cup Crisco Oil
1   tablespoon Dijon mustard
1   tablespoon dried parsley flakes
1   tablespoon grated Parmesan cheese
1   clove garlic, minced or ⅛ to ¼ teaspoon garlic
    powder
    Salt and pepper

1. Cook potatoes until just tender. Drain. Slice into large
   salad bowl.
2. Add green beans, cucumber, celery, carrot and olives.
3. Combine vinegar, Crisco Oil, mustard, parsley flakes,
   Parmesan cheese and garlic in container with tight-
   fitting lid. Shake well. Pour dressing over vegetables.
   Toss to mix well. Season with salt and pepper to taste.

8 Servings

210 CALORIES / FAT 8 g (72 CAL or 34% of total calories) / SAT FAT 1 g (<5% of total calories) / CARB 32 g / PROTEIN 3 g / CHOL 0 mg / SODIUM 150 mg

(continued)

including my three daughters, are Deltas. Later, as we talked, took photographs and remembered days past, Dr. Height told us how she became head of the NCNW. As I remember it, she said, "It was in 1941 in Chicago that Mrs. Bethune stood up and publicly thanked the previous Executive Director for her hard work and service. Then, Mrs. Bethune said it was time for a younger woman to get a chance to serve and then she said, "Dorothy Height, wouldn't you like to do it?" Dr. Height told me when she found out she had been selected, she said, "How could I say no before Mrs. Bethune and God and everyone else?" She told me from that day to this, she has asked young people to try tasks they may be afraid to tackle because she believes in the ability of young women to rise to the challenge. I'll never forget that and I shall never forget the memorable day we had dinner with her.

Carolyn Bolden Rhodes

CRUNCHY CABBAGE APPLE SLAW

½ cup nonfat sour cream
  alternative
1 tablespoon Crisco Oil
2 tablespoons cider vinegar
1 tablespoon plus 2 teaspoons
  sugar
1 teaspoon celery seed
¾ teaspoon salt

¼ teaspoon dry mustard
4 cups shredded cabbage
1 medium red apple, chopped
¼ cup finely chopped green bell
  pepper
2 tablespoons finely chopped
  onion

1. Combine "sour cream", Crisco Oil, vinegar, sugar, celery seed, salt and dry mustard in small bowl.
2. Combine cabbage, apple, green pepper and onion in large bowl. Pour creamy mixture over vegetables. Toss to mix. Cover. Refrigerate until ready to serve. Toss again just before serving.

8 Servings

60 CALORIES / FAT 2 g (18 CAL or 29% of total calories) / SAT FAT <1 g (<5% of total calories) / CARB 10 g / PROTEIN 2 g / CHOL 0 mg / SODIUM 215 mg

LIMA BEAN SALAD

2 packages (10 ounces each)
  frozen baby lima beans
¼ cup sliced green onions
¼ cup minced parsley
1 chopped hard-cooked egg
¼ cup nonfat mayonnaise dressing
¼ cup nonfat sour cream
  alternative

1 tablespoon tarragon vinegar
1 teaspoon dried dill weed
½ teaspoon salt
⅛ teaspoon pepper
8 lettuce leaves
4 tomatoes, cut in wedges

1. Cook lima beans according to package directions. Cool under cold running water. Drain well. Place in large bowl. Add onions, parsley and egg.
2. Combine mayonnaise dressing, "sour cream", vinegar, dill weed, salt and pepper. Add to lima beans. Toss to mix. Serve on lettuce with tomato wedges.

6 to 8 Servings

110 CALORIES / FAT 1 g (11 CAL or 10% of total calories) / SAT FAT <1 g (<5% of total calories) / CARB 20 g / PROTEIN 7 g / CHOL 25 mg / SODIUM 255 mg

THREE BEAN SALAD

1 can (16 ounces) red kidney beans, drained
1 can (16 ounces) cut green beans, drained
1 can (16 ounces) cut wax beans, drained
1 medium onion, diced or thinly sliced
1 cup sliced celery

¼ cup chopped green bell pepper
¼ cup chopped red bell pepper
¾ cup sugar
⅔ cup vinegar
¼ cup Crisco Oil
¾ teaspoon salt
½ teaspoon pepper
6 lettuce leaves (optional)

1. Combine kidney beans, green beans and wax beans, onion, celery, green pepper and red pepper in large bowl.
2. Combine sugar and vinegar. Stir until dissolved. Add Crisco Oil, salt and pepper. Stir to blend. Pour over vegetables. Toss to coat. Cover. Refrigerate overnight, stirring occasionally, if desired.
3. To serve, drain vegetables. Serve on lettuce, if desired.

8 to 10 Servings

170 CALORIES / FAT 6 g (53 CAL or 31% of total calories) / SAT FAT <1 g (<5% of total calories) / CARB 28 g / PROTEIN 3 g / CHOL 0 mg / SODIUM 660 mg

FROZEN FRUIT SALAD

1 cup thawed frozen light whipped topping
1 cup nonfat mayonnaise dressing
1 can (20 ounces) pineapple chunks in heavy syrup, drained and quartered

1½ cups miniature marshmallows
1 cup maraschino cherries, quartered
¾ cup natural sliced almonds
9 lettuce leaves

1. Combine whipped topping, mayonnaise dressing, pineapple, marshmallows, cherries and nuts. Pack into 8-inch square glass dish. Cover. Freeze several hours or overnight, stirring once after first hour of freezing. Cut in squares. Serve on lettuce.

9 Servings

180 CALORIES / FAT 5 g (46 CAL or 26% of total calories) / SAT FAT 4 g (<5% of total calories) / CARB 29 g / PROTEIN 2 g / CHOL 0 mg / SODIUM 235 mg

A Citizen of the World

You know how it is sometimes when you travel abroad. If you eat or drink anything, you're very likely to develop a painful upset stomach or worse. I had dinner once with Dr. Height before I was planning a trip out of the country. I told her of my plans and asked her how she fared when she traveled. She told me she had been to nearly every continent in the world and she had never been sick once. When I asked her how she managed such a feat, she told me about her first trip to India. It was back in the fifties. She told me that when she returned, everyone she knew asked her how her digestive system had fared, expecting to hear harrowing tales from her. She said on the trip she had seen nearly one hundred Americans in the hospital, but that she was never sick a day nor ever had a minute's trouble because she always carried her food with her. When she went out to the villages to work, she would take three or four boiled eggs, a few tangerines or bananas. When she could get it she would take her own bottled water too. I asked her why she did this and she said she didn't (continued)

BETHUNE FRUIT SALAD

Fruit Mixture
1   cup cubed cantaloupe (½-inch cubes)
1   cup cubed honeydew melon (½-inch cubes)
1   cup cubed fresh pineapple (½-inch cubes)
2   peaches, sliced
½   pound grapes, whole or halved lengthwise
2   oranges, peeled and sliced
1   can (11 ounces) mandarin orange segments, drained
2   bananas, sliced

Sauce
1   carton (16 ounces) nonfat sour cream alternative
1   cup firmly packed brown sugar
    Juice of 1 orange
    Juice of ½ lemon
3   tablespoons pineapple juice
1   teaspoon cinnamon
4 to 6 maraschino cherries, cut (optional)

1.   For fruit mixture, combine cantaloupe, honeydew, pineapple, peaches, grapes, oranges and mandarin orange segments in large bowl. Refrigerate.
2.   For sauce, combine "sour cream", brown sugar, orange juice, lemon juice, pineapple juice and cinnamon in medium bowl. Refrigerate.
3.   To serve, add bananas to fruit mixture. Spoon into individual dishes. Top with sauce.
4.   Garnish with maraschino cherry piece, if desired.

14 to 16 Servings

150 CALORIES / FAT <1 g (3 CAL or <5% of total calories) / SAT FAT <1 g (<5% of total calories) / CARB 34 g / PROTEIN 3 g / CHOL 0 mg / SODIUM 30 mg

WALDORF CHICKEN SALAD

    8   boneless, skinless chicken breast halves
    2   tablespoons melted butter
   ¼   teaspoon salt
  ¹⁄₁₆ teaspoon white pepper
    1   cup chopped celery
    1   cup chopped apple
   ¼   cup nonfat sour cream alternative
   ¼   cup cider vinegar
   ¼   cup nonfat mayonnaise dressing
    2   tablespoons plus 1½ teaspoons confectioners sugar
    2   tablespoons brown spicy mustard

1. Heat oven to 350°.
2. Season chicken breast with butter, salt and pepper. Place in baking pan. Bake at 375° until done, about 15 to 20 minutes.
3. Cool. Refrigerate until cold. Dice.
4. Combine celery, apple, "sour cream", vinegar, mayonnaise dressing, confectioners sugar and mustard, in large bowl. Mix well. Fold in chicken.

8 servings

180 CALORIES / FAT 4 g (40 CAL or 22% of total calories) / SAT FAT 1 g (5% of total calories) / CARB 7 g / PROTEIN 27 g / CHOL 65 mg / SODIUM 305 mg

**Adaptation from Recipe by
Johnny Rivers, Executive Chef
Walt Disney World**

(continued)

have time to be sick because she was determined that nothing so avoidable as stomach trouble would spoil her opportunity to meet people and learn from them.

Kathleen Arnold

CHILLED SHRIMP PASTA SALAD

1 cup lowfat plain yogurt	3 ribs celery, chopped
2 tablespoons salt substitute seasoning	3 large tomatoes, diced
	1 bunch green onions, chopped
2 tablespoons brown spicy mustard	1 pound cooked shrimp
	1 pound shell macaroni, cooked (without salt or fat)
2 teaspoons salt	
½ teaspoon pepper	

1. Combine yogurt, seasoning, mustard, salt and pepper in chilled large bowl. Mix well.
2. Add celery, tomatoes and green onions. Mix well.
3. Add shrimp and macaroni. Mix well.
4. Refrigerate about 2 hours before serving.

8 Servings

170 CALORIES / FAT 2 g (16 CAL or 9% of total calories) / SAT FAT 1 g (<5% of total calories) / CARB 22 g / PROTEIN 17 g / CHOL 110 mg / SODIUM 750 mg

**Adaptation from Recipe by
Johnny Rivers, Executive Chef
Walt Disney World**

JUANITA'S SEAFOOD MOUSSE

1 package (4-serving size) lemon flavor gelatin	2 tablespoons lemon juice
	2 tablespoons grated onion
¼ teaspoon salt	2 cups cooked, shrimp shelled and deveined
¾ cup boiling water	
1 cup nonfat sour cream alternative	2 tablespoons chopped fresh dill* Fresh dill (optional)
½ cup nonfat mayonnaise dressing	Assorted crackers (optional
2 tablespoons horseradish	

1. Dissolve gelatin and salt in boiling water. Stir in "sour cream", mayonnaise dressing, horseradish, lemon juice and onion. Refrigerate until slightly thickened.
2. Fold in shrimp and 2 tablespoons dill. Spoon into 4-cup mold. Refrigerate about 3 hours or until firm. Unmold on serving plate.
3. To serve, garnish with additional dill and serve with crackers, if desired.

4-Cup Mold (8 servings)
*1 teaspoon dried dill weed may be substituted for fresh.

70 CALORIES / FAT <1 g (3 CAL or <5% of total calories) / SAT FAT <1 g (<5% of total calories) / CARB 8 g / PROTEIN 8 g / CHOL 55 mg / SODIUM 285 mg

CHEF'S SALAD MOLD

2 packages (4-serving size each)
or 1 package (8-serving size)
lemon or lime flavor gelatin
2 cups boiling water
1 cup cold water
3 tablespoons cider vinegar
⅛ teaspoon hot pepper sauce
6 slices (¾-ounces each) fat free
process cheese product, cubed

¾ cup diced tomato
½ cup shredded lettuce
½ cup diced green bell pepper
½ cup diced cooked lean ham
½ cup diced cooked turkey
3 tablespoons thinly sliced green
onions
Salad greens (optional)
Tomato wedges (optional

1. Dissolve gelatin in boiling water. Add cold water, vinegar and hot pepper sauce. Refrigerate until thick and syrupy.
2. Fold in cheese, diced tomato, lettuce, green pepper, ham, turkey and green onions. Pour into 5-cup mold. Refrigerate 6 hours or overnight. Unmold on serving plate.
3. Serve on salad greens and garnish with tomato wedges, if desired.

4 to 6 Servings

100 CALORIES / FAT 1 g (13 CAL or 13% of total calories) / SAT FAT <1 g (<5% of total calories) / CARB 10 g / PROTEIN 12 g / CHOL 20 mg / SODIUM 990 mg

DAISY'S MOLDED BEET SALAD

1 can (16 ounces) whole or sliced
beets
1 package (4-servings) lemon or
orange flavor gelatin
¼ cup sugar

¼ cup cider vinegar
1½ cups finely chopped celery
1 tablespoon prepared
horseradish

1. Brush 4-cup mold lightly with Crisco Oil.
2. Drain beets, reserving liquid. Add enough water to liquid to make 1½ cups. Bring to a boil. Add gelatin, sugar and vinegar. Stir until dissolved. Cool to room temperature. Refrigerate until thick and syrupy.
3. Dice beets. Stir beets, celery and horseradish into gelatin. Pour into mold. Refrigerate 2 to 3 hours or until set. Unmold on serving plate.

6 Servings

75 CALORIES / FAT <1 g (<5 CAL or <5% of total calories) / SAT FAT <1 g (<5% of total calories) / CARB 18 g / PROTEIN 1 g / CHOL 0 mg / SODIUM 245 mg

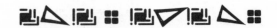

MOLDED ORANGE-PINEAPPLE SALAD

1 package (8-serving size) orange flavor gelatin
2 cups boiling water
1¾ cups cold water
1 can (11 ounces) mandarin orange segments, drained
1 can (8 ounces) crushed pineapple, well drained
1 cup nonfat cottage cheese
½ cup raisins
¼ cup coarsely chopped pecans
1 container (8 ounces) frozen light whipped topping, thawed
Lettuce leaves

1. Dissolve gelatin in boiling water. Add cold water. Stir in oranges, pineapple, cottage cheese, raisins and nuts.* Add whipped topping. Stir to blend.
2. Pour mixture into 8-cup mold or 12 X 7½ X 1½-inch glass dish. Refrigerate several hours or overnight, stirring 3 or 4 times during first 4 hours so that mixture is blended and creamy and fruit is evenly distributed.
3. To serve, unmold onto lettuce-lined plate or cut into squares and serve on individual lettuce-lined plates.

12 Servings.
*Alternate Method: Refrigerate fruit and gelatin mixture until thick and syrupy. Fold in whipped topping. Transfer to mold. Refrigerate until firm.

120 CALORIES / FAT 4 g (37 CAL or 31% of total calories) / SAT FAT <1 g (<5% of total calories) / CARB 20 g / PROTEIN 3 g / CHOL 0 mg / SODIUM 75 mg

HONEY MANDARIN CHICKEN TOSS

1   head iceburg lettuce, chopped
1   cup grated raw carrot
1   cup shredded red cabbage
1   cup julienned green bell pepper
1   cup julienned red bell pepper
1   cup julienned yellow onion
¾   cup honey
¾   cup Dijon mustard
4   boneless, skinless chicken breast halves, cooked
    and cut into bite-size pieces
½   cup slivered almonds
1   can (11 ounces) mandarin orange segments

1.   Combine lettuce, carrot and cabbage in large salad
     bowl.
2.   Blanch green pepper, red pepper and onion in 2 cups
     boiling water for 5 minutes. Drain.
3.   Combine honey and mustard in large saucepan. Heat
     until warm.
4.   Toss chicken, peppers, onion and mustard sauce.
     Spoon over lettuce. Garnish with nuts and orange
     segments.

4 servings

560 CALORIES / FAT 14 g (122 CAL or 22% of total calories) / SAT FAT 1 g (<5% of total calories) / CARB 81 g / PROTEIN 36 g / CHOL 70 mg / SODIUM 695 mg

Adaptation from Recipe
Tim Lightning
Royol Oak Country Club, Ohio

(continued)

sweet tasting, not limp and bitter the way it gets when you boil it for hours on end. And that's how she got Dorothy to eat cabbage. Until this day it is her favorite green vegetable.

Josephine Ryals

MACARONI-FRANK SALAD BOWL

2 cups (8-ounce package) macaroni
1 cup nonfat sour cream alternative
¼ cup nonfat French dressing
½ teaspoon salt
2 cups romaine lettuce pieces

1 cup diced celery
¼ cup thinly sliced radishes
¼ cup sliced green onions
2 turkey frankfurters, sliced
2 medium tomatoes, cut in wedges

1. Cook macaroni according to package instructions (without salt or fat). Combine hot macaroni, "sour cream", French dressing and salt. Cover. Place in refrigerator to chill thoroughly.
2. Combine romaine, celery, radishes, green onions and sliced frankfurters in large salad bowl. Add macaroni mixture and tomato wedges. Toss lightly. Serve.

8 servings

165 CALORIES / FAT 3 g (31 CAL or 19% of total calories) / SAT FAT 1 g (<5% of total calories) / CARB 26 g / PROTEIN 8 g / CHOL 10 mg / SODIUM 350 mg

GARDEN CHICKEN SALAD

3 cups cut-up cooked chicken breast
½ cup chopped zucchini
¼ cup chopped carrot
2 tablespoons chopped onion
2 tablespoons snipped fresh parsley

⅓ cup nonfat mayonnaise dressing
¼ cup lowfat sour cream alternative
½ teaspoon celery salt
⅛ teaspoon pepper

1. Combine chicken, zucchini, carrot, onion and parsley in large serving bowl.
2. Combine mayonnaise dressing, "sour cream", celery salt and pepper in small bowl. Add to chicken mixture. Mix well. Cover. Refrigerate at least 2 hours.

6 servings

170 CALORIES / FAT 4 g (38 CAL or 22% of total calories) / SAT FAT 1 g (<5% of total calories) / CARB 5 g / PROTEIN 28 g / CHOL 75 mg / SODIUM 360 mg

TODAY'S POKE SALAD

1 package (10 ounces) raw spinach, torn in bite-size pieces
1 pound raw mustard greens, torn in bite-size pieces
1 cup chopped watercress (3 ounces)
1 cup chopped onion
4 slices turkey bacon, cooked and crumbled

1. Wash greens. Pat dry.
2. Combine greens, onion and turkey bacon in salad bowl. Toss well.
3. Serve with nonfat Italian dressing.

8 Servings

50 CALORIES / FAT 1 g (10 CAL or 21% of total calories) / SAT FAT <1 g (6% of total calories) / CARB 6 g / PROTEIN 5 g / CHOL <5 mg / SODIUM 285 mg

CURRY DRESSING

1 tablespoon Crisco Oil
¼ cup finely chopped onion
2 tablespoons apple juice
2 teaspoons curry powder
½ cup nonfat sour cream alternative
3 tablespoons chutney
1 tablespoon lemon juice
1 teaspoon soy sauce
1 clove garlic, sliced

1. Heat Crisco Oil in small saucepan on low heat. Add onion. Sauté until tender. Add apple juice. Cook 3 minutes. Stir in curry powder. Cook and stir one minute. Cool slightly.
2. Combine onion mixture, "sour cream", chutney, lemon juice, soy sauce and garlic in container of blender or food processor. Process until smooth. Serve with green salad, raw vegetables ham or chicken.

One Cup Dressing (6 One-Tablespoon Servings)

25 CALORIES / FAT 1 g (8 CAL or 34% of total calories) / SAT FAT <1 g (<5% of total calories) / CARB 3 g / PROTEIN 1 g / CHOL 0 mg / SODIUM 35 mg

SAUCY & SAVORY HERB DRESSING

1 cup nonfat cottage cheese
¼ cup skim milk
2 tablespoons red wine vinegar
2 teaspoons Crisco Oil
¼ cup chopped green onions
¼ cup chopped fresh parsley
1 clove garlic, minced
¼ teaspoon dried oregano leaves
¼ teaspoon dried basil leaves
¼ teaspoon black pepper
⅛ teaspoon cayenne pepper

1. Combine cottage cheese, milk, vinegar and Crisco Oil in container of electric blender or food processor. Process until smooth.
2. Add green onions, parsley, minced garlic, oregano, basil, black pepper and cayenne. Process until blended. Serve over crisp greens.

1⅔ Cups (26 One-Tablespoon Servings)

10 CALORIES / FAT <1 g (<5 CAL or 28% of total calories) / SAT FAT <1 g (<5% of total calories) / CARB 1 g / PROTEIN 1 g / CHOL 0 mg / SODIUM 30 mg

Luncheon with Mrs. Bethune

I was standing in line at the post office the other day when a young friend of mine asked me if I planned to send Dr. Height a food memory for her new cookbook. Her question reminded me of the time I had a luncheon in honor of Mrs. Mary McLeod Bethune. It was in the early fifties when my children were very young. Mrs. Marion Seymour, who was assistant superintendent of nurses at Freedman's Hospital and my daughter's godmother, asked me to do a ladies luncheon. One of the guests is now 103 years old, Mrs. Charlotte May who lives in Kansas. There were about a dozen of us for luncheon that day. I remember I served "Hinton Delight" which was my special dish for company in those days. It was dressing spread in a casserole dish with sliced chicken topped with a creamy wine dressing and grated cheese. I also served a black cherry gelatin mold, string beans and sliced tomatoes with caramel pie for dessert. It was in October, 1954. Mrs. Bethune sat at the head of the table because she was the guest of honor. What I remember most clearly is how she talked about her

(continued)

CLASSIC CREAM DRESSING

2 cups nonfat cottage cheese
⅓ cup skim milk
¼ cup fresh lemon juice
2 teaspoons Crisco Oil

1. Place cottage cheese, milk, lemon juice and Crisco Oil in blender jar. Blend at medium speed until smooth.

Alternate Method: Mash cheese with fork or potato masher. Place in jar with screw top. Add milk, lemon juice and Crisco Oil. Shake well.

2½ Cups Dressing (40 One-Tablespoon Servings)

10 CALORIES / FAT <1 g (<5 CAL or 18% of total calories) / SAT FAT <1 g (<5% of total calories) / CARB 1 g / PROTEIN 1 g / CHOL 0 mg / SODIUM 40 mg

Variations:
HERB N' SPICE DRESSING
4 green onions and half of tops, sliced
2 tablespoons fresh minced parsley
1 teaspoon Worcestershire sauce
¼ teaspoon dry mustard
¼ teaspoon dried oregano leaves
⅛ teaspoon garlic powder
1¼ cups Classic Cream Dressing

1. Stir onions, parsley, Worcestershire sauce, dry mustard, oregano and garlic powder into Classic Cream Dressing.

1¼ Cups Dressing (20 One-Tablespoon Servings)

10 CALORIES / FAT <1 g (<5 CAL or 18% of total calories) / SAT FAT <1 g (<5% of total calories) / CARB 1 g / PROTEIN 2 g / CHOL 0 mg / SODIUM 45 mg

HONEY BANANA DRESSING
1¼ cups Classic Cream Dressing
½ medium banana, cut in chunks
2 tablespoons honey
1 teaspoon lemon juice

1. Combine Classic Cream Dressing, banana, honey and lemon juice in blender jar. Blend at medium speed until smooth.

1½ Cups Dressing (24 One-Tablespoon Servings)

15 CALORIES / FAT <1 g (<5 CAL or 11% of total calories) / SAT FAT <1 g (<5% of total calories) / CARB 3 g / PROTEIN 1 g / CHOL 0 mg / SODIUM 35 mg

(continued)

dreams for the National Council of Negro Women. She said she wanted it to become a great organization to help improve the lives of our women. She wanted women all over the country to join because she believed that by working together we could accomplish great things. Mrs. Bethune talked about the young people and how they were moving on and how all of us needed to think about children, not just our own children but all the children in the country. She talked to us about Dorothy Height who she described as a bright young woman full of energy who would lead NCNW to great things. The affection and respect that she had for Miss Height was tangible. We all knew that if Mrs. Bethune believed in Dorothy, then Dorothy must be on the ball. All in all, it was a very moving speech, but Mrs. Bethune didn't talk to us as if we were an audience, she talked to us the way you talk to friends. It was an afternoon that I'll always remember.

Mrs. Vi Curtis Hinton

THOUSAND ISLAND DRESSING

1 cup nonfat sour cream
  alternative
1 cup chili sauce
¼ cup sweet pickle relish, well
  drained

1 tablespoon Crisco Oil
½ cup sliced green onions
½ cup chopped celery
1 hard-cooked egg, finely
  chopped

1. Combine "sour cream", chili sauce, pickle relish, Crisco Oil, green onions, celery and hard-cooked egg. Stir with fork to blend. Cover. Refrigerate until ready to use.
2. Stir again just before serving.

3 Cups Dressing (48 One-Tablespoon Servings)

15 CALORIES / FAT 1 g (<5 CAL or 25% of total calories) / SAT FAT <1 g (<5% of total calories) / CARB 2 g / PROTEIN 1 g / CHOL 5 mg / SODIUM 90 mg

CREAMY SPICED DRESSING

1¼ cups plain nonfat yogurt or
   nonfat sour cream alternative
2 tablespoons cider vinegar
2 teaspoons Crisco Oil
1 teaspoon sugar
½ teaspoon chili powder

¼ teaspoon salt
⅛ teaspoon black pepper
⅛ teaspoon cayenne pepper
1 tablespoon minced fresh parsley
  or 1 teaspoon dried

1. Combine yogurt, vinegar, Crisco Oil, sugar, chili powder, salt, black pepper and cayenne in small bowl. Stir until smooth. Stir in parsley.
2. Serve over sliced cucumbers, tomatoes or avocados.

1⅓ Cups (21 One-Tablespoon Servings)
Note: Omit vinegar. Serve as a potato topper or vegetable dip.

15 CALORIES / FAT <1 g (<5 CAL or 30% of total calories) / SAT FAT <1 g (<5% of total calories) / CARB 1 g / PROTEIN 1 g / CHOL 0 mg / SODIUM 35 mg

"Reprise" by Marie Wilson (Brooklyn, NY)

"Reprise" is my answer to the question, "What is a woman?" This work celebrates the lives of twelve women of unique achievement. They include a physicist; an astronomer; an anthropologist; an outlaw and a gloriously eccentric explorer. Gertrude Benham spent thirty years walking around the world; she was the first woman to climb Mt. Kilimanjaro and she always carried her knitting, pocket Shakespeare, Bible and umbrella. The thirteen silhouettes represent "generic women"... the nubile Eve; maidservant; mother; witch; crusader; teacher, etc.

Marie Wilson

While quilts were present in the Americas from the earliest days, the African influenced quilts took a unique form. Some share characteristics with Euro-American quilts while others are made in an improvisational patchwork style. The improvisational quilt reflects evidence of African aesthetics. Some scholars relate this type of quilt to the textiles of West Africa. Motifs and structural principles similar to African strip weaving and Fon appliqués can be seen in African-American quilts. They are colorful with bold, asymmetrical piecing, multiple patterns, symbolic forms and casual randomly placed quilt stitches...the very opposite of the symmetrical, precision pieced, soft colored Euro-American quilt with its small and intricate quilt stitches.

LITE N' LEAN OVEN FRIED CHICKEN BREAST

¾ cup fine dry bread crumbs
¼ cup all-purpose flour
1 teaspoon paprika
1 teaspoon poultry seasoning
1 teaspoon onion salt
½ teaspoon garlic powder

½ teaspoon dried thyme leaves
¼ teaspoon pepper
1 tablespoon plus 1½ teaspoons Crisco Oil
4 whole chicken breasts, skinned and split (about 4 pounds)

1. Heat oven to 400°.
2. Combine bread crumbs, flour, paprika, poultry seasoning, onion salt, garlic powder, thyme and pepper. Stir with fork until well blended. Add Crisco Oil slowly. Toss with fork to distribute. Stir until well blended.
3. Moisten chicken with water. Roll in coating mixture. Place in single layer in 15½ X 10½-inch jelly roll pan or other large pan. Sprinkle any remaining crumb mixture over chicken.
4. Bake at 400° for 30 minutes or until no longer pink in center.

8 Servings

200 CALORIES / FAT 5 g (41 CAL or 21% of total calories) / SAT FAT <1 g (<5% of total calories) / CARB 11 g / PROTEIN 28 g / CHOL 65 mg / SODIUM 145 mg

CRISPY BAKED CHICKEN BREASTS

8 boneless, skinless chicken breast halves (about 2 pounds)
2 egg whites
½ cup skim milk
½ cup all-purpose flour
1 tablespoon paprika

1 teaspoon dried basil leaves
½ teaspoon salt
¼ teaspoon pepper
1 cup fine dry bread crumbs
¼ cup Crisco Oil

1. Heat oven to 425°.
2. Rinse chicken breast halves. Pat dry with paper towels.
3. Beat egg whites until frothy. Beat in milk.
4. Combine flour, paprika, basil, salt and pepper in large plastic food storage bag. Place bread crumbs in another bag. Dip breast halves, one or two at a time, in flour mixture, then in egg white mixture, then in crumbs.
5. Place Crisco Oil in 15¼ X 10¼ X ¾-inch jelly roll pan or other shallow pan. Place in 425° oven for 3 or 4 minutes or until Crisco Oil is hot, but not smoking. Add chicken breasts in single layer.
6. Bake at 425° for 10 minutes. Turn chicken over. Bake for 5 minutes.

8 Servings

240 CALORIES / FAT 8 g (73 CAL or 30% of total calories) / SAT FAT 1 g (<5% of total calories) / CARB 11 g / PROTEIN 29 g / CHOL 65 mg / SODIUM 220 mg

COUNTRY CHICKEN 'N BISCUITS

Malcolm X

We were all talking over dinner about events which made a major impression on us when Dr. Height told us about a meeting she had with Malcolm X, Whitney Young, James Farmer, Betty Shabazz, Ossie Davis, Lorraine Hansberry, Andrew Young and several other people at Sidney Poitier's home in Pleasantville, NY. She said the meeting came about at a time when the press was having a field day with the idea that all sorts of Black organizations were battling against each other for leadership and for who would determine the route Black America should take in pursuit of equality. According to Dr. Height, the meeting, which really was more of a summit session than a plain old meeting, led to an agreement to disagree privately, to fuss and fight among themselves if need be, but to project unity in public. It was only through presenting a unified front, Dr. Height reported, that any gains could be made. That part of the story was very powerful, but what was utterly delightful, was when Dr. Height told us how Sidney Poitier came to pick her up in a sports car himself and take her to his house — everyone was

(continued)

Base

1	tablespoon Crisco Oil
1	cup chopped onion
¼	cup all-purpose flour
½	teaspoon salt
¼	teaspoon pepper
¼	teaspoon dried basil leaves
¼	teaspoon dried thyme leaves
2½	cups skim milk
1	chicken flavor bouillon cube
1	tablespoon Worcestershire sauce
2	cups cubed, cooked chicken
1	bag (16 ounces) frozen mixed vegetables
2	tablespoons grated Parmesan cheese

Biscuits

1	cup all-purpose flour
1	tablespoon sugar
1½	teaspoons baking powder
1	tablespoon snipped fresh parsley
⅛	teaspoon salt
⅓	cup skim milk
3	tablespoons Crisco Oil

1. Heat oven to 375°.
2. For base, heat Crisco Oil in 2-quart saucepan. Add onion. Sauté until tender. Remove from heat. Stir in flour, salt, pepper, basil and thyme. Add milk, bouillon cube and Worcestershire sauce. Cook and stir on medium-high heat until mixture comes to a boil and is thickened. Stir in chicken, vegetables and cheese. Heat. Pour into ungreased 2-quart casserole.
3. For biscuits, combine flour, sugar, baking powder, parsley and salt in medium bowl. Add milk and Crisco Oil. Stir with fork, until dry ingredients are just moistened. Drop dough by well-rounded measuring tablespoonfuls onto hot chicken mixture to form 8 biscuits.
4. Bake at 375° for 35 to 45 minutes or until chicken mixture is bubbly and biscuits are golden brown.

8 Servings

280 CALORIES / FAT 9 g (84 CAL or 30% of total calories) / SAT FAT 1 g (5% of total calories) / CARB 30 g / PROTEIN 18 g / CHOL 30 mg / SODIUM 485 mg

SOUTHERN STYLE OVEN BARBECUED CHICKEN

6   boneless, skinless chicken breast halves (about 1½ pounds)

Barbecue sauce
2   tablespoons Crisco Shortening or Crisco Oil
1   cup finely chopped onion
1   clove garlic, minced
1   cup ketchup
¼   cup lemon juice
¼   cup honey
2   tablespoons Worcestershire sauce
1   teaspoon dry mustard
1 to 2 teaspoons hot pepper sauce
½   teaspoon salt
2   drops liquid smoke (optional)

1. Heat oven to 450°.
2. Place chicken in 11¾ X 7½-inch baking dish.
3. For barbecue sauce, heat Crisco Shortening or Crisco Oil in medium skillet on medium heat. Add onion and garlic. Stir-fry until soft but not browned. Remove from heat. Cool slightly. Stir in ketchup, lemon juice, honey, Worcestershire sauce, dry mustard, hot pepper sauce, salt and liquid smoke, if used. Stir until well blended. Pour over chicken.
4. Bake at 450° for 20 minutes or until chicken is no longer pink in center.

6 Servings

275 CALORIES / FAT 6 g (57 CAL or 20% of total calories) / SAT FAT 1 g (3% of total calories) / CARB 26 g / PROTEIN 28 g / CHOL 70 mg / SODIUM 820 mg

(continued)

jealous! A long time fan of his, I can just bet everyone was.

Beverly Coleman
BC Associates
  Enterprises, Inc.

VELMA'S CHICKEN BROCCOLI CASSEROLE

5 ounces uncooked macaroni
2 teaspoons Crisco Shortening or Crisco Oil
⅔ cup chopped onion
2 large cloves garlic, minced
1 pound boneless, skinless chicken breast, cut into 1-inch pieces
2 cans (14½ ounces each) tomatoes, undrained and coarsely chopped
1 can (8 ounces) tomato sauce
¼ cup ketchup
1¼ teaspoons dried basil leaves
¾ teaspoon dried oregano leaves
¼ teaspoon salt
1 package (10 ounces) frozen broccoli cuts, thawed, well drained
½ cup grated Parmesan cheese, divided

1. Heat oven to 350°.
2. Cook macaroni following package directions, omitting salt and fat. Drain.
3. Heat Crisco Shortening or Crisco Oil in large skillet on medium-high heat. Add onion and garlic. Sauté until tender. Add chicken. Cook and stir just until chicken is no longer pink. Stir in tomatoes, tomato sauce, ketchup, basil, oregano and salt. Bring to a boil. Reduce heat. Simmer, uncovered, 5 minutes, stirring occasionally.
4. Combine macaroni, broccoli, chicken mixture and ¼ cup cheese. Stir well. Spoon into 13 X 9 X 2-inch baking dish. Sprinkle with remaining ¼ cup cheese.
5. Bake at 350° for 20 minutes.

8 Servings

215 CALORIES / FAT 4 g (37 CAL or 17% of total calories) / SAT FAT 1 g (5% of total calories) / CARB 26 g / PROTEIN 20 g / CHOL 35 mg / SODIUM 485 mg

HERBED CHICKEN & RICE

1½ teaspoons low sodium chicken flavor instant
     bouillon granules
1½ cups boiling water
2½ pound broiler-fryer chicken, cut up and skinned
     Pepper
 2 tablespoons Crisco Oil
 1 cup uncooked long grain rice*
 1 cup sliced fresh mushrooms
⅓ cup chopped celery
¼ cup chopped onion
½ teaspoon ground poultry seasoning
½ teaspoon dried rosemary leaves (optional)
 2 teaspoons dried parsley flakes or 2 tablespoons
     chopped fresh parsley
 2 tablespoons toasted sliced almonds (optional)

1. Dissolve bouillon in boiling water.
2. Heat oven to 350°. Line 13 X 9 X 2-inch pan with foil.
3. Sprinkle chicken pieces with pepper. Heat Crisco Oil
   in large skillet on medium-high heat. Add chicken.
   Brown on all sides.
4. Sprinkle rice over bottom of lined pan. Top with
   mushrooms, celery, onion, poultry seasoning and
   rosemary (if used). Pour chicken bouillon over top.
   Arrange chicken on top. Sprinkle with parsley flakes.
   Cover tightly with additional foil.
5. Bake at 350° about one hour or until rice is tender.
   Uncover. Sprinkle with almonds, if desired.

6 Servings
*Brown rice may be substituted for white rice. Cooking
time should be increased to 1½ hours.*

520 CALORIES / FAT 14 g (126 CAL or 25% of total calories) / SAT FAT 2 g (<5%
of total calories) / CARB 47 g / PROTEIN 48 g / CHOL 135 mg / SODIUM 490 mg

(continued)
had gone to those kinds of
schools. Talking to Dr.
Height opened my eyes.
She told me she was shy in
school, but she made
herself get involved in
speaking contests and she
won too. She told me she
had asthma as a child but
that she still played sports,
basketball in fact. The one
thing that really made a
big impression on me was
Dr. Height telling me when
she was growing up how
young people, my age and
older, were involved in
changing the country
through the Christian
Youth Movement.

Lauren Cooper

CREAMY MUSTARD CHICKEN WITH RICE

6   boneless, skinless chicken breast
    halves (about 1½ pounds)
    Salt and pepper
2   tablespoons Crisco Shortening
    or Crisco Oil
1   chicken flavor bouillon cube
1   cup boiling water
2   tablespoons all-purpose flour

½   cup nonfat sour cream
    alternative
2   tablespoons Dijon mustard
4   cups cooked rice (without salt
    or fat)
2   tablespoons chopped fresh
    parsley

1. Sprinkle chicken with salt and pepper.
2. Heat Crisco Shortening or Crisco Oil in large skillet on medium-high heat. Sauté chicken about 5 minutes per side or until golden brown and center is no longer pink. Remove chicken.
3. Dissolve bouillon cube in water. Stir well.
4. Add flour to skillet. Cook and stir 2 minutes on medium heat. Stir in chicken bouillon slowly. Stir until thickened and smooth. Reduce heat to low. Stir in "sour cream" and mustard. Return chicken to skillet. Turn to coat with sauce. Serve with rice. Sprinkle with parsley.

6 Servings

375 CALORIES / FAT 7 g (61 CAL or 16% of total calories) / SAT FAT <1 g (<5% of total calories) / CARB 42 g / PROTEIN 33 g / CHOL 70 mg / SODIUM 330 mg

COUNTRY CRISPED CHICKEN SKILLET

¼   cup Crisco Shortening or Crisco
    Oil
⅓   cup skim milk
⅔   cup all-purpose flour
1   teaspoon paprika

¾   teaspoon salt
½   teaspoon garlic powder
½   teaspoon pepper
4   whole chicken breasts, split and
    skinned (about 4 pounds)

1. Heat Crisco Shortening or Crisco Oil in large nonstick skillet on medium-high heat.
2. Pour milk into shallow bowl. Combine flour, paprika, salt, garlic powder and pepper in large plastic food bag.
3. Dip chicken into milk and then shake one piece at a time in flour mixture to coat.
4. Fry chicken 25 minutes or until meat near the bone is no longer pink.

8 Servings

230 CALORIES / FAT 9 g (77 CAL or 34% of total calories) / SAT FAT 1 g (<5% of total calories) / CARB 9 g / PROTEIN 28 g / CHOL 65 mg / SODIUM 280 mg

TURKEY SPAGHETTI

1	pound chopped or ground turkey breast	¼	pound light margarine
½	cup onion, chopped	1	teaspoon black pepper
1	cup green bell pepper, chopped	1	teaspoon salt
1	tablespoon garlic, chopped	1½	pounds spaghetti, cooked (without salt or fat)
4	tomatoes, chopped		

1. Heat margarine in large skillet on medium heat.
2. Add chopped or ground turkey breast. Cook about 5 minutes.
3. Add garlic, onion and peppers. Cook 5 minutes
4. Add salt, pepper and tomatoes. Cook slowly on low heat about 20 minutes. Serve over spaghetti.

6 Servings

380 CALORIES / FAT 14 g (124 CAL or 33% of total calories) / SAT FAT 3 g (8% of total calories) / CARB 39 g / PROTEIN 24 g / CHOL 45 mg / SODIUM 600 mg

**Adapation from Recipe
Johnny Rivers, Executive Chef
Walt Disney World**

SAUCY TURKEY CUTLETS

3	tablespoons all-purpose flour	3	medium tomatoes, diced
½	teaspoon salt	1	small onion, thinly sliced
¼	teaspoon dried rosemary leaves	2	teaspoons capers (optional)
1	package (16-ounce) turkey cutlets	8	small unpeeled red potatoes, cooked
2	tablespoons Crisco Shortening or Crisco Oil		

1. Combine flour, salt and rosemary on waxed paper. Coat turkey cutlets lightly.
2. Heat Crisco Shortening or Crisco Oil in large non stick skillet on medium-high heat.
3. Sauté turkey on both sides until lightly browned and no longer pink in center. Remove from skillet. Reduce heat to medium-low.
4. Add tomatoes, onion and capers to skillet. Cover. Cook 10 minutes or until vegetables are tender. Return turkey to skillet. Heat through.
5. To serve, arrange potatoes and turkey on 4 dinner plates. Spoon sauce over turkey.

4 Servings

300 CALORIES / FAT 9 g (83 CAL or 28% of total calories) / SAT FAT 1 g (5% of total calories) / CARB 24 g / PROTEIN 30 g / CHOL 70 mg / SODIUM 350 mg

LOUISIANA PEPPER CHICKEN

Let Us Break Bread Together

Dr. Benjamin Hooks, Executive Director of the National Association for the Advancement of Colored People (NAACP), dispatched me to the Washington Bureau in the late summer of 1990 in the wake of the grave illness of legendary lobbyist Althea T.L. Simmons. I quickly discovered that our civil rights coalition met frequently, and often over brown bag or cold box lunches or simply snacks and coffee. I also discovered that Dr. Dorothy Height followed a different method of eating and meeting.

I recall, specifically, my first meeting in her downtown Washington, DC office. It was a meeting of the Black Leadership Forum in September, 1990. Dr. Height's style and stature left a positive, lasting impression on me. During this meeting, civil rights leaders sought strength through strategy. There was a full plate of legislative initiatives to discuss, including the Civil Rights Act of 1990 and the National Voter Registration Act (the "Motor Voter" bill). There was much food for thought on the subject of deteriorating race relations in the nation, and (continued)

6   boneless, skinless chicken breast halves (about 1½ pounds)
¾   teaspoon salt
½   teaspoon cayenne pepper
⅓   cup all-purpose flour
⅓   cup Crisco Shortening or Crisco Oil
1   medium green bell pepper, cut lengthwise into ¼-inch strips
1   medium red bell pepper, cut lengthwise into ¼-inch strips
¼   cup chopped green onions
3   tablespoons minced fresh parsley
1½ cups chicken broth
1   tablespoon lemon juice
1   teaspoon dried basil leaves
½   teaspoon dried thyme leaves
4   cups hot cooked rice (without salt or fat)

1. Rinse and dry chicken.
2. Combine salt and cayenne. Sprinkle on chicken. Coat with flour.
3. Heat Crisco Shortening or Crisco Oil in large skillet on medium-high heat. Sauté chicken on both sides until browned and center is no longer pink. Drain on paper towels. Remove to serving plate. Keep warm.
4. Add green and red peppers and green onions to skillet. Stir-fry 2 to 3 minutes or until crisp-tender. Stir in parsley. Spoon over chicken.
5. Add chicken broth, lemon juice, basil and thyme to skillet. Cook on high heat until reduced to about one-half cup. Pour over chicken breasts. Serve with rice.

6 Servings

460 CALORIES / FAT 15 g (132 CAL or 29% of total calories) / SAT FAT 2 g (<5% of total calories) / CARB 47 g / PROTEIN 33 g / CHOL 70 mg / SODIUM 540 mg

CREAMY CHICKEN 'N NOODLES

2 tablespoons Crisco Shortening or Crisco Oil
2½ pounds broiler-fryer, skin removed, cut into pieces
1 medium green bell pepper, chopped
1 medium onion, chopped
1 tablespoon plus 1¼ teaspoons paprika
2 cups chicken broth
Parsley sprigs
1 container (16 ounces) nonfat sour cream alternative
1 tablespoon all-purpose flour
4 cups hot cooked noodles
Salt and pepper (optional)

1. Heat Crisco Shortening or Crisco Oil in large deep skillet on medium heat. Add chicken. Brown on all sides. Remove from skillet.
2. Add green pepper and onion to skillet. Stir-fry until softened. Stir in paprika. Cook one minute.
3. Return chicken to skillet. Add broth (add water if needed). Add parsley. Reduce heat. Cover. Simmer about 20 minutes or until chicken is tender. Remove from heat. Remove chicken from skillet.
4. Combine "sour cream" and flour. Stir into hot broth. Puree small amount at a time in food processor or blender. Return chicken and sauce to skillet. Return to heat to warm. Serve with noodles. Season with salt and pepper, if desired.

4 Servings

725 CALORIES / FAT 19 g (171 CAL or 23% of total calories) / SAT FAT 3 g (<5% of total calories) / CARB 54 g / PROTEIN 80 g / CHOL 250 mg / SODIUM 670 mg

(continued)

there were many other items on the civil rights menu to digest.
As this important meeting came to a close, the unmistakable, irresistible aroma of some serious "down home" cooking wafted through the stately conference room where the meeting took place. The customary formalities for adjournment were minimized. Minds and mouths that were focused upon civil rights priorities were now attuned to the midday meal provided by Dr. Height. The freedom fighters hastened to tables now filled with chicken, ribs, smoked ham, greens, candied yams, potato salad, hot rolls, sweet potato pie and much more. Thanks to Dr. Dorothy Height, we would truly break bread together and gain strength for the journey.

**Edward A Hailes, Jr.
Counsel
Washington Bureau of
the NAACP**

LEMONY MUSHROOM TURKEY BREAST

½ teaspoon chicken flavor instant bouillon granules
½ cup boiling water
1 pound turkey breast cutlets, pounded thin
3 tablespoons all-purpose flour
2 tablespoons Crisco Shortening or Crisco Oil, divided

¼ pound fresh mushrooms, thinly sliced
¼ cup dry white wine
1 tablespoon plus 1½ teaspoons lemon juice
1 tablespoon minced fresh parsley
2⅔ cup cooked rice (without salt or fat)

1. Dissolve bouillon in boiling water.
2. Coat turkey slices with flour. Shake off excess.
3. Heat one tablespoon Crisco Shortening or Crisco Oil in large non-stick skillet on medium-high heat. Add mushrooms. Sauté 2 minutes. Remove mushrooms.
4. Add remaining one tablespoon Crisco Shortening or Crisco Oil to skillet. Add turkey slices. Brown 2 minutes per side. Remove turkey.
5. Add wine, chicken broth and lemon juice to skillet. Boil 3 minutes until slightly reduced.
6. Return turkey to skillet. Turn slices to coat with sauce. Add mushrooms. Simmer to reheat. Stir in parsley.
7. Place turkey on platter. Spoon sauce over turkey. Garnish with additional parsley, if desired.

4 Servings

405 CALORIES / FAT 9 g (84 CAL or 21% of total calories) / SAT FAT 1g (<5% of total calories) / CARB 46 g / PROTEIN 32 g / CHOL 70 mg / SODIUM 190 mg

QUICK TURKEY HASH

1 tablespoon vegetable oil
1 cup sliced mushrooms
½ cup finely chopped onion
2 cups diced cooked turkey
2 cups diced cooked potatoes

1 tablespoon snipped parsley
1 teaspoon salt
⅛ teaspoon black pepper
⅔ cup undiluted skim evaporated milk

1. Heat oil in large saucepan on medium heat. Add mushrooms and onion. Sauté about 5 minutes.
2. Remove from heat. Stir in turkey, potatoes, parsley, salt and pepper. Stir in evaporated milk. Reduce heat to low. Heat mixture thoroughly (about 5 minutes).

6 servings

160 CALORIES / FAT 5 g (45 CAL or 28% of total calories) / SAT FAT 1 g (7% of total calories) / CARB 12 g / PROTEIN 16 g / CHOL 35 mg / SODIUM 405 mg

SPICY TURKEY CUTLETS

1 can (8 ounces) tomato sauce
1 tablespoon Crisco Oil
1½ teaspoons dried oregano leaves
1 tablespoon dried parsley flakes
1 teaspoon dried thyme leaves

½ teaspoon salt
1 clove garlic, minced or ½
    teaspoon garlic powder
¼ teaspoon crushed red pepper
1 pound turkey breast cutlets

1. Combine tomato sauce, Crisco Oil, oregano, parsley, thyme, salt, garlic and crushed red pepper in small bowl.
2. Spread one tablespoon sauce over each cutlet. Roll up. Place seam side down in baking dish. Spoon remaining sauce over cutlets. Refrigerate at least 30 minutes.
3. Heat oven to 350°.
4. Bake uncovered at 350° for 25 minutes.

4 Servings

180 CALORIES / FAT 5 g (49 CAL or 27% of total calories) / SAT FAT 1 g (<5% of total calories) / CARB 5 g / PROTEIN 28g / CHOL 70 mg / SODIUM 680 mg

HENRIETTA'S SPICY FRIED CHICKEN BREASTS

1 to 2 teaspoons black pepper
½ teaspoon poultry seasoning
½ teaspoon paprika
½ cayenne pepper
¼ teaspoon dry mustard
4 whole chicken breasts, split and skinned (about 4 pounds)

⅔ cup all-purpose flour
2¼ teaspoons garlic salt
¼ teaspoon salt
¼ teaspoon celery salt
¼ cup Crisco Shortening or Crisco Oil

1. Combine black pepper, poultry seasoning, paprika, cayenne and dry mustard. Sprinkle on fleshy part of chicken. Press lightly.
2. Combine flour, garlic salt, salt and celery salt in paper or plastic bag. Add chicken, one piece at a time. Shake to coat. Shake all pieces a second time for more even coating.
3. Heat Crisco Shortening or Crisco Oil in large nonstick skillet on medium heat. Add chicken, skinned side down. Sprinkle with remaining flour mixture. Fry 30 minutes. Turn every 10 minutes. Increase heat to medium-high. Fry 5 minutes longer or until chicken is no longer pink. Drain on paper towels.

8 Servings

225 CALORIES / FAT 9 g (77 CAL or 34% of total calories) / SAT FAT 1 g (<5% of total calories) / CARB 9 g / PROTEIN 27 g / CHOL 65 mg / SODIUM 785 mg

COLORFUL CHICKEN CORN SAUTÉ

1   tablespoon chili powder
½   teaspoon salt
4   boneless skinless chicken breast
    halves, cut in 2 X ½-inch strips
    (about 1 pound)
2   tablespoons Crisco Shortening
    or Crisco Oil, divided
1   cup chopped onion

2   medium green bell peppers, cut
    in 2 X ½-inch strips
1   medium red bell pepper, cut in
    2 X ½-inch strips
1   package (10 ounces) frozen
    corn, thawed
    Red pepper sauce (optional)

1.   Combine chili powder and salt in bowl. Add chicken. Toss to coat.
2.   Heat one tablespoon Crisco Shortening or Crisco Oil in large skillet on
     medium-high heat. Add chicken. Stir-fry until center is no longer pink.
     Remove to serving dish.
3.   Heat remaining one tablespoon Crisco Shortening or Crisco Oil in skillet. Add
     onion. Stir-fry about 2 minutes or until softened. Add green and red peppers.
     Stir-fry 3 to 4 minutes or until crisp-tender. Add corn. Stir to mix and heat.
     Return chicken to skillet to reheat. Season with hot pepper sauce, if desired.

6 Servings

190 CALORIES / FAT 6 g (54 CAL or 28% of total calories) / SAT FAT 1 g (<5% of total calories) / CARB 15 g /
PROTEIN 20 g / CHOL 45 mg / SODIUM 245 mg

CHICKEN VEGGIE PASTA TOSS

2   tablespoons Crisco Shortening
    or Crisco Oil
6   boneless, skinless chicken breast
    halves, cut in 1-inch pieces
    (about 1½ pounds)
1   clove garlic, minced
3   cups broccoli flowerets
2   cups sliced fresh mushrooms
1   fresh tomato, diced

1   package (8 ounces) linguine or
    spaghetti, cooked (without salt
    or fat)
¾   cup grated Parmesan cheese
1   tablespoon dried basil leaves
½   teaspoon salt
¼   teaspoon pepper
¾   cup evaporated skim milk

1.   Heat Crisco Shortening or Crisco Oil in large skillet on medium-high heat.
     Add chicken and garlic. Stir-fry about 5 minutes or until no longer pink in
     center. Transfer to serving dish.
2.   Add broccoli, mushrooms and tomato to skillet. Stir-fry 3 to 5 minutes until
     crisp-tender. Return chicken to skillet to heat. Transfer mixture to large
     serving bowl. Add linguine, Parmesan cheese, basil, salt and pepper. Toss to
     mix. Add milk. Toss. Serve immediately.

6 Servings

315 CALORIES / FAT 10 g (88 CAL or 28% of total calories) / SAT FAT 3 g (8% of total calories) / CARB 20 g /
PROTEIN 37 g / CHOL 75 mg / SODIUM 490 mg

LANA'S CHICKEN SUPREME

6 boneless, skinless chicken breast halves
¾ teaspoon salt
½ teaspoon cayenne pepper
½ cup all-purpose flour
¼ cup Crisco Shortening or Crisco Oil
2 medium yellow onions, chopped
2 cloves garlic, finely chopped
1 medium green bell pepper, coarsely chopped

2 medium ripe tomatoes, coarsely chopped*
2 tablespoons ketchup
1 teaspoon dried thyme leaves
1 bay leaf
1 cup chicken broth, canned or homemade
3 tablespoons chopped fresh parsley
4 cups hot cooked rice (without salt or fat)

1. Cut chicken into 1-inch strips. Combine salt and cayenne pepper. Sprinkle on chicken. Place flour in plastic bag. Add chicken pieces one at a time. Shake to coat lightly.
2. Heat Crisco Shortening or Crisco Oil in large skillet on medium-high heat. Cook and stir chicken until no longer pink. Remove to side dish with slotted spoon.
3. Add onion, garlic and green pepper to skillet. Cook and stir on medium-high heat 3 minutes.
4. Stir in tomatoes, ketchup, thyme, bay leaf and chicken broth. Reduce heat to medium. Cook, uncovered, 10 minutes, stirring occasionally.
5. Add chicken and parsley. Reduce heat. Simmer 5 minutes longer. Remove bay leaf. Serve over hot rice.

6 Servings
*Substitute one can (1-pound) plum tomatoes, drained and coarsely chopped if fresh tomatoes are unavailable.

460 CALORIES / FAT 12 g (108 CAL or 23% of total calories) / SAT FAT 1 g (<5% of total calories) / CARB 54 g / PROTEIN 33 g / CHOL 65 mg / SODIUM 540 mg

Women in the Military

Dr. Height and I had a long talk over dessert once about her role in helping women in the armed services. She told me that right after World War II, she was invited by General George Marshall to serve on a committee. She was the first Black woman to be asked to serve on what was called the Defense Advisory Committee on Women in the Services. Her service on the committee lasted three or four years and she was able to look as issues ranging from food and shelter to racism and promotions. Dr. Height went to the Pentagon and to bases all over the country… she even went to Camp Lejeune.
The committee was assigned the task of finding out what women in all branches of the service felt about their treatment. The committee looked at health issues, the way meals were planned for male servicemen and not for female soldiers. Dr. Height told me her committee also had to consider housing so when they visited bases, they stayed in the barracks where the young women in the services lived. This gave the committee first

(continued)

RAINBOW CHICKEN 'N VEGGIE SPAGHETTI

½ teaspoon chicken flavor instant bouillon granules
½ cup boiling water
2 tablespoons Crisco Shortening or Crisco Oil
2 medium onions, peeled and sliced into thin rings
2 cloves garlic, minced
1 teaspoon dried oregano leaves
½ teaspoon dried thyme leaves
¼ teaspoon pepper
4 boneless, skinless chicken breast halves, cut into 1¼-inch squares (about 1 pound)
4 medium carrots, peeled and cut crosswise into ⅛-inch thick slices
1 pound zucchini, cut crosswise into ¼-inch thick slices
½ pound mushrooms, cut in half lengthwise (optional)
1 pound spaghetti, cooked (without salt or fat)
¼ cup grated Parmesan cheese

1. Dissolve bouillon in boiling water.
2. Heat Crisco Shortening or Crisco Oil in large skillet on high heat. Stir in onions, garlic, oregano, thyme and pepper. Add chicken. Stir-fry 2 to 3 minutes or until center of chicken is no longer pink. Reduce heat to low. Stir in carrots, zucchini, mushrooms (if used) and bouillon. Cover. Simmer 3 minutes. Stir occasionally.
5. Toss chicken-vegetable mixture and spaghetti with cheese. Serve immediately.

6 Servings

295 CALORIES / FAT 8 g (68 CAL or 23% of total calories) / SAT FAT 1 g (<5% of total calories) / CARB 33 g / PROTEIN 25 g / CHOL 45 mg / SODIUM 210 mg

SKILLET CHICKEN & MACARONI SALAD

3 tablespoons Crisco Shortening or Crisco Oil, divided
¾ pound fresh green beans, cut into 1-inch pieces
½ teaspoon salt, divided
¼ cup water
4 boneless, skinless chicken breast halves, cut into ¾-inch cubes (about 1 pound)
½ teaspoon ground ginger
8 ounces (3 cups) uncooked medium shell macaroni, cooked (without salt or fat)
1 can (15¼ to 19 ounces) red kidney beans, drained
2 tablespoons soy sauce
2 tablespoons lime juice

1. Heat one tablespoon Crisco Shortening or Crisco Oil in large skillet on medium-high heat. Add green beans and ¼ teaspoon salt. Stir-fry until beans are coated. Add water. Stir-fry until beans are crisp-tender. Remove from skillet.
2. Heat remaining 2 tablespoons Crisco Shortening or Crisco Oil in skillet. Add chicken, ginger and remaining ¼ teaspoon salt. Stir-fry about 4 minutes or until no longer pink in center. Remove from heat. Stir in macaroni, kidney beans, green beans, soy sauce and lime juice. Stir until well blended and heated through. Serve warm.

6 Servings

435 CALORIES / FAT 9 g (81 CAL or 19% of total calories) / SAT FAT <1 g (<5% of total calories) / CARB 58 g / PROTEIN 30 g / CHOL 45 mg / SODIUM 885 mg

(continued)

hand experience with the problems in housing. She told me that what impressed her most about the entire experience was how decisions were made. Her committee would make suggestions and see the results much more quickly than they expected. Dr. Height found that influencing policy in the military had far reaching consequences. I look forward to talking to her very soon about her views on women in combat.

J. Gary Cooper
Major General, USMCR
(Retired)
Assistant Secretary of the Air Force for Manpower, Reserve Affairs, Installations and Environment

AUNT BEE'S HOT STUFF CHICKEN

1   pound boneless, skinless chicken breast, cut into 1 X 1-inch pieces
1   tablespoon cornstarch
2   teaspoons Crisco Shortening or Crisco Oil
3   tablespoons chopped green onions
2   cloves garlic, minced

¼   to 1½ teaspoons crushed red pepper
¼   to ½ teaspoon ground ginger
2   tablespoons wine vinegar
2   tablespoons soy sauce
2   teaspoons sugar
⅓   cup unsalted dry roasted peanuts
4   cups hot cooked rice (without salt or fat)

1. Combine chicken and cornstarch in small bowl. Toss to coat.
2. Heat Crisco Shortening or Crisco Oil in large skillet or wok on medium-high heat. Add chicken. Stir-fry 5 to 7 minutes or until center is no longer pink. Remove from skillet.
3. Add onions, garlic, crushed red pepper and ginger. Stir-fry 15 seconds. Remove from heat.
4. Combine vinegar, soy sauce and sugar. Stir well. Add to skillet. Return chicken to skillet. Stir until chicken is coated with mixture. Stir in peanuts. Return to heat to warm. Serve over rice.

4 Servings

500 CALORIES / FAT 10 g (92 CAL or 19% of total calories) / SAT FAT 2 g (<5% of total calories) / CARB 65 g / PROTEIN 36 g / CHOL 65 mg / SODIUM 595 mg

"GARLICKY" CHICKEN 'N RICE

1   2½-pound broiler-fryer chicken, skin removed
6   cups water
1   tablespoon Crisco Oil
1¾   cups chopped celery

1¼   cups chopped carrot
1   medium onion, chopped
5   cloves garlic, minced
2   cups uncooked brown rice
   Salt and pepper (optional)

1. Place chicken in large saucepan. Add water. Simmer, covered, until tender. Remove from heat. Remove chicken from broth. Reserve broth. Cool chicken enough to remove from bones. Cut into bite-size pieces.
2. Measure 4½ cups broth. Add water if needed. Place broth and chicken back in large pan.
3. Heat Crisco Oil in large skillet on medium heat. Add celery, carrot, onion and garlic. Sauté until slightly softened. Add to chicken and broth. Bring to a boil. Add rice. Reduce heat to low. Cover. Cook 30 to 50 minutes or until rice is tender. Season with salt and pepper, if desired.

6 Servings

505 CALORIES / FAT 10 g (90 CAL or 18% of total calories) / SAT FAT 2 g (<5% of total calories) / CARB 54 g / PROTEIN 46 g / CHOL 135 mg / SODIUM 200 mg

CHICKEN JERUSALEM

3 tablespoons olive oil
2 pounds frying chicken, skinned, cut in serving pieces
½ cup all-purpose flour
½ cup Sherry wine
3 artichoke bottoms, quartered
1 cup sliced mushrooms
⅛ teaspoon salt
⅛ teaspoon white pepper
1 cup coffee cream
  Nutmeg
3⅓ cups cooked rice (without salt or fat)
  Chopped parsley

1. Heat olive oil in large skillet on medium heat.
2. Coat chicken with flour. Sauté until browned, about 15 minutes. Add wine, artichokes, mushrooms, salt and pepper. Reduce heat to low. Cover and simmer about 15 minutes or until chicken is tender.
3. Place coffee cream in small saucepan on very low heat. Bring to a simmer. Season with nutmeg. Pour over chicken. Serve with rice. Garnish with parsley.

5 servings

680 CALORIES / FAT 23 g (210 CAL or 31% of total calories) / SAT FAT 8 g (10% of total calories) / CARB 61 g / PROTEIN 47 g / CHOL 155 mg / SODIUM 225 mg

**Adaptation from Recipe
J. B. Thomas, CEO
Edgemont Country Club**

Sharing a Good Meal with Dr. Dorothy Height

There is something about sharing a good meal with good friends. Beyond the culinary aspect, the setting produces the ingredients of Fellowship, a sense of Well Being, and promotes Family Spirit. For the past several years, my family has had the pleasure of hosting Dr. Dorothy Height and members of the "NCNW/Black Family Reunion Celebration " during their annual visits to Cincinnati. On each occasion, Dr. Height absolutely mesmerized us with her clear and concise recollections from her wonderful treasure chest of experiences. These anecdotes range from meetings with presidents and world leaders to her work with Dr. Bethune and Dr. King and even back to her childhood.
I guess the best "Dr. Height stories" are those that grew out of her childhood. My favorite of all centers on her role as organizer, booking agent and soloist for the "Jolly Three" -- a versatile and "awesome" trio. While I will always cherish the opportunities that I have had to share Dr. Height's experiences, her stories about her youth are truly special to me. There is always that certain smile and twinkle in her eye when she recalls those special times.

O. LaVelle Bond

A Woman of Vision

From the moment I met Dorothy Height, I knew I had come into contact with one of the superior minds of our era. There was a piercing understanding which showed from her bright, gleaming eyes and a forthright "knowing" which emanated from her measured gestures. Her aura is one of being at home and in touch with our space and time. After chatting casually about current events, we discussed the photography of Brian Lanker, a New York photographer who presented, with panache, a study of women of color who through their careers have added to the well-being of our society. His work appeared in *I Dream A World*. Dorothy Height was one of the women presented. She related in great detail how this photographer of the spirit was able to come very close to showing hers to all of us. Photography is one of the pleasures of my spare time and I am always interested in knowing how souls are captured on photographic printing paper.
Ms. Height said Mr. Lanker chose daybreak to photograph her in Lincoln Park in front of the statue of Mary McLeod Bethune

(continued)

NUTTY SPICED CHICKEN SKILLET

3   tablespoons Crisco Oil, divided
5   teaspoons soy sauce, divided
3   teaspoons cornstarch, divided
¼   to ½ teaspoon dried crushed red pepper
4   boneless, skinless chicken breast halves, cut into
     1-inch pieces (about 1 pound)
½   cup boiling water
½   teaspoon chicken flavor instant bouillon granules
½   teaspoon ginger
1   medium onion, cut into 1-inch pieces
1   clove garlic, minced
1   red bell pepper, cut into 1-inch pieces (optional)
½   pound fresh broccoli, cut into 1-inch pieces
¼   cup coarsely chopped walnuts
2⅔   cups hot cooked rice (without salt or fat)

1. Combine one tablespoon Crisco Oil, 2 teaspoons soy sauce, one teaspoon cornstarch and red pepper flakes in medium bowl. Add chicken. Stir to coat. Refrigerate 30 minutes.
2. Combine water and bouillon in small bowl. Stir until granules are dissolved. Add ginger, remaining 3 teaspoons soy sauce and remaining 2 teaspoons cornstarch.
3. Heat one tablespoon Crisco Oil in large skillet or wok on medium-high heat. Add onion, garlic, red bell pepper and broccoli. Stir-fry until crisp-tender. Remove to serving dish.
4. Heat remaining one tablespoon Crisco Oil in skillet. Add chicken mixture. Stir-fry until chicken is no longer pink in center.
5. Return vegetables to skillet. Add bouillon mixture. Cook and stir until thickened. Stir in nuts. Serve with rice.

4 Servings

480 CALORIES / FAT 17 g (153 CAL or 32% of total calories) / SAT FAT 2 g (<5% of total calories) / CARB 48 g / PROTEIN 34 g / CHOL 65 mg / SODIUM 635 mg

FAVORITE BRUNSWICK STEW

3   whole chicken breasts, split and skinned
3   tablespoons Crisco Shortening or Crisco Oil
2   onions, chopped
3   cups water
3   tomatoes, peeled and quartered
½   cup sherry wine
2   teaspoons hot pepper sauce
1   pound fresh lima beans
    Kernels cut from 3 ears of corn
½   cup sliced okra
½   cup bread crumbs
1   garlic clove, minced
1   tablespoon minced parsley
1   teaspoon chopped fresh or freeze dried chives
¼   teaspoons salt
¼   teaspoon black pepper
¼   teaspoon dried oregano leaves
¼   teaspoon dill seed

1. Heat Crisco Oil or Crisco Shortening in Dutch oven
    on medium heat. Add chicken breasts brown on both
    sides. Remove chicken. Add onions. Sauté. Return
    chicken to Dutch oven. Add water, tomatoes, sherry
    and hot pepper sauce. Cover. Cook on low heat for
    30 minutes. Remove chicken. Remove chicken from
    bone. Return chicken to Dutch oven.
2. Add lima beans, corn and okra. Simmer one hour.
3. Add bread crumbs, garlic, parsley, chives, salt,
    pepper, oregano and dill seed. Simmer 30 minutes.

8 Servings

310 CALORIES / FAT 8 g (73 CAL or 23% of total calories) / SAT FAT 2 g (6% of total calories) / CARB 30 g / PROTEIN 26 g / CHOL 50 mg / SODIUM 190 mg

(continued)

and of children dancing. She arose at a very early hour so that Mr. Lanker could capture the sun in the perfect juxtaposition so as to capture the perfect shadow, on the perfect face of a legend of our time. I will not forget the sight of her face in the photograph or at our meeting. It was my pleasure.

**Brenda Devroaux
National Institutes of
Health**

HERITAGE
RECIPE

KWANZAA JOLLOF RICE

2	tablespoons plus 1½ teaspoons Crisco Oil, divided
1½	pounds boneless, skinless chicken breast
3	medium onions, chopped
2	small green bell peppers, chopped
½	pound raw shrimp, shelled and deveined
6	cups water
¾	cup chopped carrots
¾	cup cut green beans
¾	cup peas
3	medium tomatoes, cut up
1	teaspoon salt
½	teaspoon black pepper
½	teaspoon cayenne pepper
1	sprig thyme, crushed, or 1 teaspoon dried
1½	cups uncooked long-grain rice
¼	cup tomato paste

1. Heat 2 tablespoons Crisco Oil in stock pot or kettle. Brown chicken. Add onions and green peppers. Cook on medium heat 5 to 10 minutes.
2. Sauté shrimp in remaining 1½ teaspoons oil in small skillet.
3. Bring 6 cups water to a boil in large saucepan. Add carrots, green beans and peas. Cook about 5 minutes.
4. Drain vegetables, reserving 3 cups cooking liquid. Add to chicken in stock pot along with shrimp, tomatoes, salt, black pepper, cayenne and thyme. Reduce heat to low. Simmer 5 minutes.
5. Combine rice and tomato paste in bowl. Stir until rice is coated. Stir into stock pot. Add small amounts of water as needed to prevent sticking. Cook about 20 minutes or until chicken, vegetables and rice are tender.

6 Servings

445 CALORIES / FAT 9 g (78 CAL or 18% of total calories) / SAT FAT 1 g (<5% of total calories) / CARB 50 g / PROTEIN 40 g / CHOL 125 mg / SODIUM 590 mg

HERITAGE
RECIPE

Leave No One Behind

I remember several years ago, as concern about black men was coming to the forefront of public attention, discussing with Dorothy a desire to form a national organization of black males similar to the National Council of Negro Women. Dorothy came to a small meeting of interested men to support and encourage us in forming such a group. She felt the the NCNW had played a very significant role for black women in America, particularly in their participation in the civil rights movement and in the recognition they bestowed on black female leadership.

Ms. Height spoke of some of the pitfalls and jealousies that might develop among competing male groups if a national organization appeared. For that reason, she felt that forming networks and coalitions under the umbrella of a "council" would be appropriate. Dorothy attended the first national conference of African-American men as a keynote speaker. At the conclusion of the conference, the National Council of African-American Men, Incorporated was established. Thus, Ms. Height has not

(continued)

JAMAICAN JERKED CHICKEN

1½ cups soy sauce
1 cup freshly squeezed lime juice
1 cup thinly sliced fresh ginger
½ cup chopped fresh garlic
4 green onions, trimmed and roughly cut
2 jalapeño peppers, seeded
1 cup apple cider vinegar
½ to ¾ cup dark brown sugar
½ cup Crisco Oil
¼ cup ground allspice
2 tablespoons light molasses
2 teaspoons cinnamon
2 teaspoons freshly chopped thyme (or 1 teaspoon dried)
1 teaspoon pepper
½ teaspoon ground nutmeg
½ teaspoon ground cloves
16 to 24 chicken thighs (about 6 pounds) with skin removed

1. Place soy sauce, lime juice, ginger, garlic, onions and peppers in food processor bowl. Puree until smooth.
2. Transfer to mixing bowl. Stir in vinegar, brown sugar, Crisco Oil, allspice, molasses, cinnamon, thyme, pepper, nutmeg and cloves. Let stand 30 minutes.
3. Adjust seasonings with soy sauce, lime juice and brown sugar. Marinade should be spicy, gingery and slightly sweet and sour.
4. Place chicken in large heavy resealable plastic bag. Pour marinade over chicken. Seal bag. Refrigerate two days. Turn bag over occasionally.
5. Remove chicken from marinade. Grill or broil. Turn frequently to avoid charring.

12 Servings

390 CALORIES / FAT 9 g (79 CAL or 20% of total calories) / SAT FAT 2 g (<5% of total calories) / CARB 45 g / PROTEIN 31 g / CHOL 115 mg / SODIUM 795 mg

(continued)

only demonstrated herself to be a leader among black women but also a leader in encouraging black male empowerment.

Alvin Poussaint, MD
Harvard Medical School
Department of Psychiatry

Putting An End to the Slave Markets

Whenever you sit down to a meal with Dr. Height, you can be sure you'll get some history with your meal. We were at a luncheon in New York one afternoon when she told me about the "slave markets" which flourished all over the City after the Depression. Women were leaving the South in droves looking for work. They would gather on street corners and white people would drive by and pick out domestic workers, take them home and work them nearly to death for very low wages, if they paid them at all.

Dr. Height told me the women were treated horribly, taken advantage of and even abused. Her work with the YWCA got her involved in trying to get a law passed about the "slave markets". Unfortunately, the City Council refused to believe that such a thing existed, even though Dr. Height and others had stood with the women, witnessed what happened and talked to women who had been mistreated. I asked her if the failure to get a law passed had frustrated her. She told me that it had made her even more determined to tackle big problems in small pieces

(continued)

ORANGE MUSTARD GLAZED CHICKEN BREASTS

Marinade
- ⅓ cup Crisco Oil
- ¼ cup lemon juice
- 2 tablespoons orange juice

- 6 boneless, skinless chicken breast halves (about 1½ pounds)

Glaze
- ¼ cup firmly packed light brown sugar
- 2 tablespoons orange marmalade
- ⅛ teaspoon dry mustard
  Salt and pepper (optional)

Topping
- 1 can (11 ounces) Mandarin orange segments

1. For marinade, combine Crisco Oil, lemon juice and orange juice in shallow baking dish. Stir well. Place chicken in marinade. Turn to coat. Refrigerate 30 minutes. Turn once.
2. For glaze, combine brown sugar, marmalade and dry mustard. Stir until well blended.
3. For topping, heat orange segments in small saucepan on low heat.
4. Heat broiler or prepare grill.
5. Remove chicken from marinade. Broil or grill 3 to 5 minutes per side until center is no longer pink. Spread glaze on chicken. Broil until glaze is bubbly and melts. Salt and pepper, if desired. Transfer to serving plate.
6. Drain orange segments. Spoon over chicken breasts.

6 Servings

220 CALORIES / FAT 6 g (50 CAL or 23% of total calories) / SAT FAT 1 g (<5% of total calories) / CARB 16 g / PROTEIN 26 g / CHOL 65 mg / SODIUM 80 mg

ZESTY CARIBBEAN CHICKEN BREAST

¼ cup Crisco Oil
1 teaspoon grated lemon peel
¼ cup lemon juice
1 tablespoon paprika
1 tablespoon honey
1 teaspoon garlic salt
1 teaspoon ginger
1 teaspoon dried oregano leaves
¼ teaspoon hot pepper sauce
6 boneless, skinless chicken breast halves (about 1½ pounds)
Lemon slices (optional)
Parsley sprigs (optional)

1. Combine Crisco Oil, lemon peel, lemon juice, paprika, honey, garlic salt, ginger, oregano and hot pepper sauce in shallow baking dish. Stir well. Add chicken. Turn to coat. Refrigerate 30 minutes or up to 4 hours. Turn occasionally.
2. Heat broiler or prepare grill.
3. Remove chicken from marinade. Broil or grill 3 to 5 minutes per side or until center is no longer pink. Garnish with lemon slices and parsley, if desired.

6 Servings

170 CALORIES / FAT 6 g (51 CAL or 30% of total calories) / SAT FAT 1 g (<5% of total calories) / CARB 2 g / PROTEIN 26 g / CHOL 65 mg / SODIUM 230 mg

(continued)

and solve them step by step. That idea made an impression on me that I have never forgotten.

Leslie Gaffney, Director, Community Affairs SONY Corporation of America

No More Asterisks For Us

When Dorothy Height was hospitalized in 1985 for a broken hip, we shared a standard bedside meal... a carton of milk and Jello pudding. Not exactly the meal someone of Dr. Height's stature or talent might create or enjoy. But she was good-natured about the surroundings and the menu. Urged to talk about how black people had been treated by the policy makers of her times, she remembered a story that became her litmus test. "I used to hear the men in World War II say that on all the lists of names in the Army, beside all those who were black they put an asterisk. They said that every once in a while they would get all the asterisks together. That's what we have been so often," she said. She paused. The metaphor of being an asterisk, the afterthought of a broader agenda, was disheartening. But not for long. It became a challenge. "If the reports are about what is happening to the family, then there's an asterisk about the black family. When the report is about women, there's an asterisk about black women. We don't want and we will not be asterisks. We will define ourselves."

Jacqueline Trescott
The Washington Post

COUNTRY CHICKEN & GRAVY

Microwave

Chicken
- ½ teaspoon paprika
- ½ teaspoon poultry seasoning
- ¼ teaspoon dried thyme leaves
- ¼ teaspoon salt
- ¼ teaspoon pepper
- 1½ pounds boneless, skinless chicken breast halves
- 1½ cups corn flakes, crushed to yield ½ cup

Creamy Gravy
- 1 tablespoon Crisco Oil
- 1 tablespoon all-purpose flour
- ½ cup skim milk
- ¼ cup condensed chicken broth, undiluted
- ¼ teaspoon salt
- ⅛ teaspoon pepper
- 2 tablespoons chopped fresh chives

1. For chicken, combine paprika, poultry seasoning, thyme, salt and pepper. Sprinkle half of mixture over chicken. Turn chicken over. Sprinkle with remaining seasoning mixture. Coat with corn flakes.
2. Place in 11¾ X 7½-inch glass dish with thickest portions toward outside of dish. Cover with waxed paper. Microwave at HIGH for 8 minutes or until chicken is no longer pink in center, rotating dish half turn after 4 minutes. Remove chicken to serving platter. Keep warm.
3. For gravy, combine Crisco Oil and flour in 4-cup glass measure. Stir until smooth. Add milk and broth gradually. Stir until smooth.
4. Microwave at HIGH for 3 to 5 minutes or until thickened, stirring once. Stir in salt, pepper and chives. Spoon over chicken.

6 Servings

185 CALORIES / FAT 4 g (36 CAL or 19% of total calories) / SAT FAT <1 g (<5% of total calories) / CARB 7 g / PROTEIN 28 g / CHOL 65 mg / SODIUM 385 mg

SOUTHERN STYLE CHICKEN & DUMPLINGS

Microwave

Chicken Mixture

1 cup thinly sliced carrots
1 cup peeled, cubed red potato
½ cup chopped onion
½ cup sliced celery
¼ teaspoon salt

1 cup canned condensed chicken broth
1¼ pounds boneless, skinless chicken breast halves
2 tablespoons all-purpose flour
½ cup water

Dumplings

1 cup all-purpose flour
2 teaspoons dried parsley flakes
1 teaspoon baking powder
½ teaspoon dried thyme leaves

¼ teaspoon salt
⅓ cup plus 1 tablespoon buttermilk
2 tablespoons Crisco Oil

1. For chicken mixture, combine carrots, potato, onion, celery and salt in 2-quart round casserole or baking dish. Pour broth over top. Arrange chicken on vegetables with thickest part towards outside of dish. Cover with waxed paper.
2. Microwave at HIGH for 12 minutes or until chicken is tender. Rotate dish half turn every 4 minutes. Turn chicken over. Microwave 2 minutes. Remove chicken.
3. Recover vegetables. Microwave at HIGH for 3 minutes.
4. Combine flour and water. Stir well. Stir into vegetables. Recover. Microwave at (HIGH) 4 minutes, stirring after 2 minutes.
5. Chop chicken. Stir into vegetables.
6. For dumplings, combine flour, parsley flakes, baking powder, thyme and salt. Add buttermilk and Crisco Oil all at once. Stir with fork, just until moistened and dough forms. Drop from spoon into 6 mounds around edge of chicken-vegetable mixture. Recover.
7. Microwave at HIGH for 4 minutes, rotating dish half turn after 2 minutes. Let stand, covered, 5 minutes.

6 Servings

310 CALORIES / FAT 7 g (63 CAL or 20% of total calories) / SAT FAT 1 g (<5% of total calories) / CARB 33 g / PROTEIN 28 g / CHOL 55 mg / SODIUM 600 mg

CHICKEN PARMESAN ON COUNTRY HAM

I Leave You Racial Dignity

It was 1942 and like most of the girls who worked in Washington, DC in the war service, I had never really lived on my own. So naturally enough, I had always eaten Christmas dinner with my family. But this year was different. There was no way to travel all the way to my home and get back to work even if I had the money to make the trip, which I surely did not. So I resigned myself to a lonely holiday. Then out of the blue, I received a wondrous invitation to have dinner with Mrs. Eleanor Roosevelt. For a little country girl that was the most exciting thing that had ever happened to me. The catch was that even with the invitation, you still had to apply to attend the meal because only 300 girls could participate. So I put in my bid right away and hoped for the best. I was one of the lucky ones selected to go!
It was a most unusual gathering for that day and age because it was for everybody — colored and white girls alike! We all came to the YWCA and I tell you, there was no more dressed up group of girls in the entire city. I had put on my Sunday

(continued)

1   cup dry bread crumbs
½   cup Parmesan cheese
⅛   teaspoon pepper
6   boneless, skinless chicken breast halves
1   cup skim milk
6   small slices country ham or ham steak (about 2 ounces each)
2   tablespoons margarine
1   clove garlic, minced

1.   Heat oven to 400°. Line 13 X 9 X 2-inch pan with foil.
2.   Combine crumbs, cheese and pepper.
3.   Dip chicken in skim milk. Coat with crumb mixture.
4.   Place ham in pan. Top with chicken.
5.   Melt margarine in small saucepan on medium heat. Add garlic. Sauté until lightly browned. Sprinkle over chicken.
6.   Bake at 400° for 30 minutes or until chicken is no longer pink in center.

6 servings

345 CALORIES / FAT 11 g (100 CAL or 29% of total calories) / SAT FAT 4 g (10% of total calories) / CARB 13 g / PROTEIN 46 g / CHOL 105 mg / SODIUM 1120 mg

MEAT ROLL-UPS

Roll-Ups
- 1 pound ground beef round
- ¼ cup water
- 1 teaspoon salt, divided
- Pepper
- 2 cups fine dry bread crumbs
- 2 tablespoons minced onion
- 1 tablespoon melted margarine
- ½ teaspoon poultry seasoning
- Hot water

Vegetable Sauce
- 2 cups canned tomatoes
- ½ cup chopped green bell pepper
- ½ cup chopped celery
- ¼ cup chopped onion
- Salt and pepper

1. Heat oven to 375°. Grease 13 X 9 X 2-inch baking dish.
2. For roll-ups, combine meat, ¼ cup water, ½ teaspoon salt and pepper. Mix well. Divide meat mixture into 6 portions. Place one on waxed paper. Cover with waxed paper. Press into 5 X 5-inch squares. Repeat.
3. Combine bread crumbs, onion, melted margarine, poultry seasoning and remaining ½ teaspoon salt, and enough hot water to moisten. Spread spoonful of stuffing on each meat square. Roll up. Place in baking dish seam side down.
4. Bake at 375° for 45 minutes.
5. For vegetable sauce, combine undrained tomatoes, green pepper, celery, onion, salt and pepper in large saucepan. Heat to boiling. Reduce heat. Simmer 30 minutes. Serve hot over meat roll-ups.

6 servings

315 CALORIES / FAT 9 g (85 CAL or 27% of total calories) / SAT FAT 3 g (9% of total calories) / CARB 30 g / PROTEIN 27 g / CHOL 65 mg / SODIUM 725 mg

(continued)
best, hat and gloves and the nicest dress I owned. Mrs. Roosevelt came by and greeted all of us. There were girls assigned to be roving reporters who went from table to table asking all of us where we were from and how it felt to have dinner with the wife of the President of the United States. We were all just as giddy as geese at our good fortune. I never shall forget that meal. It was served family style so we could all serve ourselves at the table and eat just as much as we wanted.

We had turkey and ham and dressing and sweet potatoes with meringue on top and stewed vegetables and the best bread I had ever tasted. No one had butter during the war but even the margarine tasted good that day. What made it even more impressive was that 200 other girls had come just for the tomato juice cocktail hour before the dinner and while we ate, they sat up in the balcony and watched as happy as you please. I never realized then that the meal was historic. I just knew that it was great fun and so exciting!

It was only in later years when I became active with the National Council of Negro Women that I learned the YWCA was only

(continued)

HOME PRIDE MEAT LOAF

2 teaspoons Crisco Oil
¼ cup chopped onion
1½ pounds ground beef round
1 cup quick oats (not instant or old fashioned)
1 cup tomato juice
½ cup ketchup or barbecue sauce, divided
1 egg white
1 teaspoon Worcestershire sauce
¼ teaspoon salt
¼ teaspoon pepper
¼ teaspoon garlic salt

1. Heat oven to 350°.
2. Heat Crisco Oil in small skillet on medium heat. Add onion. Sauté until softened.
3. Combine onion, meat, oats, tomato juice, ¼ cup ketchup, egg white, Worcestershire sauce, salt, pepper and garlic salt. Stir until well blended. Press into 8½ X 4½ X 2½-inch loaf pan (or shape into loaf). Turn out into larger baking pan.
4. Bake at 350° for 50 minutes. Remove from oven. Spread remaining ¼ cup ketchup over top. Return to oven. Bake 10 minutes.
5. Remove from oven. Let stand 5 minutes. Place on serving plate. Slice. Serve.

8 Servings

240 CALORIES / FAT 9 g (78 CAL or 32% of total calories) / SAT FAT 3 g (10% of total calories) / CARB 13 g / PROTEIN 27 g / CHOL 70 mg / SODIUM 495 mg

(continued)

the second place in all of Washington, DC to serve people of both races. I also learned later that not only had I shared Christmas dinner with Mrs. Roosevelt, I had also shared a very special meal with someone who became an important part of my life, Dorothy Height. It was just like her to get something big and important like that off the ground and never take a bit of credit for it.

Mildred Speights

CHEESY TOMATO & BEEF CASSEROLE

1   tablespoon Crisco Shortening or Crisco Oil
1   cup chopped celery
1   cup chopped onion
1   medium green bell pepper, chopped
1   pound ground beef round
1   can (14½ ounces) Italian style stewed tomatoes
1   can (8 ounces) tomato sauce
1   can (6 ounces) tomato paste
1   cup water
1   bay leaf
1½ teaspoons dried basil leaves
1¼ teaspoons salt
¼   teaspoon pepper
1   package (12 ounces) cholesterol free, yolk free
    noodle style pasta, cooked (without salt or fat)
½   cup dry fine bread crumbs
1   cup (4 ounces) shredded ⅓ less fat sharp Cheddar
    cheese

1. Heat oven to 375°. Oil 12½ X 8½-inch baking dish.
2. Heat Crisco Shortening or Crisco Oil in large skillet on
    medium heat. Add celery, onion and green pepper.
    Sauté until softened but not browned. Push veg-
    etables to one side of skillet. Add meat. Sauté until
    browned. Add undrained tomatoes, tomato sauce,
    tomato paste, water, bay leaf, basil, salt and pepper.
    Reduce heat. Simmer 5 minutes. Remove bay leaf.
3. Place noodles in casserole. Spoon meat mixture over
    noodles. Sprinkle bread crumbs and cheese over top.
4. Bake at 375° for 15 to 20 minutes or until cheese
    melts.

8 Servings

410 CALORIES / FAT 10 g (93 CAL or 23% of total calories) / SAT FAT 3 g (8% of total calories) / CARB 49 g / PROTEIN 28 g / CHOL 60 mg / SODIUM 935 mg

We Worked All Hours

Once, when Dr. Height was preparing for her national convention, we talked over a late night snack about her work with Mrs. Bethune. She told me, "Many a night I would finish my job at the Phyliss Wheatley Y at Ninth and Rhode Island and walk up to 9th and Westminster where Mrs. Bethune lived with the Smith family. I was the first volunteer executive director for the National Council of Negro Women then. It would be 10:30 or 11 o'clock at night by the time I would get there and we'd work until one or two o'clock in the morning and then I'd walk back home. That shows you how the streets have changed since then. But I learned an important lesson. I'm not an AM or a PM person. I'm a whenever I need to be person. Thanks to Mrs. Bethune, I can work at all hours."

**Roseline McKinney
Executive Director, Delta Sigma Theta Sorority**

CLASSIC MEAT LASAGNA

A Delta Pearl

Dr. Height and I shared a soul food meal during the dedication of AfricaTown in Prichard, Alabama when I was 1st Vice President of Delta Sigma Theta Sorority. It was in the mid eighties and although I had known about Dr. Height all my life, I had never really had the opportunity to talk with her in such an informal and personable manner. It was a delightfully unforgettable meal. Our conversation was wide ranging. She has the wonderful ability to make you feel as if you are old friends right away, so of course I asked her about her Delta involvement. She told me she had wanted to be a Delta since she was a child. There were several women from Pittsburgh who used to go to her hometown of Rankin and work with the little black girls there. These women made such an impression on Dr. Height that she decided when she went to college, she just had to be a Delta. But there was not an undergraduate chapter at NYU when she was a student there and her efforts to organize one were unsuccessful. Thus, she later became a member of the Rho City

(continued)

1 cup chopped onion
3 cloves garlic, minced
2 tablespoons Crisco Shortening or Crisco Oil
1 pound ground beef round
2 cans (14½ ounces each) no salt added stewed tomatoes
1 can (6 ounces) no salt added tomato paste
2 teaspoons dried basil leaves
1 teaspoon dried oregano leaves
½ teaspoon sugar
¼ teaspoon pepper
2 cups lowfat (1%) cottage cheese
½ cup grated Parmesan cheese, divided
¼ cup chopped fresh parsley
8 ounces wide lasagna noodles
1 cup (4 ounces) shredded low moisture part-skim mozzarella cheese, divided

1. Sauté onion and garlic in Crisco Shortening or Crisco Oil in large skillet on medium heat until soft. Push to one side of skillet. Add meat. Crumble and cook. Drain, if necessary. Add tomatoes. Break into smaller pieces. Add tomato paste, basil, oregano, sugar and pepper. Simmer 30 minutes.
2. Combine cottage cheese, ¼ cup Parmesan cheese and parsley in separate bowl.
3. Cook lasagna noodles 7 minutes in unsalted boiling water. Drain well.
4. Heat oven to 350°.
5. Place thin layer of meat sauce in 13 X 9 X 2-inch pan. Add in layers half the noodles, half the cottage cheese mixture, 2 tablespoons Parmesan cheese, ⅓ cup mozzarella and thin layer of sauce. Repeat noodle and cheese layers. Top with remaining sauce and remaining ⅓ cup mozzarella.
6. Bake at 350° for 45 minutes. Let stand 15 minutes before serving. Cut in rectangles about 3 X 4 inches.

12 Servings

245 CALORIES / FAT 7 g (69 CAL or 28% of total calories) / SAT FAT 2 g (8% of total calories) / CARB 24 g / PROTEIN 21 g / CHOL 35 mg / SODIUM 265 mg

MARGO'S STUFFED GREEN PEPPERS

5   green bell peppers
1   tablespoon Crisco Shortening or Crisco Oil
½   cup chopped onion
2   tablespoons diced celery
1   clove garlic, minced
½   pound ground beef round
1   cup cooked long grain rice (without salt or fat)
1   can (8 ounces) tomato sauce
1   jar (2-½ ounces) sliced mushrooms, drained, chopped
1   tablespoon Worcestershire sauce
1½ teaspoons Italian herb seasoning
¼   teaspoon sugar
⅛   teaspoon salt
⅛   teaspoon pepper

1. Heat oven to 350°.
2. Remove tops and seeds from peppers. Cook in boiling water 5 minutes. Drain upside-down.
3. Heat Crisco Shortening or Crisco Oil in large skillet on medium heat. Add onion, celery and garlic. Sauté until onion is tender. Push to one side of skillet. Add meat. Sauté until browned. Remove from heat.
4. Add rice, tomato sauce, mushrooms, Worcestershire sauce, Italian herb seasoning, sugar, salt and pepper. Stir until well blended. Spoon into green peppers.
5. Place peppers upright in baking dish. Add boiling water to barely cover bottom of dish.
6. Bake at 350° for 30 to 40 minutes or until heated through.

5 Servings

215 CALORIES / FAT 7 g (63 CAL or 29% of total calories) / SAT FAT 2 g (8% of total calories) / CARB 22 g / PROTEIN 16 g / CHOL 35 mg / SODIUM 470 mg

(continued)

Wide Chapter in New York. Dr. Height told me that in the early forties, the National President of Delta, Elsie Austin, invited her to work with a group that was looking at ways to make Greek letter organizations more effective in improving the race. She started thinking about areas of concern and out of that came Delta's Five Point Program Thrust which guides our mission to this day. I relished the story of how Dr. Height became National President. She became a Delta in 1939 and at the convention in 1947, she was elected president. Dr. Height told me the conventions had met in church basements because hotels and convention facilities were all still segregated. When she was elected president after the 1947 meeting in San Antonio, she said, "We have to get Delta out of the basement." Well, as you know, she did just that and the rest is a beautiful history!

**Dr. Yvonne Kennedy
Immediate Past
President, Delta Sigma
Theta Sorority,
Incorporated
President, Bishop State
Community College
House Majority Floor
Leader, Alabama State
Legislature**

SALISBURY STEAK WITH ONIONS & PEPPERS

1 tablespoon Crisco Oil	1 egg white
4 medium onions, sliced	1 teaspoon salt, divided
3 bell peppers (red, green or	¼ teaspoon black pepper, divided
yellow) cut into thin strips	1 tablespoon all-purpose flour
1 pound ground beef round	1 cup water
2 slices white bread, crumbled	⅓ cup ketchup
(about 1¼ cups)	½ teaspoon soy sauce

1. Heat Crisco Oil in large (at least 12-inch) skillet on medium heat. Add onions and bell peppers. Cook and stir until tender. Remove to serving platter. Cover to keep warm.
2. Combine meat, bread crumbs, ½ teaspoon salt and ⅛ teaspoon pepper. Mix in egg white. Shape into four ½-inch thick oval patties.
3. Place patties in same skillet. Cook on low heat on both sides until desired doneness. Transfer to serving platter with onions and peppers. Recover.
4. Stir flour, remaining ½ teaspoon salt and remaining ⅛ teaspoon pepper into skillet. Cook one minute. Add water, ketchup and soy sauce. Cook and stir until mixture thickens. Pour over patties and vegetables.

4 Servings

360 CALORIES / FAT 13 g (117 CAL or 33% of total calories) / SAT FAT 4 g (10% of total calories) / CARB 23 g / PROTEIN 36 g / CHOL 95 mg / SODIUM 980 mg

CHILI CON CARNE

1 tablespoon Crisco Shortening or	1 tablespoon chili powder
Crisco Oil	1 teaspoon salt
1 cup chopped onion	¼ teaspoon pepper
1 cup chopped green bell pepper	Dash hot pepper sauce
1 pound ground beef round	(optional)
1 can (28 ounces) tomatoes	1 can (30 ounces) kidney beans
1 can (8 ounces) tomato sauce	

1. Heat Crisco Shortening or Oil in large saucepan or Dutch oven on medium heat. Add onion and green pepper. Sauté until softened. Add meat. Brown lightly. Stir in undrained tomatoes, tomato sauce, chili powder, salt, pepper and hot pepper sauce, if desired. Bring to a boil. Reduce heat. Simmer 45 minutes.
2. Add undrained kidney beans. Bring to a boil to heat beans.

8 One-Cup Servings

185 CALORIES / FAT 5 g (51 CAL or 28% of total calories) / SAT FAT 1 g (7% of total calories) / CARB 18 g / PROTEIN 17 g / CHOL 35 mg / SODIUM 505 mg

FAMILY FAVORITE SPAGHETTI WITH MEAT SAUCE

1 pound ground beef round
2 tablespoons Crisco Shortening or Crisco Oil
½ cup chopped carrot
½ cup chopped celery
⅓ cup chopped onion
2 cloves garlic, minced
1 can (14½ ounces) no salt added tomatoes
1 can (10¾ ounces) condensed reduced-sodium tomato soup

1 can (6 ounces) no salt added tomato paste
2 teaspoons sugar
1½ teaspoons Italian herb seasoning
1 teaspoon dried basil leaves
¼ teaspoon salt
¼ teaspoon crushed red pepper
1 bay leaf
1 pound spaghetti, cooked (without salt or fat)

1. Heat large skillet on medium-high heat. Add meat. Sauté until browned. Remove meat. Drain and wipe out skillet.
2. Heat Crisco Shortening or Crisco Oil in skillet on medium heat. Add carrot, celery, onion and garlic. Sauté until carrot is tender.
3. Add meat, undrained tomatoes, tomato soup, tomato paste, sugar, Italian herb seasoning, basil, salt, red pepper and bay leaf. Stir to blend. Break apart tomatoes. Bring to a boil. Reduce heat. Cover. Simmer 45 minutes to one hour, stirring occasionally. Remove bay leaf. Serve over spaghetti.

8 Servings

To Microwave:
1. Combine Crisco Shortening or Crisco Oil, carrot, celery, onion, and garlic in large microwave-safe dish. Cover with plastic wrap. Microwave at HIGH for 4 minutes. Stir after 2 minutes. Crumble meat into dish. Cover. Cook at HIGH for 4 minutes. Stir after 2 minutes. Use fork to break up any large meat pieces. Drain.
2. Follow step 3, above, for adding remaining ingredients. Cover. Microwave at HIGH for 8 minutes. Stir every 2 minutes.

285 CALORIES / FAT 9 g (84 CAL or 30% of total calories) / SAT FAT 2 g (7% of total calories) / CARB 31 g / PROTEIN 21 g / CHOL 45 mg / SODIUM 400 mg

FAMILY SWISS STEAK & POTATOES

<table>
<tr><td>½</td><td>cup all-purpose flour</td></tr>
<tr><td>1½</td><td>teaspoons salt</td></tr>
<tr><td>½</td><td>teaspoon pepper</td></tr>
<tr><td>2½</td><td>pounds round steak, cut about 1½ inches thick</td></tr>
<tr><td>2</td><td>tablespoons Crisco Shortening or Crisco Oil</td></tr>
<tr><td>2</td><td>cups sliced onion</td></tr>
<tr><td>1</td><td>can (14½ ounces) tomatoes</td></tr>
<tr><td>½</td><td>cup water</td></tr>
<tr><td>½</td><td>teaspoon dried thyme leaves</td></tr>
<tr><td>1</td><td>bay leaf</td></tr>
<tr><td>8</td><td>medium potatoes, peeled</td></tr>
</table>

1. Combine flour, salt and pepper. Spread half on large cutting board or other flat surface. Place meat on flour. Sprinkle with remaining flour. Pound meat on both sides with mallet or edge of heavy saucer or small plate until all flour is worked in.
2. Heat Crisco Shortening or Crisco Oil in large deep skillet or Dutch oven on medium heat. Add meat. Brown on both sides, adding onion during last 2 to 3 minutes.
3. Add undrained tomatoes, water, thyme and bay leaf. Heat to a boil. Reduce heat. Cover. Simmer one hour 15 minutes. Turn meat over. Add potatoes. Simmer until meat is tender and potatoes are done.
4. Arrange meat and potatoes on platter. Remove bay leaf from sauce. Pour sauce over meat and potatoes.

8 Servings

445 CALORIES / FAT 15 g (138 CAL or 31% of total calories) / SAT FAT 4 g (9% of total calories) / CARB 31 g / PROTEIN 44 g / CHOL 115 mg / SODIUM 580 mg

I Leave You the Challenge of Developing Confidence in One Another

The first time I met Dr. Height, we went down to the Washington waterfront and had a seafood dinner at the Channel Inn. Our conversation revolved around me becoming part of the National Council of Negro Women and working on the Fund for the Future. I was very excited about that relationship but I was even more excited about actually being in the presence of Dr. Height. I felt that I was part of history just listening to her stories about the events that she had been a part of over the years.

I was floored by her enthusiasm and by her extraordinary memory. But the thing that made the greatest impression on me was how much she felt I could do on behalf of NCNW. Her confidence in me inspired me to want to work as she has worked to really help people.

She talked about Mrs. Bethune's emphasis on self sufficiency and about her own plans for taking NCNW into the twenty-first century. She wants to move the Council into a

(continued)

SLOW COOKED BAKED STEW

2   pounds lean beef round, cut into bite size pieces
2   cups chopped onion
2   cups quartered potatoes
2   cups carrot chunks
2   cups large cut celery
1   can (8 ounces) sliced mushrooms, drained
½   teaspoon salt
½   teaspoon pepper
5   tablespoons tapioca
1   teaspoon sugar
3   cups tomato juice

1. Heat oven to 250°.
2. Place meat, onions, potatoes, carrots, celery, mush-
    rooms, salt, pepper, tapioca and sugar in roaster or
    Dutch oven. Pour tomato juice over top. Cover tightly.
3. Bake at 250° for 5 hours.

6 servings

435 CALORIES / FAT 12 g (106 CAL or 24% of total calories) / SAT FAT 4 g (9% of total calories) / CARB 35 g / PROTEIN 48 g / CHOL 125 mg / SODIUM 950 mg

NEW ORLEANS STEW

1   pound ground beef round
1   medium onion, chopped
1½ cups water
1   can (10¾ ounces) golden mushroom soup
1   package (10 ounces) frozen whole kernel corn
½   teaspoon salt
1   teaspoon chili powder
1½ cups quick cooking rice
1   medium tomato, cut in wedges
1   green bell pepper, cut in strips

1. Brown meat in skillet, leaving in large chunks. Add
    onion. Cook until tender. Add water, soup, corn, salt
    and chili powder. Bring to a boil.
2. Stir in rice, tomato and green pepper. Cover. Simmer
    5 minutes. Fluff with fork.

5 servings

485 CALORIES / FAT 11 g (97 CAL or 20% of total calories) / SAT FAT 4 g (7% of total calories) / CARB 63 g / PROTEIN 33 g / CHOL 75 mg / SODIUM 655 mg

(continued)

building that it owns rather than rents. In that headquarters, her dream is to have a Women's Resource Center. She talked about it having an auditorium so that women could gather for meetings and performances and readings. As I listened to her describe the library and the art collections and all the other dreams she has for the Women's Resource Center, I knew that I would do whatever I could to help make those dreams a reality.

Juanita Leonard
Bowie, Maryland

PEPPERS, ONIONS & STEAK OVER RICE

¼ cup Crisco Shortening or Crisco Oil

1½ pounds ½-inch thick lean boneless round steak, cut into 2-inch strips

2 cloves garlic, minced

1 can (14½ ounces) whole tomatoes, drained and diced

1 can (10½ ounces) condensed, double strength, beef broth (bouillon), undiluted, divided*

2 medium green bell peppers, cut into 2 X ¼-inch strips

1 cup sliced green onions and tops

2 tablespoons cornstarch

2 tablespoons soy sauce

4 cups hot cooked rice (without salt or fat)

1. Heat Crisco Shortening or Crisco Oil in large skillet on medium-high heat. Add steak and garlic. Cook until browned.
2. Add tomatoes and one cup beef broth. Cover. Simmer 15 minutes.
3. Stir in green pepper and green onions. Cover. Simmer 5 minutes.
4. Combine remaining beef broth, cornstarch and soy sauce. Stir until well blended. Add to skillet. Stir until thickened. Serve over rice.

6 Servings

Note: 1¼ cups reconstituted beef broth made with double amount of very low sodium beef broth granules may be substituted for beef broth (bouillon).

520 CALORIES / FAT 19 g (171 CAL or 33% of total calories) / SAT FAT 4 g (7% of total calories) / CARB 47 g / PROTEIN 39 g / CHOL 95 mg / SODIUM 900 mg (*535)

WILMA'S SKILLET HASH

2 tablespoons Crisco Oil

3 large potatoes, cut into ½-inch cubes

1 cup chopped green bell pepper

2 medium onions, chopped

2 cloves garlic, minced

½ cup beef broth

3 cups cubed leftover cooked lean beef (1¼ pound)

Hot pepper sauce

Black pepper

1. Heat Crisco Oil in large skillet on medium heat. Add potatoes, onions, green pepper and garlic. Cook on medium heat, turning occasionally until potatoes are tender.
2. Add broth, meat, salt, hot pepper sauce and pepper to taste. Cook until meat is hot.

8 Servings

230 CALORIES / FAT 9 g (81 CAL or 35% of total calories) / SAT FAT 2 g (9% of total calories) / CARB 15 g / PROTEIN 22 g / CHOL 60 mg / SODIUM 100 mg

COUNTRY STEAK WITH GRAVY & BISCUITS

Meat

- 2 pounds thinly sliced, trimmed, round steak, cut in serving pieces
- ½ teaspoon salt
- ¼ teaspoon pepper
- ½ cup all-purpose flour

- 1 tablespoon Crisco Oil
- 1 cup chopped onion
- 1 cup water
- 1 cup low fat buttermilk
- 5 slices (¾ ounce each) fat free process cheese product

Biscuits

- 1¾ cups all-purpose flour
- 2 tablespoons plus 2 teaspoons granulated sugar
- 1 tablespoon baking powder

- ½ teaspoon salt
- ⅔ cup skim milk
- ¼ cup Crisco Oil

1. For meat, season with salt and pepper. Dredge in flour.
2. Heat Crisco Oil in large non-stick skillet on medium heat. Brown meat on both sides. Add onion. Cook until onion is softened but not brown. Add water. Simmer a few minutes until browned bits are loosened from skillet. Stir in buttermilk. Simmer, covered, until meat is almost tender, about one hour.
3. Break cheese into small pieces. Add to juices in skillet. Stir until melted. Serve meat and gravy over biscuits.
4. For biscuits, heat oven to 425°.
5. Combine flour, sugar, baking powder and salt in medium bowl.
6. Combine milk and Crisco Oil. Add to flour mixture. Stir with fork just until dough forms. Place on well floured surface. Pat into circle about one-half inch thick. Cut with floured 2½-inch round cutter. (Press dough scraps together to form some biscuits to make total of 8.) Place on ungreased baking sheet.
7. Bake at 425° for 10 to 12 minutes or until golden brown.

8 Servings

490 CALORIES / FAT 19 g (167 CAL or 34% of total calories) / SAT FAT 4 g (7% of total calories) / CARB 38 g / PROTEIN 41 g / CHOL 95 mg / SODIUM 730 mg

SMOTHERED COUNTRY STEAK

3 pounds beef round steak, pounded
Pepper
½ cup all-purpose flour, divided
3 tablespoons Crisco Shortening or Crisco Oil
2 cups chopped onion
1 cup chopped green bell pepper

2 cloves garlic, minced
2 cups beef broth, divided
1 cup ketchup
½ teaspoon dried thyme leaves
Hot pepper sauce
14 ounces cholesterol free, yolk free noodle style pasta, cooked (without salt or fat)

1. Cut meat into 8 servings. Season with pepper if desired. Dredge with 6 tablespoons flour.
2. Heat Crisco Shortening or Crisco Oil in large skillet on medium heat. Add meat. Brown well on both sides. Remove meat from skillet. Add onions, green pepper and garlic to skillet. Sauté until onions are softened. Add 1½ cups beef broth, ketchup, thyme and season with hot pepper sauce. Stir well. Return meat to skillet. Cover. Simmer until meat is tender.
3. Combine remaining ½ cup broth and 6 tablespoons flour. Stir well. Stir into skillet. Simmer and stir until thickened. Serve over pasta.

8 Servings

630 CALORIES / FAT 20 g (181 CAL or 29% of total calories) / SAT FAT 6 g (8% of total calories) / CARB 53 g / PROTEIN 57 g / CHOL 140 mg / SODIUM 670 mg

SKILLET BEEF WITH CABBAGE & RED POTATOES

6 cups water
8 red skin potatoes, cut in half (3 cups)
1 pound lean beef round, cut in thin pieces
1 large onion, chopped

1 tablespoon garlic, chopped
2 teaspoons salt
¼ tablespoon pepper
½ small head cabbage, coarsely chopped
2 large carrots, cut in thirds

1. Place heavy large skillet on high heat. Add water, potatoes, beef, onion, garlic, salt and pepper. Cook until half the liquid is reduced.
2. Add cabbage and carrots. Cook 35 minutes or until cabbage and carrots are tender.

6 Servings

Adaptation from Recipe
Johnny Rivers, Executive Chef
Walt Disney World

245 CALORIES / FAT 6 g (57 CAL or 23% of total calories) / SAT FAT 2 g (8% of total calories) / CARB 23 g / PROTEIN 25 g / CHOL 60 mg / SODIUM 785 mg

SUNDAY DINNER POT ROAST

1   2½-pound boneless eye of or round beef roast
½   teaspoon salt
¼   teaspoon pepper
2   tablespoons Crisco Shortening or Crisco Oil
1   small onion, coarsely chopped
1   clove garlic, chopped

1   tablespoon Worcestershire sauce
1   teaspoon dried basil leaves
2¼ cups water, divided
2   tablespoons all-purpose flour
1   package (12 ounces) cholesterol free yolk free noodle style pasta, cooked (without salt or fat)

1.   Heat oven to 325°.
2.   Sprinkle roast with salt and pepper. Heat Crisco Shortening or Crisco Oil in ovenproof Dutch oven on medium-high heat. Brown roast on all sides. Add onion and garlic. Cook until slightly softened. Add Worcestershire sauce and basil leaves. Pour one cup water over roast. Cover.
3.   Bake at 325° for 3 hours or until tender. Remove roast. Slice.
4.   Combine flour and remaining 1¼ cups water. Stir until smooth. Stir into pan drippings. Cook and stir until bubbly and thickened. Serve over pot roast and noodles.

6 Servings

630 CALORIES / FAT 20 g (180 CAL or 28% of total calories) / SAT FAT 6 g (8% of total calories) / CARB 46 g / PROTEIN 63 g / CHOL 155 mg / SODIUM 340 mg

FAMILY FAVORITE HAMBURGER CASSEROLE

1   tablespoon Crisco Shortening or Crisco Oil
1   cup chopped onion
1   pound ground beef round
1   package (9 ounces) frozen cut green beans
3   cups frozen southern style hash brown potatoes

1   can (10¾ ounces) zesty tomato soup
½   cup water
1   teaspoon dried basil leaves
¾   teaspoon salt
¼   teaspoon pepper
¼   cup fine dry bread crumbs

1.   Heat oven to 350°. Oil 11¾ X 7½-inch baking dish.
2.   Heat Crisco Shortening or Crisco Oil in large skillet on medium-high heat. Add onion. Sauté until softened. Push to one side of skillet. Add meat. Sauté until browned. Add green beans. Cook and stir about 5 minutes or until thawed. Add potatoes.
3.   Combine tomato soup and water. Stir until well blended. Stir into skillet. Stir in basil, salt and pepper. Spoon into casserole. Sprinkle with bread crumbs.
4.   Bake at 350° for 30 minutes or until potatoes are tender. Let stand 5 minutes before serving.

4 Servings

460 CALORIES / FAT 15 g (135 CAL or 29% of total calories) / SAT FAT 4 g (7% of total calories) / CARB 44 g / PROTEIN 38 g / CHOL 95 mg / SODIUM 830 mg

VEGETABLE PORK SKILLET

1 tablespoon Crisco Shortening or Crisco Oil

4 4-ounce, lean, boneless, center cut loin pork slices, ½-inch thick (about 1 pound)

2 medium onions, thinly sliced and separated into rings

1 can (14½ ounces) tomatoes

¾ cup water

2 teaspoons paprika

1 teaspoon salt

½ teaspoon celery seed

¼ teaspoon pepper

¼ teaspoon garlic powder

3 medium unpeeled potatoes, diced

1 package (9 ounces) frozen cut green beans

1. Heat Crisco Shortening or Crisco Oil in large skillet on medium heat. Sauté meat until browned on both sides. Remove from skillet.
2. Add onions to skillet. Cook until tender. Add undrained tomatoes, water, paprika, salt, celery seed, pepper and garlic powder. Bring to a boil.
3. Return meat to skillet. Reduce heat. Cover. Simmer 10 to 15 minutes.
4. Add potatoes. Cover. Simmer 15 minutes.
5. Add beans. Cover. Simmer 5 to 7 minutes or until potatoes and beans are tender.

4 Servings

405 CALORIES / FAT 12 g (111 CAL or 28% of total calories) / SAT FAT 3 g (7% of total calories) / CARB 44 g / PROTEIN 31 g / CHOL 70 mg / SODIUM 800 mg

ORANGE-GLAZED FRESH HAM

4 pound boneless fresh ham (rump end)

1 jar (12 ounces) orange marmalade

1 tablespoon soy sauce

¼ teaspoon ginger

¼ teaspoon cloves

1 Heat oven to 325°.
2. Place ham on rack in open roasting pan. Insert meat thermometer in thickest part of ham.
3. Bake, uncovered, at 325° for 1 to 1½ hours (allow 20 minutes per pound) or until meat thermometer registers 155°.
4. Combine marmalade, soy sauce, ginger and cloves. Mix well. Brush on ham several times during last 45 minutes of cooking time. Let ham stand 10 to 15 minutes before slicing.

16 Servings

215 CALORIES / FAT 6 g (55 CAL or 26% of total calories) / SAT FAT 2 g (9% of total calories) / CARB 15 g / PROTEIN 24 g / CHOL 75 mg / SODIUM 145 mg

DOC'S BARBECUED PORK CHOPS

2 tablespoons Crisco Shortening or Crisco Oil

6 4-ounce, lean, boneless, center cut loin pork chops, trimmed

1 medium onion, chopped

3 cloves garlic, minced

1 can (6 ounces) no salt added tomato paste

½ cup cider vinegar

¼ cup plus 2 tablespoons firmly packed light brown sugar

¼ cup water

3 tablespoons Worcestershire sauce

1 teaspoon dry mustard

1 teaspoon chili powder

¼ teaspoon salt

¼ teaspoon pepper

1 package (12 ounces) cholesterol free yolk free noodle style pasta, cooked (without salt or fat)

1. Heat oven to 350°.
2. Heat Crisco Shortening or Crisco Oil in large skillet on medium-high heat. Sauté pork chops until lightly browned. Remove chops from skillet. Place in baking dish in single layer.
3. Add onion and garlic to skillet. Sauté on medium heat until soft. Stir in tomato paste, vinegar, brown sugar, water, Worcestershire sauce, dry mustard, chili powder, salt and pepper. Bring to a boil. Reduce heat. Simmer 5 minutes. Pour sauce over chops. Turn to coat. Cover.
4. Bake at 350° for 45 to 60 minutes or until chops are tender. Serve with noodles.

6 Servings

To Microwave:
1. Combine Crisco Shortening or Crisco Oil, onion and garlic in 11¾ X 7½-inch microwave-safe dish. Cover with plastic wrap. Microwave at HIGH for 3 minutes. Stir after 1 minute, 30 seconds.
2. Follow step 3, above, for adding remaining ingredients. Stir well. Place uncooked chops in sauce. Turn to coat. Cover. Microwave at HIGH for 16 minutes. Turn dish every 4 minutes. Rearrange chops after 8 minutes. Let stand 5 minutes, covered. Serve with noodles.

525 CALORIES / FAT 14 g (128 CAL or 24% of total calories) / SAT FAT 3 g (5% of total calories) / CARB 65 g / PROTEIN 34 g / CHOL 70 mg / SODIUM 310 mg

PORK ROAST GUADELOUPE & RICE

Marinade

½ cup finely chopped onion
¼ cup water
3 tablespoons lime juice
2 large cloves garlic, minced
1 tablespoon Crisco Oil
1 to 2 teaspoons finely chopped jalapeño pepper (½ small)
¾ teaspoon dried thyme leaves, crushed, divided
¼ teaspoon salt
⅛ teaspoon pepper

1½ pound boneless pork loin
1 cup beef broth, divided
2 teaspoons sugar
1 tablespoon cornstarch
2 tablespoons minced parsley
4 cups hot cooked rice (without salt or fat)

1. For marinade, combine onion, water, lime juice, garlic, Crisco Oil, jalapeño pepper, ½ teaspoon thyme, salt and pepper.
2. Place roast in large resealable plastic bag. Pour marinade over meat. Seal. Refrigerate 4 to 6 hours.
3. Heat oven to 350°.
4. Remove meat from marinade, reserving marinade. Place meat in baking pan.
4. Roast at 350° for 40 to 50 minutes or until meat thermometer registers 155 to 160°. Remove meat from pan. Cover with foil. Let stand 10 minutes.
5. Pour ½ cup beef broth in pan.
6. Strain reserved marinade. Add to pan along with sugar and remaining ¼ teaspoon thyme. Stir well.
7. Combine remaining ½ cup broth and cornstarch. Stir well. Add to pan. Cook and stir on medium heat until thickened and bubbly. Cook one minute. Stir in parsley. Slice meat to serve. Serve with sauce and cooked rice.

6 Servings

385 CALORIES / FAT 11 g (103 CAL or 27% of total calories) / SAT FAT 3 g (8% of total calories) / CARB 41 g / PROTEIN 28 g / CHOL 70 mg / SODIUM 290 mg

PARTY PORK CHOPS 'N YAMS

1 tablespoon plus 1½ teaspoons
Crisco Shortening or Crisco Oil
6 smoked pork loin chops, cut ¾-
inch thick, about 6 ounces each
2 cups cooked, mashed fresh
yams or sweet potatoes

1 can (8 ounces) crushed
pineapple, drained, reserve
liquid
3 tablespoons maple syrup
¼ teaspoon cinnamon
⅛ teaspoon salt

1. Heat oven to 350°.
2. Heat Crisco Shortening or Crisco Oil in large skillet on medium heat. Brown
meat.
3. Place meat in 13 X 9-inch baking pan.
4. Combine yams, pineapple, maple syrup, cinnamon and salt. Mix well. Spoon
mixture over meat. Pour pineapple liquid into pan.
5. Bake, uncovered, at 350° for 25 to 30 minutes or until yams are thoroughly
heated.

6 Servings

360 CALORIES / FAT 9 g (82 CAL or 23% of total calories) / SAT FAT 2 g (5% of total calories) / CARB 34 g /
PROTEIN 34 g / CHOL 105 mg / SODIUM 115 mg

TEXAS-STYLE BARBECUE PORK CHOPS

1 tablespoon Crisco Shortening or
Crisco Oil
½ cup finely chopped onion
½ cup finely chopped celery
1 cup ketchup
½ cup molasses
½ cup water

2 tablespoons red wine vinegar
2 teaspoons dry mustard
¼ teaspoon cayenne pepper, or to
taste
¼ teaspoon salt
6 center loin pork chops, cut ¾-
inch thick, about 6 ounces each

1. Heat Crisco Shortening or Crisco Oil in medium saucepan on medium heat.
Add onion and celery. Cook 5 minutes. Stir in ketchup, molasses, water,
vinegar, dry mustard, cayenne and salt. Mix well. Bring to a boil. Reduce
heat. Simmer 15 minutes, stirring occasionally.
2. Heat broiler.
3. Place meat on broiler pan 5 inches from heat. Broil about 8 minutes on each
side, brushing frequently with sauce. Serve with remaining sauce, if desired.

6 Servings

310 CALORIES / FAT 11 g (96 CAL or 31% of total calories) / SAT FAT 3 g (9% of total calories) / CARB 28 g /
PROTEIN 26 g / CHOL 70 mg / SODIUM 685 mg

Home Made Pie as a Leadership Training Tool

I was with Miss Height so many times over the years... I spent so many evenings with her... so many memorable times. She is just a fantastic woman. I remember how we would just sit and talk. One time we were in Alabama, up in Tuskegee, where we had a workshop to train women. Well, we were supposed to go to this woman's house to have dinner that evening. She had cooked okra and green peas and corn... all kinds of fresh vegetables. And she had homemade pie with ice cream for dessert. One of the other women at the table was trying to lose weight, so when dessert was offered, she sent it back. Miss Height turned to her, regal as a queen with a smile on her face and said, "There are other people at the table. You should have consulted us before you did that. Don't ever take drastic actions without consulting the people that you work with." We all laughed because Miss Height had a way of using her sense of humor to teach and that pie experience taught us an important leadership lesson. It was just precious

(continued)

GEORGIA'S PORK JAMBALAYA

1	tablespoon Crisco Oil
¾	cup (4 ounces) smoked ham, diced
1	kielbasa sausage (6 ounces), cut in ½-inch slices
1	pound boneless pork loin, cubed
1½	cups chopped onion
1	cup chopped celery
1	large green bell pepper, chopped
2	cloves garlic, minced
½	teaspoon hot pepper sauce
2	bay leaves
1½	teaspoons salt
1½	teaspoons dried oregano leaves
1½	teaspoons pepper
1	teaspoon dried thyme leaves
4	medium tomatoes, peeled and chopped
1	can (8 ounces) tomato sauce
1	can (14½ ounces) chicken broth
½	cup chopped green onion
2	cups long grain rice

1. Heat oven to 350°.
2. Heat Crisco Oil in large Dutch oven on medium heat. Stir in ham, sausage and pork. Sauté until lightly browned, stirring frequently. Stir in onion, celery and green pepper. Sauté until crisp-tender, about 5 minutes. Stir in garlic, hot pepper sauce, bay leaves, salt, oregano, pepper and thyme. Cook and stir 5 minutes. Stir in tomatoes. Cook 5 to 8 minutes. Stir in tomato sauce and chicken broth. Bring to a boil. Stir in green onion and rice.
3. Bake, covered, at 350° for 20 to 25 minutes or until rice is tender. Remove bay leaves before serving.

10 Servings

330 CALORIES / FAT 11 g (101 CAL or 31% of total calories) / SAT FAT 4 g (10% of total calories) / CARB 37 g / PROTEIN 19 g / CHOL 45 mg / SODIUM 970 mg

STUFFED PORK CHOPS

6   chops, ¾ inch or more thick, 6 ounces each (4
    ounces cooked)
1   cup dry bread or cracker crumbs
½   cup chopped green onion tops
½   cup finely chopped celery
½   cup whole kernel corn
½   cup chopped green bell pepper
1   tablespoon poultry seasoning
1   tablespoon prepared mustard
½   cup all-purpose flour
½   teaspoon paprika
1   teaspoon salt
½   teaspoon pepper
2   teaspoons vegetable oil

1.   Heat oven to 325°.
2.   Make pocket in side of each chop.
3.   Combine bread crumbs, onion, celery, corn, green
    pepper and poultry seasoning. Fill each pocket with
    dressing. Close openings with small skewers. Rub
    with mustard. Sprinkle both sides with flour and
    paprika. Place in 13 X 9 X 2-inch baking pan. Add
    small amount of water.
4.   Sprinkle with salt and pepper. Drizzle oil over chops.
5.   Bake at 325° for 1 hour 30 minutes. Brown under
    broiler before serving.

6 servings

320 CALORIES / FAT 11 g (99 CAL or 31% of total calories) / SAT FAT 3 g (9% of
total calories) / CARB 25 g / PROTEIN 29 g / CHOL 70 mg / SODIUM 630 mg

(continued)

for her to talk that way
over dinner, as if we were
still having a business
meeting. Whenever I've
been with Miss Height, I've
learned something
important.

**Unita Z. Blackwell
1992 MacArthur
Foundation Award
Winner**

SAVORY PORK SKILLET WITH NOODLES

1   tablespoon Crisco Shortening or Crisco Oil
1   pound boneless pork loin, cut in ¾-inch cubes
1   cup chopped onion
1   can (14½ ounces) stewed tomatoes
1   teaspoon chili powder

½   cup green bell pepper, cut into 1-¼ inch squares
½   cup ¼-inch diagonally sliced celery
4   cups cooked yolk free, cholesterol free noodle style pasta (without salt or fat)

1. Heat Crisco Shortening or Crisco Oil in large skillet on medium-high heat. Add meat. Brown on all sides.
2. Push pork to one side of skillet. Add onion to cleared side. Sauté 2 minutes. Stir onion and pork occasionally.
3. Stir in tomatoes and chili powder. Cover. Simmer about 17 minutes.
4. Stir in green pepper and celery. Cover and simmer 5 minutes. Serve over noodles.

4 Servings

675 CALORIES / FAT 14 g (130 CAL or 19% of total calories) / SAT FAT 4 g (5% of total calories) / CARB 95 g / PROTEIN 41 g / CHOL 70mg / SODIUM 260 mg

CAJUN CHOPS WITH CREOLE BEANS & RICE

1   tablespoon paprika
1   teaspoon seasoned salt
1   teaspoon rubbed sage
½   teaspoon cayenne pepper
½   teaspoon black pepper
½   teaspoon garlic powder

2   pounds boneless pork loin chops, ½-inch thick, about 4 ounces each
2   teaspoons Crisco Shortening or Crisco Oil
    Creole Beans & Rice (see recipe on page 115)

1. Combine paprika, seasoned salt, sage, cayenne, pepper and garlic powder. Coat chops with seasoning mixture on both sides.
2. Heat Crisco Shortening or Crisco Oil in large non-stick skillet on high heat. Put chops in pan. Reduce heat to medium. Fry on both sides 6 to 8 minutes or until dark brown. Serve with Creole Beans & Rice.

8 Servings

485 CALORIES / FAT 15 g (139 CAL or 29% of total calories) / SAT FAT 3 g (6% of total calories) / CARB 53 g / PROTEIN 36 g / CHOL 70 mg / SODIUM 1085 mg

JESSICA'S JAMAICAN PORK

1 tablespoon Crisco Shortening or
   Crisco Oil
1 teaspoon curry powder
2 medium bananas
1 pound pork tenderloin, cubed

½ cup pineapple juice
¼ cup minced onion
¼ cup flake coconut
2⅔ cups hot cooked rice (without
   salt or fat)

1. Heat Crisco Shortening or Crisco Oil in large skillet on medium heat. Stir in
    curry powder. Cut bananas into ½-inch slices. Add to skillet. Sauté until
    golden brown. Remove from skillet.
2. Add meat to skillet. Sauté until golden brown. Stir in pineapple juice and
    minced onion. Cover. Reduce heat. Simmer 10 minutes or until meat is
    tender. Stir in coconut and bananas. Toss lightly. Serve with rice.

4 Servings

495 CALORIES / FAT 12 g (106 CAL or 21% of total calories) / SAT FAT 4 g (8% of total calories) / CARB 59 g /
PROTEIN 37 g / CHOL 105 mg / SODIUM 95 mg

WEST INDIAN PORK

1 pound pork tenderloin
1 tablespoon Crisco Shortening or
   Crisco Oil, divided

2 medium bananas, peeled and
   sliced
¼ cup brown sugar
¼ cup brandy or rum

1. Slice tenderloin into 1-inch pieces. Flatten slightly with heel of hand.
2. Heat one teaspoon Crisco Shortening or Crisco Oil in large skillet on medium
    heat. Add meat. Brown quickly on both sides, about 4 to 5 minutes. Remove
    meat from skillet. Keep warm.
3. Heat remaining 2 teaspoons Crisco Shortening or Crisco Oil in skillet. Add
    bananas. Sauté 2 to 3 minutes. Add brown sugar and brandy. Cook and stir
    until sauce is thick and bubbly. Return meat to skillet. Heat through.

4 Servings

355 CALORIES / FAT 9 g (83 CAL or 23% of total calories) / SAT FAT 2 g (6% of total calories) / CARB 32 g /
PROTEIN 33 g / CHOL 105 mg / SODIUM 85 mg

TEXAS-STYLE PORK BARBECUE

The Only National Organization Ever to Actually Put Housing Into the Ground

When Miss Height came down to Mississippi in 19 and 66, she came to work with local organizers like me on how we were to do what we had to do in organizing women to reach out for real solutions to real problems. I was working on housing. Miss Height taught me that my skills are important and worth a lot. She encouraged me and she is truly part of the reason I am what I am today. There she was, Dr. Dorothy Height, a woman who had talked with presidents and there I was, a little community organizer from Mayersville, Mississippi, and she always called me "Miss Blackwell". She knew me well enough to be on a first name basis, but she has such dignity that she gives you dignity. She lets you feel as if you are somebody as special as she is. Her genius is that she doesn't put restraints on the people who work with her. She gives you free rein to be creative while still offering you the drive and the inspiration you need to get the job done. Working on housing

(continued)

2 teaspoons Crisco Shortening or Crisco Oil
¼ cup coarsely chopped onion
1 clove garlic, minced
¾ cup chili sauce
1 tablespoon firmly packed brown sugar
1 tablespoon cider vinegar
1 tablespoon molasses
1 tablespoon water
1 teaspoon lemon juice
1 teaspoon prepared mustard
¼ teaspoon liquid smoke
⅛ teaspoon cayenne pepper
⅛ teaspoon salt
¾ pound boneless cooked pork loin, thinly sliced
4 onion rolls, split and toasted

1. Heat Crisco Shortening or Crisco Oil in medium saucepan on medium heat. Add onion and garlic. Sauté until tender. Stir in chili sauce, brown sugar, vinegar, molasses, water, lemon juice, mustard, liquid smoke, cayenne and salt. Bring to a boil. Reduce heat. Simmer, uncovered, about 15 minutes.
2. Add meat slices to saucepan. Stir gently to coat with sauce. Heat about 5 minutes or until meat is heated through.
3. Place meat on bottom half of rolls. Cover with tops. Serve with extra sauce on the side.

4 Servings

330 CALORIES / FAT 9 g (78 CAL or 24% of total calories) / SAT FAT 2 g (6% of total calories) / CARB 34 g / PROTEIN 28 g / CHOL 80 mg / SODIUM 930 mg

COUNTRY-FRIED PORK, PEPPERS & RICE

4   boneless pork loin chops, about 6 ounces each
2   tablespoons yellow cornmeal
1   tablespoon all-purpose flour
1   teaspoon paprika
½   teaspoon garlic salt
½   teaspoon onion powder
¼   teaspoon pepper
¼   teaspoon ground cumin
1   tablespoon Crisco Oil
1   medium green bell pepper, cut in strips
1   medium red bell pepper, cut in strips
2⅔ cups hot cooked rice (without salt or fat)

1. Pound meat to ¼-inch thickness.
2. Combine cornmeal, flour, paprika, garlic salt, onion powder, pepper and cumin.
3. Dip meat in water. Allow excess to drip off.
4. Coat with cornmeal mixture on both sides.
5. Heat Crisco Oil in large skillet on medium heat. Add meat. Sauté 4 minutes. Turn over. Add pepper strips. Cook 4 minutes or until pork is nicely browned and just slightly pink in the center. Remove pork from skillet. Cook peppers 1 to 2 minutes or until tender. Serve pork and peppers with rice.

4 Servings

515 CALORIES / FAT 16 g (147 CAL or 29% of total calories) / SAT FAT 5 g (8% of total calories) / CARB 47 g / PROTEIN 42 g / CHOL 105 mg / SODIUM 375 mg

(continued)

with the NCNW we put 200 units of homes in Gulfport, Mississippi. The first home ownership program in America run by a national organization was put together by Miss Height so we named it Forest Height. We made sure to leave a lot of trees standing so the neighborhoods would look nice. Then we put 264 two, three, four and five bedroom houses in the ground in Indianola, Mississippi. You can only imagine what that meant to the people who were finally able to own their own homes... decent homes with modern conveniences thanks to Miss Height.

Mayor Unita Z. Blackwell
Mayersville, Mississippi

SPICY PORK CHILI

1 tablespoon Crisco Oil
1½ pounds boneless pork loin, cut into 1-inch cubes
1 medium onion, coarsely chopped
1 medium green bell pepper, coarsely chopped
1 clove garlic, minced
1 tablespoon all-purpose flour
2 cans (14½ ounces each) whole peeled tomatoes, no salt added, crushed

1 can (16 ounces) red kidney beans
1 can (8 ounces) tomato sauce
3 tablespoons chili powder
1 tablespoon ground cumin
½ teaspoon salt
½ teaspoon black pepper
1½ cups (6 ounces) shredded ⅓ less fat sharp Cheddar cheese
16 warm flour tortillas

1. Heat Crisco Oil in Dutch oven on medium heat. Add meat, onion, green pepper and garlic. Cook until meat is browned. Stir in flour. Add undrained tomatoes, kidney beans, tomato sauce, chili powder, cumin, salt and pepper. Simmer, uncovered, one hour.
2. Sprinkle with cheese. Serve with tortillas.

8 Servings

530 CALORIES / FAT 19 g (167 CAL or 31% of total calories) / SAT FAT 6 g (10% of total calories) / CARB 59 g / PROTEIN 28 g / CHOL 65 mg / SODIUM 1015 mg

APPLE ORCHARD PORK CHOPS

2 teaspoons Crisco Oil
6 pork loin chops, cut ½-inch thick, about 6 ounces each
2 cups apple cider or apple juice
⅓ cup German-style mustard

3 apples, unpared, cored, sliced ½-inch thick
½ cup currants or raisins
½ cup sliced green onions
¼ cup water
2 tablespoons cornstarch

1. Heat Crisco Oil in large skillet on medium heat. Add meat. Brown on both sides.
2. Combine apple cider and mustard. Pour over meat. Cover. Cook on medium-low 45 minutes.
3. Add apples, currants and green onions. Cover. Cook 5 to 10 minutes.
4. Place meat and apples on serving platter. Keep warm.
4. Combine water and cornstarch. Stir into cider liquid gradually. Cook and stir until thickened. Serve sauce over meat and apples.

6 Servings

325 CALORIES / FAT 11 g (96 CAL or 29% of total calories) / SAT FAT 3 g (8% of total calories) / CARB 33 g / PROTEIN 26 g / CHOL 70 mg / SODIUM 255 mg

CRISPY OVEN FRIED FISH

½ cup seasoned dry, fine bread crumbs

1 tablespoon grated Parmesan cheese

2 teaspoons grated lemon peel

¾ teaspoon dried marjoram leaves

½ teaspoon paprika

¼ teaspoon dried thyme leaves

⅛ teaspoon garlic powder

4 flounder or sole fillets (about 1 pound)

3 tablespoons lemon juice

2 tablespoons white wine

1 tablespoon Crisco Oil

1. Heat oven to 425°. Oil 13 X 9 X 2-inch pan.
2. Combine bread crumbs, Parmesan cheese, lemon peel, marjoram, paprika, thyme and garlic powder in shallow pan.
3. Rinse fish fillets. Pat dry.
4. Combine lemon juice and wine in shallow pan. Dip each fillet in lemon mixture, then in crumb mixture, coating well.
5. Place fish in pan. Drizzle with Crisco Oil.
6. Bake at 425° for 20 to 25 minutes or until fish flakes easily when tested with fork.

4 Servings

175 CALORIES / FAT 6 g (50 CAL or 28% of total calories) / SAT FAT 1 g (<5% of total calories) / CARB 7 g / PROTEIN 24 g / CHOL 60 mg / SODIUM 180 mg

CRISPY OVEN FRIED FISH FINGERS

½ cup seasoned fine, dry bread crumbs

1 tablespoon grated Parmesan cheese

2 teaspoons grated lemon peel

¾ teaspoon dried marjoram leaves

½ teaspoon paprika

¼ teaspoon dried thyme leaves

⅛ teaspoon garlic powder

4 cod fillets (about 1 pound)

3 tablespoons lemon juice

2 tablespoons white wine

1 tablespoon Crisco Oil

1. Heat oven to 425°. Oil 13 X 9 X 2-inch pan.
2. Combine bread crumbs, Parmesan cheese, lemon peel, marjoram, paprika, thyme and garlic powder in shallow pan.
3. Combine lemon juice and wine in shallow pan. Cut fish into desired size "fingers" or "sticks". Dip each finger into lemon mixture, then in crumb mixture, coating well.
4. Place fish fingers on lightly oiled baking sheet. Drizzle with Crisco Oil.
5. Bake at 425° for 10 to 12 minutes or until fish flakes easily when tested with fork. Let stand 2 to 3 minutes on baking sheet.
6. Serve with tartar sauce, page 92.

4 Servings

175 CALORIES / FAT 6 g (50 CAL or 28% of total calories) / SAT FAT 1 g (<5% of total calories) / CARB 7 g / PROTEIN 24 g / CHOL 60 mg / SODIUM 180 mg

CRISPY SPICY OVEN FRIED CATFISH WITH TARTAR SAUCE

Savory Ongoing Memories

Sitting with Dr. Height at her annual Christmas "Get-Together" in the basement party room of her Washington apartment, surrounded mostly by women and a few men who are loyal to "Queen Dorothy" as I fondly and respectfully think of her... fingers, hers and mine deep in collard greens, chittlins with hot sauce, potato salad and other soul food standards... steeped in savory spices and pot liquors, floating in paper plates anchored over paper napkins in sturdy laps.... Whether it be the pomp and circumstance, formal wear and people care at the Christmas party, the Black Family Reunion reception at the National Museum of American History, the Smithsonian Festival of American Folklife Foodways, or future courses she may share with and for all of us — I pause for a moment to think that great food that sustained us through slavery and in freedom goes well with this great lady of African-American life and leadership.

**James Early
Assistant Secretary for Education & Public Service
The Smithsonian Institute**

1 tablespoon Crisco Oil
¾ cup cornmeal
1 teaspoon pepper
1 teaspoon garlic salt
1 teaspoon lemon pepper seasoning
1 teaspoon Cajun spice
1 egg, beaten
2 tablespoons water
1 pound catfish fillets
Tartar Sauce recipe (optional)

1. Heat oven to 425°. Coat bottom of 13 X 9 X 2-inch pan with Crisco Oil.
2. Combine cornmeal, pepper, garlic salt, lemon pepper and Cajun spice in large flat dish.
3. Combine egg and water.
4. Rinse fish. Dip in egg mixture. Coat with cornmeal mixture. Place in pan.
5. Bake at 425° for 22 to 25 minutes or until fish flakes easily when tested with fork. Serve with tartar sauce, if desired.

4 Servings

370 CALORIES / FAT 11 g (103 CAL or 28% of total calories) / SAT FAT 2 g (5% of total calories) / CARB 36 g / PROTEIN 29 g / CHOL 120 mg / SODIUM 855 mg

Tartar Sauce
1 cup nonfat sour cream alternative
½ cup sweet pickle relish
¼ cup finely chopped green onions
1 teaspoon Crisco Oil

1. Combine "sour cream", pickle relish, green onions and Crisco Oil in small bowl. Stir to blend. Serve with fish. Cover and refrigerate leftover sauce.

1¼ Cups Sauce (20 One-Tablespoon Servings)
Hint: Prepare and refrigerate at least 2 hours before serving to allow flavors to blend.

**Adaptation from Recipe
Ronald H. Brown, Chairman
Democratic National Committee**

19 CALORIES / FAT <1 g (<1 CAL or <1% of total calories) / SAT FAT <1 g (<1% of total calories) / CARB 3 g / PROTEIN 1 g / CHOL 0 mg / SODIUM 50 mg

SISTER SARA'S TUNA POTPIES

Filling

2 tablespoons Crisco Oil
3 medium carrots, thinly sliced
1 small onion, diced
2 tablespoons all-purpose flour
1 can (12 ounces) evaporated
   skim milk
1 cup water
1 package (9 ounces) frozen cut
   green beans or peas

1 can (16 ounces) whole potatoes,
   drained and diced
1 can (12½ to 13 ounces) solid
   white tuna in water, drained and
   broken up
1 tablespoon minced fresh dill or
   ¼ teaspoon dried dill weed
¼ teaspoon salt

Crust

1¼ cups all-purpose flour
1 teaspoon baking powder

3 tablespoons Crisco Oil
¼ cup cold water

1. For filling, heat Crisco Oil in large saucepan on medium heat. Add carrots and onion. Cook until tender. Stir in flour. Cook one minute. Stir in milk and water gradually. Cook and stir until mixture thickens slightly.
2. Add green beans, stirring to separate. Remove saucepan from heat. Stir in potatoes, tuna, dill and salt. Spoon into four 14-ounce ramekins.*
3. Heat oven to 400°.
4. For crust, combine flour and salt in medium bowl.
5. Combine Crisco Oil and water. Add to flour mixture. Stir with fork until mixture forms large clumps. Press with fingers to form ball. Divide into 4 sections. Flatten between hands to form four "pancakes".
6. Roll each "pancake" between unfloured sheets of waxed paper (or plastic wrap) on dampened countertop. Peel off top sheet.
7. Trim one inch larger than top of ramekin. Moisten outside edge of ramekin with water. Flip dough over onto ramekin. Fold edge under. Flute. Cut slits in crust for escape of steam. Place ramekins on baking sheet.
8. Bake at 400° for 25 to 30 minutes or until filling is bubbly and crust is golden brown.

4 servings
*Note: Use 2-quart casserole if ramekins are unavailable. Roll pastry to fit top of casserole. Bake at 400° for 30 to 35 minutes.

605 CALORIES / FAT 19 g (172 CAL or 28% of total calories) / SAT FAT 2 g (3% of total calories) / CARB 68 g / PROTEIN 41 g / CHOL 55 mg / SODIUM 895 mg

LETTY'S TUNA NOODLE CASSEROLE

1 tablespoon Crisco Shortening or Crisco Oil
1 cup sliced celery
⅓ cup chopped onion
¼ cup diced green bell pepper
1 can (6⅛ ounces) water packed tuna, drained
6 ounces cholesterol free, yolk free noodle style pasta (3½ cups dry), cooked (without salt or fat)

½ cup nonfat sour cream alternative
1 jar (2 ounces) sliced pimientos, drained
½ teaspoon salt
1 can (10¾ ounces) condensed cream of celery soup
½ cup skim milk
4 slices (¾ ounces each) reduced fat process American cheese, diced
2 tablespoons dry bread crumbs

1. Heat oven to 425°. Oil 2-quart baking dish.
2. Heat Crisco Shortening or Crisco Oil in large skillet on medium heat. Add celery, onion and green pepper. Stir-fry until softened. Combine with noodles, tuna, "sour cream", pimientos and salt.
3. Combine soup and milk in small saucepan on medium heat. Warm. Add cheese. Stir until cheese melts. Combine with noodle mixture. Turn into baking dish. Sprinkle with bread crumbs.
4. Bake at 425° for 20 to 25 minutes or until hot and bubbly.

6 Servings

310 CALORIES / FAT 8 g (68 CAL or 22% of total calories) / SAT FAT 3 g (7% of total calories) / CARB 38 g / PROTEIN 21 g / CHOL 30 mg / SODIUM 975 mg

SPICY SIZZLIN' CATFISH

½ teaspoon Crisco Oil
1 cup onion, thinly sliced, divided
1 pound boneless catfish
½ teaspoon pepper

½ teaspoon garlic powder
2 medium tomatoes, chopped
Tabasco sauce

1. Heat oven to 425°. Coat 13 X 9 X 2-inch baking pan lightly with oil.
2. Layer in bottom of pan half the onion slices. Place fish on top of onion. Sprinkle with pepper and garlic powder. Cover with chopped tomato and remaining onion slices. Dot top onion with Tabasco sauce.
3. Bake at 425° for 20 to 25 minutes or until fish flakes easily with fork.

4 Servings

165 CALORIES / FAT 6 g (51 CAL or 31% of total calories) / SAT FAT 1 g (6% of total calories) / CARB 6 g / PROTEIN 22 g / CHOL 65 mg / SODIUM 80 mg

CAVEY'S SEAFOOD/RICE CASSEROLE

1¾ cups instant rice
1 can (7½ ounces) salmon, drained
1 can (6 ounces) crab meat, drained
1 cup chopped celery
½ cup chopped green bell pepper
1 tablespoon instant minced onion

1 can (10¾ ounces) condensed cream of mushroom soup
1 cup nonfat mayonnaise dressing
1½ cups skim milk
1 teaspoon Worcestershire sauce
¾ teaspoon lemon juice
¼ teaspoon pepper
Paprika

1. Heat oven to 350°.
2. Combine uncooked rice, salmon, crab meat, celery, green pepper, onion, soup, mayonnaise dressing, milk, Worcestershire sauce, lemon juice, and pepper. Stir until well blended. Pour into 8 or 9-inch square pan or glass baking dish. Sprinkle with paprika.
3. Bake at 350° for one hour or until hot and bubbly.

6 Servings

275 CALORIES / FAT 7 g (61 CAL or 22% of total calories) / SAT FAT 3 g (8% of total calories) / CARB 38 g / PROTEIN 17 g / CHOL 55 mg / SODIUM 665 mg

SINFULLY DELICIOUS SALMON

2 ten ounce salmon steaks
2 teaspoons cracked black pepper
1 teaspoon seafood seasoning
¼ cup green onions, chopped
½ cup celery, chopped

2 shallots
½ lemon
3 bay leaves
1½ cups water

1. Heat oven to 350°.
2. Grease bottom of 8-inch square pan with butter.
3. Lay steaks in pan. Sprinkle pepper and seafood seasoning over the steaks. Place celery, onions, shallots, and lemon slices around fish in bottom of pan. Add bay leaves. Pour water in pan.
4. Cover pan tightly with plastic wrap, forming a seal. Cover pan with tin foil. Fold over edges tightly so that plastic is completely covered.
5. Bake at 350° for 22 minutes.

2 Servings

**Adaptation from Recipe
Kym Gibson
Blair House, President's Guest House**

345 CALORIES / FAT 10 g (89 CAL or 26% of total calories) / SAT FAT 2 g (<5% of total calories) / CARB 3 g / PROTEIN 57 g / CHOL 145 mg / SODIUM 220 mg

SALMON LASAGNA

From Poverty to Pig Farming

The summer of 1985 was my first year as Executive Director of PUSH for EXCELLENCE. On one of my trips to Chicago, I was a guest in the Constance Avenue home of Reverend and Mrs. Jackson. Early one Sunday morning, Mrs. Jackson told me that Dr. Height would join us that day for lunch. As we stood around the butcher block counter top that sits in the middle of the kitchen, Reverend Jackson filled me in on Dr. Height. I marveled at the tremendous respect he had for Dr. Height's accomplishments and began to anticipate her arrival with the spirit befitting a queen. Dr. Height arrived earlier than expected, giving me a chance to talk with her before lunch. We sat in the living room in the high back tapestry chairs next to the fireplace. Dr. Height told me that she had met my parents, Rachel and Jackie Robinson many years ago when my father was still a professional baseball player. I was struck by Dr. Height's poise and urged her to talk about the beginnings of the National Council of Negro Women. This led to the topic of raising pigs in Mississippi.

During the late sixties, Dr. (continued)

Lasagna

4   lasagna noodles
1   cup part skim ricotta cheese
½   cup low moisture, part skim mozzarella cheese, shredded
2   egg whites
2   teaspoons chopped fresh parsley
4   salmon fillets (four ounces each)
4   slices low fat Swiss flavor process cheese

Spinach Pine Nut Sauce

½   cup chopped spinach
2   tablespoons chopped onion
1½ strips turkey bacon, chopped
1   tablespoon toasted pine nuts
1½ tablespoons all-purpose flour
1½ cups 2% milk
¼   cup white wine
    Dash nutmeg

1. Heat oven to 350°.
2. For lasagna, cook lasagna noodles to al dente. Drain.
3. Combine ricotta, mozzarella, egg whites and parsley in medium bowl.
4. Lay each lasagna flat. Place salmon fillet in center. Top with 2 tablespoons ricotta mixture. Fold one side of pasta over. Spoon two more tablespoons of mixture on. Fold other side over. Top with slice of Swiss cheese. Place each individual lasagna in baking dish.
5. Bake at 350° for 15 to 20 minutes or until cheese is browned and lasagna is bubbling.
6. For sauce, heat skillet on medium heat. Add spinach, onion, bacon and pine nuts. Sauté until onions are clear. Stir in flour. Cook and stir until flour is blended. Stir in milk. Simmer 5 minutes. Stir occasionally. Add wine and nutmeg.
7. To serve, pour ½ cup spinach sauce on each plate. Place lasagna on top of sauce.

4 Servings

**Adaptation from Recipe
Johnny Rivers, Executive Chef
Walt Disney World**

565 CALORIES / FAT 16 g (140 CAL or 25% of total calories) / SAT FAT 6 g (10% of total calories) / CARB 54 g / PROTEIN 49 g / CHOL 90 mg / SODIUM 610 mg

OLD FASHIONED SALMON PATTIES WITH CHEESY BROCCOLI SAUCE

Salmon patties
  1   can (15½ ounces) salmon, drained and flaked
  2   egg whites, lightly beaten
  ½   cup fine dry bread crumbs
  ⅓   cup finely chopped onion
  ¼   teaspoon seasoned salt
  ⅛   teaspoon pepper
  2   tablespoons all-purpose flour
  2   tablespoons Crisco Shortening or Crisco Oil

Cheesy Broccoli Sauce (Optional)
  2   tablespoons Crisco Shortening or Crisco Oil
  2   tablespoons all-purpose flour
  ½   teaspoon salt
  1⅔   cups skim milk
  5   slices fat free American process cheese, diced
  1   package (10 ounces) frozen chopped broccoli, cooked and drained
  1   tablespoon lemon juice
  ½   teaspoon Worcestershire sauce
  4   cups cooked rice (without salt or fat)

1. For salmon patties, combine salmon, egg whites, bread crumbs, onion, seasoned salt and pepper in medium bowl. Mix well. Divide into 6 portions. Shape into patties. Coat well with flour.
2. Heat Crisco Shortening or Crisco Oil in large skillet on medium heat. Sauté patties 5 to 10 minutes per side on medium to low heat or until golden brown.
3. For Cheesy Broccoli Sauce, heat Crisco Shortening or Crisco Oil in medium saucepan on medium heat. Blend in flour and salt. Cook and stir until bubbly. Stir in milk gradually. Cook and stir until sauce comes to a boil and is thickened. Cook and stir one minute.
4. Reduce heat to low. Stir in cheese, broccoli, lemon juice and Worcestershire sauce. Heat only until cheese melts. Serve with salmon patties and rice.

6 Servings

485 CALORIES / FAT 15 g (135 CAL or 28% of total calories) / SAT FAT 2 g (<5% of total calories) / CARB 58 g / PROTEIN 29 g / CHOL 45 mg / SODIUM 1040 mg

(continued)

Height and others called women together to meet in Sunflower and Bolivar counties in Mississippi. The question was, what did the women want and need to improve their lives. I know the response must have surprised Dr. Height as much as her telling it surprised me. The women said they wanted some meat. Thus, the Freedom Farm project was born with the assistance of Harry Belafonte.

Pigs were purchased from the Prentiss Institute. As Dr. Height tells the story, women started to raise pigs and fresh vegetables as a way to gain some measure of economic security. When the pigs reached maturity, they would be slaughtered and barbecued, salted down, smoked and preserved so that people had meat to supplement their diets. The project was based on a pig bank. When your hog gave birth, you had to return two pigs to the pig bank for someone in the community to raise. "Why pigs?" I asked, totally absorbed in the story. I learned that because raising pigs didn't require much land, it was a plan that was accessible to a large number of families. As a result of the project the women learned a great deal of economics and

(continued)

HOT 'N SPICY SHRIMP STEW

½ pound uncooked shrimp, peeled and deveined
¼ cup plus 1 tablespoon Crisco Shortening or Crisco Oil, divided
3 tablespoons white wine
½ teaspoon grated lemon peel
1 tablespoon lemon juice
½ teaspoon dried basil leaves
½ teaspoon dried oregano leaves
1 clove garlic, minced
¼ teaspoon salt
⅛ teaspoon pepper
2 drops hot pepper sauce
¾ cup uncooked, long grain rice
1½ cups water
2 tomatoes, cut into ½-inch pieces
¼ cup minced parsley
2 sliced green onions and tops

1. Place shrimp in medium glass or stainless steel bowl.
2. Combine ¼ cup Crisco Shortening or Crisco Oil, wine, lemon peel, lemon juice, basil, oregano, garlic, salt, pepper and hot pepper sauce in container with tight-fitting lid. Shake well. Remove one tablespoon. Reserve. Pour remaining marinade over shrimp. Turn to coat. Refrigerate 30 minutes. Turn once.
3. Heat remaining one tablespoon marinade in medium saucepan on medium-high heat. Add rice. Stir one minute. Pour water over rice. Stir. Bring to a boil. Reduce heat to very low. Cover. Simmer 14 to 20 minutes or until tender. Remove from heat. Fluff with fork. Stir in tomatoes. Cover.
4. Place remaining one tablespoon Crisco Shortening or Crisco Oil in large skillet on high heat. Drain shrimp. Add to skillet. Stir-fry one minute or until shrimp turn pink.
5. Spoon rice mixture onto serving platter. Pour shrimp mixture over rice. Sprinkle with parsley and green onions. Season with additional salt and pepper, if desired. Serve.

4 Servings

250 CALORIES / FAT 6 g (58 CAL or 23% of total calories) / SAT FAT 1 g (<5% of total calories) / CARB 32 g / PROTEIN 15 g / CHOL 85 mg / SODIUM 135 mg

(continued from previous page)
about health care. The Sunflower River flood, for example, taught the women the importance of inoculation. After the banks overflowed, the pigs had to be inoculated. Women realized from attending to the care of the pigs' health that immunization was important for people as well.
Being a registered nurse, I couldn't help but seize that moment to ask about pork and hypertension. Didn't the project send the wrong message? Dr. Height smiled knowingly and replied, "You can't just go in and change the culture of a community. You have to start where people are and move them to where you want them to be or where they need to be." That was the first of many valuable lessons I've come to learn from Dr. Height.

Sharon Robinson
Associate Director of Development
A Better Chance, Inc.

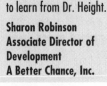

ZESTY FISH & TOMATO STEW

3 tablespoons Crisco Shortening or Crisco Oil, divided
¼ cup chopped onion
¼ cup chopped green bell pepper
1 clove garlic, minced
½ cup sliced fresh mushrooms
1 medium tomato, chopped

6 haddock or sole fillets (about 1½ pounds)
⅓ cup white wine*
1 tablespoon snipped fresh parsley
1 small bay leaf
4 cups hot cooked rice (without salt or fat)

1. Heat one tablespoon Crisco Shortening or Crisco Oil in small skillet. Add onion, green pepper and garlic. Sauté on medium heat until tender. Stir in mushrooms and tomato.
2. Heat remaining 2 tablespoons Crisco Shortening or Crisco Oil in large skillet. Add fish. Fry on medium-high heat 2 minutes per side. Remove from heat. Spread vegetable mixture on fish. Add wine, parsley and bay leaf. Cover. Cook on low heat 10 to 15 minutes, or until fish flakes easily with fork. Remove and discard bay leaf.
3. Serve with hot cooked rice.

6 Servings
*Note: For milder flavor, use water.

345 CALORIES / FAT 8 g (75 CAL or 22% of total calories) / SAT FAT 1 g (<5% of total calories) / CARB 41 g / PROTEIN 26 g / CHOL 65 mg / SODIUM 85 mg

SAVORY SHRIMP & VEGETABLE SKILLET

1 tablespoon Crisco Shortening or Crisco Oil
¾ pound shelled and deveined fresh or frozen medium shrimp, thawed
2 cups frozen broccoli cuts
1 medium red bell pepper, cut into thin 2-inch strips

½ cup boiling water
2 teaspoons chicken flavor instant bouillon granules or 2 cubes
¼ cup cold water
1 tablespoon cornstarch
1 teaspoon dried basil leaves
1 teaspoon lemon juice
½ cup sliced green onions

1. Heat Crisco Shortening or Crisco Oil in large skillet on medium heat. Add shrimp. Stir-fry about 4 minutes or until shrimp are pink. Remove to serving dish. Add broccoli and red pepper. Stir-fry until crisp-tender.
2. Combine boiling water and bouillon. Stir to dissolve. Combine cold water, cornstarch, basil and lemon juice. Stir well. Add to vegetables in skillet. Cook and stir until thickened. Add green onions and shrimp. Heat just to warm shrimp.

4 Servings

165 CALORIES / FAT 5 g (48 CAL or 29% of total calories) / SAT FAT <1 g (<5% of total calories) / CARB 10 g / PROTEIN 21 g / CHOL 130 mg / SODIUM 600 mg

CATFISH WITH VEGETABLES

1 tablespoon Crisco Shortening or Crisco Oil	3 tablespoons finely chopped pecans
1 large onion, diced	1 to 2 tablespoons soy sauce
1 tablespoon dried parsley flakes	1 to 2 teaspoons Worcestershire sauce
¼ to ½ teaspoon instant minced garlic	1 tablespoon Burgundy wine (optional) or water
1 package (24 ounces) frozen peas and carrots (5 cups)	3⅓ cups hot cooked rice (without salt or fat)
5 catfish fillets (about 1¼ pounds)	Salt and pepper (optional)

1. Heat Crisco Shortening or Crisco Oil in large skillet on medium heat. Add onion. Stir-fry until softened. Sprinkle with parsley and garlic.
2. Distribute peas and carrots over top. Reduce heat to low. Heat about 8 minutes or until vegetables are thawed.
3. Place fish on vegetables. Sprinkle with nuts. Add soy sauce and Worcestershire sauce. Cover. Simmer about 25 minutes or until fish flakes easily with fork. Add wine if skillet becomes too dry. Serve with rice. Season with salt and pepper.

5 Servings

455 CALORIES / FAT 12 g (96 CAL or 23% of total calories) / SAT FAT 2 g (<5% of total calories) / CARB 58 g / PROTEIN 30 g / CHOL 65 mg / SODIUM 625 mg

CATFISH STEW & RICE

3 cups water	1½ teaspoons salt
2 medium potatoes, diced	¾ teaspoon pepper
1 large onion, chopped	1½ pounds fresh boneless catfish fillets, cut in half
1 tablespoon garlic, chopped	
½ small head cabbage, chopped	4 cups hot cooked rice (without salt or fat)
2 large tomatoes, chopped	

1. Combine water, potatoes, onion and garlic in large pot. Cook on high heat 15 minutes. Lower heat. Add cabbage, tomatoes, salt and pepper. Cook 10 minutes. Add catfish. Cook 15 minutes. Serve over rice.

6 Servings

**Adaptation from Recipe
Johnny Rivers, Executive Chef
Walt Disney World**

375 CALORIES / FAT 6 g (50 CAL or 13% of total calories) / SAT FAT 1 g (<5% of total calories) / CARB 54 g / PROTEIN 27 g / CHOL 65 mg / SODIUM 625 mg

BEATRICE'S CREOLE SHRIMP

¼ cup Crisco Oil or Crisco Shortening
3 tablespoons all-purpose flour
⅓ cup chopped onion
¼ cup chopped celery
¼ cup chopped green bell pepper
1 can (14½ ounces) whole tomatoes
1 can (15 ounces) tomato sauce
1 package (10 ounces) frozen sliced okra
1 thin slice lemon
2 teaspoons packed brown sugar
1 teaspoon chili powder
½ teaspoon salt
¼ teaspoon garlic powder
¼ teaspoon black pepper
¼ teaspoon dried basil leaves
¼ teaspoon dried thyme leaves
1 bay leaf
⅛ teaspoon cayenne pepper
1 pound fresh medium shrimp, peeled and deveined
4 cups hot cooked rice (without salt or fat)

1. Heat Crisco Oil in large saucepan on medium heat. Add flour. Stir until smooth. Cook and stir 3 to 4 minutes, or until lightly browned.
2. Add onion, celery, and green pepper. Cook 2 to 3 minutes, or until tender.
3. Add undrained tomatoes, tomato sauce, okra, lemon, brown sugar, chili powder, salt, garlic powder, pepper, basil, thyme, bay leaf and cayenne pepper. Cover. Reduce heat. Simmer about 45 minutes, or until flavors are blended.
4. Stir in shrimp. Cover. Cook about 3 minutes, or until shrimp are opaque and firm. Remove lemon slice and bay leaf before serving. Serve with rice.

6 Servings

415 CALORIES / FAT 12 g (104 CAL or 25% of total calories) / SAT FAT 1 g (<5% of total calories) / CARB 56 g / PROTEIN 22 g / CHOL 115 mg / SODIUM 840 mg

Don't Ever Say You Are Tired

About a year and a half ago, I sat next to Dr. Height at a United Negro College Fund dinner co-sponsored by Ford at the Sheraton Washington Hotel. She had just flown in from a trip and I asked her if she was tired. My question caused her to turn to me in her majestic way and say, "Mr. Hall, one must never be tired." I remember how she dimpled and gave me a half smile as she told me, "Mary McLeod Bethune taught me long ago that since all the work of the movement is important, how can we be too tired to do it? In my opinion, none of us can afford to be tired."

I wanted to hear more so I suggested that surely, with her grueling schedule of travel, running the National Council and being on the front line of all the struggles of our era she must want to stop and rest. Dr. Height told me that on the contrary, she wanted to keep going and she would continue working as long as she could. She said she could never make any excuse to quit... there were too many people depending on her.

Elliott Hall
Vice President,
Washington Affairs
Ford Motor Company

DOCKSIDE SHRIMP GUMBO

2   tablespoons Crisco Shortening
     or Crisco Oil, divided
1   tablespoon plus 1½ teaspoons
     all-purpose flour
1   pound raw shrimp, shelled and
     deveined
1   cup chopped celery
2   onions, chopped
1½   pounds fresh okra, sliced

1   can (14½ ounces) tomatoes
4   cups water
2   bay leaves
¼   teaspoon salt
¼   teaspoon pepper
1   can (6 ounces) tomato paste
3⅓   cups hot cooked rice (without
     salt or fat)

1.   Heat 1 tablespoon plus 1½ teaspoons Crisco Shortening or Crisco Oil in
     medium skillet. Add flour. Stir constantly until rich dark brown. Stir in
     shrimp. Cook a few minutes.
2.   Heat remaining 1½ teaspoons shortening or oil in large saucepan on medium
     heat. Add celery and onions. Cook until soft and transparent. Add okra. Cook
     about 30 minutes or until okra ceases to rope. Add undrained tomatoes,
     water, bay leaves, salt and pepper. Stir in shrimp mixture. Cover. Simmer 30
     minutes, adding tomato paste after 15 minutes. Remove bay leaves before
     serving. Serve in flat bottom bowls over rice.

5 Servings

490 CALORIES / FAT 9 g (84 CAL or 17% of total calories) / SAT FAT 1 g (<5% of total calories) /
CARB 66 g / PROTEIN 37 g / CHOL 205 mg / SODIUM 745 mg

HERITAGE RECIPE

FRIDAY NIGHT CATFISH STEW

1   can (29 ounces) tomatoes,
     chopped
1   cup chopped celery
1   cup chopped green bell pepper
1   cup chopped onion

1   cup sliced carrot
1   cup ½-inch cubed zucchini
½   cup barbecue sauce
1   pound frozen catfish fillets, cut
     into 1-inch cubes

1.   Combine undrained tomatoes, celery, green pepper, onion, carrot, zucchini
     and barbecue sauce in large saucepan.
2.   Bring to a boil on medium high heat. Cover. Reduce heat. Simmer about 15
     minutes.
3.   Add fish to mixture. Cover. Cook ten minutes or until fish flakes easily with a
     fork.

6 Servings

160 CALORIES / FAT 4 g (38 CAL or 24% of total calories) / SAT FAT 1 g (5% of total calories) / CARB 15 g /
PROTEIN 16 g / CHOL 45 mg / SODIUM 465 mg

ALABAMA BARBECUED FISH

⅓ cup Crisco Oil
1 can (8 ounces) tomato sauce
2 tablespoons prepared mustard
2 tablespoons maple syrup
1 garlic clove, minced
½ teaspoon salt
¼ teaspoon pepper

3 drops hot pepper sauce
1 pound cod, halibut or haddock steak
2 tablespoons lemon juice
2 teaspoons cornstarch
2⅔ cups hot cooked rice (without salt or fat)

1. Combine Crisco Oil, tomato sauce, mustard, syrup, garlic, salt, pepper and hot pepper sauce in large shallow baking dish. Stir well. Reserve ½ cup.
2. Place fish in sauce. Turn to coat. Refrigerate 30 minutes. Turn once.
3. Heat broiler or prepare grill.
4. Remove fish from sauce. Broil or grill 3 to 5 minutes or until fish flakes easily with fork.
5. Combine reserved ½ cup sauce, lemon juice and cornstarch in small saucepan. Cook and stir until mixture comes to a boil. Reduce heat. Simmer 3 minutes. Serve with fish and rice.

4 Servings

415 CALORIES / FAT 12 g (102 CAL or 25% of total calories) / SAT FAT <1 g (<5% of total calories) / CARB 44 g / PROTEIN 30 g / CHOL 45 mg / SODIUM 370 mg

FAVORITE CAJUN CATFISH

1 pound thin catfish fillets
1 lemon
½ teaspoon salt
Garlic powder

Cajun seafood spice
2 teaspoons olive oil
2⅔ cups cooked rice (without salt or fat)

1. Place ¼ inch water in broiling pan.
2. Heat broiler.
3. Rinse fish. Place in pan.
4. Squeeze lemon juice over fish. Sprinkle with salt and garlic powder. Sprinkle with Cajun seafood spice until fish is completely covered. Sprinkle with small amount of olive oil.
5. Broil 5 minutes. Turn carefully. Broil 5 minutes or until fish flakes easily when tested with fork. Check frequently, do not overcook. Serve with rice.

4 Servings

Adaptation from Recipe
Alvin F. Poussaint, M.D.

330 CALORIES / FAT 7 g (67 CAL or 20% of total calories) / SAT FAT 2 g (<5% of total calories) / CARB 39 g / PROTEIN 24 g / CHOL 65 mg / SODIUM 340 mg

Lincoln Park Birthday Party for Mrs. Bethune

Every year, Dr. Height organizes a commemoration in honor of the birthday of Mrs. Bethune. The program is always held outdoors in Lincoln Park at the Bethune Memorial. This is the only monument to a woman and the first in a public park in Washington, DC for an African-American. Mrs. Bethune's birthday is July 10, which means the celebration always takes place on one of the hottest days in the brutally hot DC summer. The program consists of choirs and speeches and presentations and recitations of Mrs. Bethune's life history and accomplishments. It is a very moving program and I go every year. I have never been when it wasn't hot. It is so hot there you almost melt and after a few minutes, you long for a block of ice. At the conclusion of the program, all the guests go over to a nearby church for punch and cake. The care and attention the ladies of the church give to their annual refreshments are a tribute to both Mrs. Bethune and Dr. Height. I have heard the ladies talk about the cakes and each one says, "For Dorothy, it has to be the best." Even in little things, Dr. Height inspires people to excellence.

Michele Brown

BROILED SESAME FISH

¼ cup Crisco Oil
¼ cup soy sauce
¼ cup dry white wine
1½ teaspoons sesame seed
1 teaspoon sugar
½ teaspoon ginger
4 flounder, sole, or catfish fillets (about 1 pound)
½ teaspoon pepper (optional)
12 green onions

1. Combine Crisco Oil, soy sauce, wine, sesame seed, sugar and ginger in shallow baking dish. Stir until blended.
2. Place fish in marinade. Turn to coat. Refrigerate 20 minutes. Turn once.
3. Trim green onion tops to 5 to 6 inches in length. Split bottom 3 inches to give feathered look. Place in marinade for last 10 minutes of marinating time.
4. Heat broiler. Remove fish and onions from marinade. Place on broiler pan. Sprinkle with pepper, if desired.
5. Broil 3 to 5 minutes per side or until fish flakes easily with fork.

4 Servings

To Microwave:
1. Follow steps 1, 2, and 3 above.
2. Remove fish and onions from marinade. Place in 12 X 8-inch microwave-safe dish. Sprinkle with pepper, if desired. Cover with plastic wrap. Microwave at HIGH for 2 minutes. Turn dish. Microwave at HIGH for 1 minute, 30 seconds or until fish flakes easily with fork. Let stand, covered one minute.

165 CALORIES / FAT 6 g (54 CAL or 33% of total calories) / SAT FAT 1 g (<5% of total calories) / CARB 4 g / PROTEIN 22 g / CHOL 55 mg / SODIUM 425 mg

SAUCY VEGETABLE BAKED POTATOES

8 medium baking potatoes, scrubbed and dried
4 tablespoons Crisco Oil, divided
3 tablespoons all-purpose flour
¼ teaspoon pepper
2 cups skim milk

8 slices (¾ ounce each) reduced fat American pasteurized process cheese, cubed
1 package (16 ounces) frozen mixed vegetables (broccoli, cauliflower and carrot mixture), cooked and drained

1. Heat oven to 425°.
2. Use one tablespoon Crisco Oil to rub on all 8 potatoes.
3. Bake at 425° for 35 to 40 minutes or until done.
4. Blend remaining 3 tablespoons oil, flour and pepper in large saucepan until smooth. Stir in milk gradually. Cook and stir on medium or medium-high heat until mixture comes to a boil and is slightly thickened and smooth. Remove from heat. Stir in cheese until melted. Stir in vegetables. (Reheat on low, if necessary.)
5. Cut open potatoes. Top with vegetables and sauce.

8 Servings

380 CALORIES / FAT 10 g (90 CAL or 24% of total calories) / SAT FAT 3 g (7% of total calories) / CARB 60 g / PROTEIN 15 g / CHOL 10 mg / SODIUM 360 mg

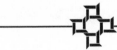

PIZZA GARDEN STYLE

Herb sauce

- 2 tablespoons Crisco Oil
- 1 cup chopped onion
- 2 cloves garlic, minced
- 2 cans (14½ ounces each) no salt added tomatoes, undrained and chopped

- 2 cans (8 ounces each) no salt added tomato sauce
- 2 tablespoons minced parsley
- 2 teaspoons dried basil leaves
- 1 teaspoon sugar
- ½ teaspoon dried oregano leaves
- ¼ teaspoon pepper

Pizza dough

- 2 cups all-purpose flour, divided
- 1 tablespoon sugar
- ½ teaspoon salt
- 1 package (¼ ounce) active dry yeast

- 1 cup warm water (110° to 115°)
- 2 tablespoons Crisco Oil
- 1 cup whole wheat flour

Fresca topping

- 1 medium zucchini, thinly sliced
- ½ large sweet red, yellow or green pepper, cut into thin strips
- 4 ounces small mushrooms, thinly sliced

- 8 ounces (2 cups) shredded low moisture part-skim mozzarella cheese
- 2 tablespoons grated Parmesan cheese

1. For sauce, combine Crisco Oil, onion and garlic in large saucepan. Cook and stir on low heat until onion is tender. Stir in tomatoes, tomato sauce, parsley, basil, sugar, oregano and pepper. Simmer, uncovered, one hour or until very thick. Cool to room temperature.
2. Heat oven to 425°. Oil two 12-inch pizza pans (or 2 baking sheets) lightly.
3. For dough, combine 1¼ cups all-purpose flour, sugar, salt and yeast in large bowl. Add water and Crisco Oil. Blend at low speed of electric mixer 30 seconds, scraping bowl constantly. Beat at high speed 3 minutes. Stir in whole wheat flour. Add enough of remaining all-purpose flour to make soft dough. Knead on lightly floured surface until smooth and elastic (about 6 to 8 minutes). Press half of dough in pan to form 13-inch circle (or roll dough on lightly floured surface and transfer to pan). Pinch edges to form rim. Prick bottom and sides with fork. Repeat for remaining dough.
4. Bake at 425° for 10 to 12 minutes or until golden brown. (Bake at 400° if using dark pizza pans or baking sheets.) Cool. Spread half of sauce evenly over each crust.
5. For topping, arrange zucchini on top. Spread pepper strips and mushrooms evenly. Sprinkle with mozzarella cheese and Parmesan cheese.
6. Bake at 425° for 12 to 15 minutes or until cheese is bubbly and lightly browned.

Two 12-Inch Pizzas (24 Slices)

Note: Herb sauce can be prepared and refrigerated for later use. One half or all of pizza dough can be lightly oiled and refrigerated in a sealed plastic bag for 2 to 3 days. Allow dough to warm to room temperature before using. Lightly browned pizza crusts can be wrapped and frozen.

125 CALORIES / FAT 4 g (40 CAL or 32% of total calories) / SAT FAT 1 g (9% of total calories) / CARB 17 g / PROTEIN 6 g / CHOL 5 mg / SODIUM 115 mg

Option — Omit Fresca Topping and use one of the following:

GOLDEN GATE CASHEW

¾ cup (3 ounces) shredded
reduced fat Monterey cheese
¾ cup (3 ounces) shredded ⅓ less
fat sharp Cheddar cheese

½ medium red bell pepper, cut
into strips
1 cup sliced fresh mushrooms
½ cup cashews
¼ cup alfalfa sprouts

1. Sprinkle Monterey cheese and Cheddar cheese over Herb Sauce.
2. Top with bell pepper strips, mushrooms and cashews.
3. Bake for 8 to 10 minutes or until cheese is bubbly and lightly browned.
   Sprinkle with sprouts. Let stand 5 minutes before serving.

135 CALORIES / FAT 5 g (48 CAL or 35% of total calories) / SAT FAT 1 g (8% of total calories) / CARB 18 g /
PROTEIN 5 g / CHOL 5 mg / SODIUM 105 mg

DEAN'S DOUBLE TOMATO

½ teaspoon garlic powder
½ teaspoon dried basil leaves
2 cups chopped, seeded, peeled
tomatoes, drained (4 medium)
½ cup sliced green onion

1½ cups (6 ounces) shredded low
moisture part-skim mozzarella
cheese
2 tablespoons grated Parmesan
cheese

1. Sprinkle garlic powder and basil over Herb Sauce. Add tomatoes and green
   onions.
2. Top with mozzarella cheese and Parmesan cheese.
3. Bake for 8 to 10 minutes or until cheese is bubbly and lightly browned.

120 CALORIES / FAT 4 g (37 CAL or 31% of total calories) / SAT FAT 1 g (8% of total calories) / CARB 17 g /
PROTEIN 5 g / CHOL 5 mg / SODIUM 100 mg

TRIPLE CHEESE WHAMMY

1 package (8 ounces) 75% less fat
Swiss flavor process cheese
product slices, cut in strips
2 cups (8 ounces) shredded low
moisture part-skim mozzarella
cheese

⅓ cup grated Parmesan cheese
½ cup snipped fresh parsley
1 teaspoon dried rosemary

1. Arrange Swiss cheese strips over Herb Sauce. Top with mozzarella cheese
   and Parmesan cheese.
2. Sprinkle with parsley and rosemary.
3. Bake for 8 to 10 minutes or until cheese is bubbly and lightly browned.

120 CALORIES / FAT 4 g (37 CAL or 30% of total calories) / SAT FAT 1 g (9% of total calories) / CARB 17 g /
PROTEIN 4 g / CHOL 5 mg / SODIUM 165 mg

SOUTH OF THE BORDER CHICKEN & PEPPER ROLL-UPS

1	teaspoon Crisco Shortening or Crisco Oil
4	boneless, skinless chicken breast halves, cut into 1½ X ¼-inch strips (about 1 pound)
2	green bell peppers, cut into 1½ X ¼-inch strips
1	large onion, cut into 1 X 1-inch pieces
2	cloves garlic, minced
½	cup fresh lime juice
1	teaspoon ground cumin
1	teaspoon dried oregano leaves
⅛	teaspoon pepper
8	medium (8-inch) flour tortillas
	Salt (optional)
½	cup salsa
¼	cup chopped green onions

1. Heat Crisco Shortening or Crisco Oil in large skillet on medium-high heat. Add chicken, green peppers, onion and garlic. Stir-fry about 2 minutes.
2. Reduce heat to low. Add lime juice, cumin, oregano and pepper. Simmer about 7 minutes or until chicken is no longer pink in center.
3. Warm tortillas, 15 seconds per side, in non-stick skillet on medium heat. Place on serving plate. Use slotted spoon to transfer chicken mixture to tortillas. Season with salt, if desired. Garnish with salsa and green onions. Fold up bottom, then fold in sides to enclose.

4 Servings

395 CALORIES / FAT 9 g (81 CAL or 20% of total calories) / SAT FAT 1 g (<5% of total calories) / CARB 49 g / PROTEIN 33 g / CHOL 65 mg / SODIUM 375 mg

CELEBRATION CHICKEN BUNS

1 tablespoon Crisco Shortening or Crisco Oil
⅓ cup finely chopped green bell pepper
⅓ cup finely chopped celery
⅓ cup finely chopped onion
1 clove garlic, minced
½ cup ketchup
2 tablespoons Worcestershire sauce

2 tablespoons cider vinegar
1 tablespoon brown sugar
½ teaspoon salt
¼ teaspoon chili powder
¼ teaspoon pepper
2 cans (5 ounces each) chicken in water, drained (1½ cups)
8 hamburger buns, split

1. Heat Crisco Shortening or Crisco Oil in large skillet on medium heat. Add green pepper, celery, onion and garlic. Sauté until crisp-tender. Add ketchup, Worcestershire sauce, vinegar, brown sugar, salt, chili powder, and pepper. Mix well. Heat to a boil. Reduce heat. Stir in chicken. Simmer 10 minutes, stirring occasionally.
2. Spoon about ¼ cup chicken mixture over bottom half of each bun. Replace top.

8 Servings

220 CALORIES / FAT 6 g (54 CAL or 24% of total calories) / SAT FAT 1 g (<5% of total calories) / CARB 30 g / PROTEIN 11 g / CHOL 20 mg / SODIUM 670 mg

SUMMER GARDEN VEGETABLE POCKET

1 tablespoon Crisco Shortening or Crisco Oil
2 cups diagonally sliced yellow squash (about ½ pound)
2 cups diagonally sliced zucchini (about ½ pound)
⅛ teaspoon dried basil leaves

⅛ teaspoon salt
⅛ teaspoon pepper
2 tablespoons grated Parmesan cheese
2 six-inch whole wheat pita breads, halved
4 leaves Boston lettuce

1. Heat Crisco Shortening or Crisco Oil in large skillet on medium-high heat. Add yellow and zucchini squash. Sauté 7 to 8 minutes or until tender. Add basil, salt and pepper. Toss to mix. Remove from heat. Sprinkle with Parmesan cheese.
2. Line pita pocket with lettuce leaf. Spoon about ½ cup vegetables into each.

4 Sandwiches

150 CALORIES / FAT 5 g (45 CAL or 30% of total calories) / SAT FAT 1 g (6% of total calories) / CARB 22 g / PROTEIN 6 g / CHOL 0 mg / SODIUM 290 mg

GROUND BEEF TOSTADAS

1	pound ground beef round
1	package (1¼ ounces) taco seasoning mix
1	cup drained canned or uncooked corn
1	can (8 ounces) kidney beans, drained
1	can (4 ounces) chopped green chilies, drained
1	tablespoon Crisco Oil
8	medium (6 to 7-inch) corn tortillas
2⅔	cups shredded iceberg lettuce
2	medium tomatoes, chopped (about 1⅓ cups)
½	cup shredded reduced fat Colby cheese (2 oz.)
½	cup chopped green onions and tops
1	cup taco sauce or salsa

1. Heat oven to 350°.
2. Sauté meat in large skillet. Drain off drippings. Follow taco seasoning mix package directions to make filling. Add corn, kidney beans and green chilies. Stir well. Keep warm.
3. Brush Crisco Oil lightly on both sides of tortillas. Place in single layer on one large or 2 small baking sheets.
4. Bake at 350° for 2½ to 3 minutes. Turn over. Bake on other side 2½ to 3 minutes longer.
5. To assemble each tostada, place tortilla on plate. Top with ½ cup meat mixture, ⅓ cup lettuce, 2 to 3 tablespoons tomato, 1 tablespoon cheese and 1 tablespoon onion. Top with 2 tablespoons taco sauce.

8 Servings

225 CALORIES / FAT 7 g (64 CAL or 29% of total calories) / SAT FAT 3 g (10% of total calories) / CARB 18 g / PROTEIN 22 g / CHOL 50 mg / SODIUM 605 mg

CHEESY VEGETABLE OMELETS

1	cup frozen mixed broccoli and cauliflower flowerets
6	egg whites
¼	cup evaporated skim milk
1½	teaspoons Crisco Oil
⅛	teaspoon turmeric
1	drop hot pepper sauce
¼	teaspoon salt
¼	teaspoon dried basil leaves
⅛	teaspoon pepper
1	teaspoon Crisco Oil, divided
4	tablespoons sliced green onions, divided
2	slices (¾-ounce each) fat free process cheese product, halved

1. Cook broccoli and cauliflower mixture according to package directions. Drain. Keep warm.
2. Combine egg whites, milk, 1½ teaspoons Crisco Oil, food color, hot pepper sauce, salt, basil and pepper in medium bowl. Stir with fork until just blended.
3. Put ¼ teaspoon Crisco Oil in small non-stick skillet. Add one tablespoon green onion. Sauté 1 or 2 minutes on low heat. Add ¼ cup egg mixture. Cook without stirring, lifting edges and tilting skillet to let uncooked mixture run underneath. Cook until barely set. Place ¼ cup vegetables on half of omelet. Top with one-half slice cheese. Fold other half of omelet over cheese. Cook about 30 seconds longer to melt cheese. Repeat for remaining omelets.

4 Servings

90 CALORIES / FAT 3 g (27 CAL or 30% of total calories) / SAT FAT <1 g (<5% of total calories) / CARB 6 g / PROTEIN 10 g / CHOL 0 mg / SODIUM 405 mg

(continued)

having access to quality care has really held black women back. It has reduced our options and made everything more difficult. To have that kind of conversation with an 80 year old woman makes you realize how broad the support for choice is in the black community.

**Kayla Jackson
Women's Reproductive
Health Program**

TOASTED "HAM" SALAD SANDWICHES

3   cups shredded cabbage
½   cup chopped unpeeled apple
    (one small)
⅓   cup nonfat sour cream
    alternative
2   tablespoons sweet pickle relish,
    drained

½   teaspoon curry powder
12 slices whole wheat bread
1   tablespoon Crisco Oil
6   slices thinly sliced turkey ham
6   slices (¾-ounce each) fat free,
    process cheese product

1. Combine cabbage, apple, "sour cream", pickle relish and curry powder in medium bowl. Stir well.
2. Brush one side of each bread slice lightly with Crisco Oil.
3. Top plain side of 6 bread slices with turkey ham slice, about ⅓ cup cabbage mixture and cheese slice. Top with remaining bread slices, plain side against cheese.
3. Heat large nonstick skillet or griddle on medium heat. Brown sandwiches on one side until brown as desired. Turn with large pancake turner. Grill on second side until brown as desired and cheese melts.

6 Sandwiches

240 CALORIES / FAT 6 g (54 CAL or 23% of total calories) / SAT FAT 1 g (5% of total calories) / CARB 34 g / PROTEIN 12 g / CHOL 15 mg / SODIUM 670 mg

SLOPPY JOES ON WHOLE WHEAT BUNS

1   tablespoon Crisco Shortening or
    Crisco Oil
½   cup minced onion
½   cup chopped celery
½   cup chopped green pepper
½   cup shredded carrots
1¼ pounds ground beef round

½   cup ketchup
½   cup water
1   teaspoon chili powder
½   teaspoon salt
¼   teaspoon pepper
    Dash hot pepper sauce
8   whole wheat sandwich buns

1. Heat Crisco Shortening or Crisco Oil in large skillet on medium heat. Add onion, celery, green pepper and carrots. Stir-fry until softened.
2. Add meat. Cook and stir until lightly browned. Stir in ketchup, water, chili powder, salt, pepper and hot pepper sauce.
3. Simmer uncovered on low heat 15 minutes or until thick enough to spoon on buns.

8 Servings

270 CALORIES / FAT 9 g (77 CAL or 28% of total calories) / SAT FAT 3 g (8% of total calories) / CARB 21 g / PROTEIN 26 g / CHOL 60 mg / SODIUM 555 mg

"The Oldham Family Quilt" by Carolyn L. Mazloomi (Cincinnati, OH)

Bettye Torrey Oldham's quilt became a reality because she has a history of travel that was initiated by her father, James Torrey, who worked for the L & N railroad all his life. Family trips on the train developed into world-wide travel. Education and a good work ethic were strongly taught by her hard working mother, Lillie Holt Torrey. Mrs. Torrey instilled in her children that family values, hard work, and education would increase their appreciation for God, life style, livelihood, and knowledge. The blocks on the quilt represent Bettye's travels to Africa, Paris, Nassau, Cairo, Rome, and Rio.

Bettye Torrey Oldham

Story quilts are narrative rather than abstract. They flow directly out of the oral tradition which used story telling as a way to impart the culture and preserve the history of a people. Story telling and the story quilt impart moral and spiritual lessons as well as personal family genealogy for future generations. To view a story quilt is to learn about the quilters, their families, values and life experiences. One has only to review West African history to understand the role of using narrative in the creation of textile pieces.

CREOLE BEANS & RICE

2 cans (14½ ounces each) peeled no salt added tomatoes
1 cup uncooked long grain rice
2 tablespoons Crisco Shortening or Crisco Oil
½ cup chopped onion
4 cloves garlic, minced
1 cup chopped celery
1 cup chopped carrots
1 cup chopped green bell pepper
1 tablespoon ground cumin

1 tablespoon chili powder
1 teaspoon dried basil leaves
½ teaspoon cayenne pepper
2 cans (16 ounces each) kidney beans, drained
1 can (6 ounces) no salt added tomato paste
3 tablespoons vinegar
1 tablespoon Worcestershire sauce
1 teaspoon sugar

1. Drain tomatoes, reserving liquid. Add enough water to make 2 cups. Pour into medium saucepan. Add rice. Bring to a boil. Reduce heat. Simmer 20 minutes or until rice is tender.
2. Heat Crisco Shortening or Crisco Oil in large saucepan on medium heat. Add onion and garlic. Cook until softened. Add celery and carrots. Cook until almost done. Add green pepper, cumin, chili powder, basil and cayenne pepper. Cook until tender.
3. Add tomatoes. Break up with spoon. Stir in kidney beans, rice, tomato paste, vinegar, Worcestershire sauce and sugar. Heat on low.

8 Servings

325 CALORIES / FAT 5 g (44 CAL or 14% of total calories) / SAT FAT <1 g (<5% of total calories) / CARB 62 g / PROTEIN 11 g / CHOL 0 mg / SODIUM 475 mg

TANGY TURNIP 'N TATERS

4 medium turnips
2 medium potatoes

1 tablespoon margarine
½ teaspoon pepper

1. Peel turnips and potatoes. Cut into quarters.
2. Place turnips and potatoes in large saucepan half filled with water. Cook on high heat until soft.
3. Drain water from vegetables. Blend with electric mixer until smooth. Stir in margarine and pepper. Serve hot.

6 Servings
Variation: Mix in 1 teaspoon horseradish before serving.

65 CALORIES / FAT 2 g (18 CAL or 28% of total calories) / SAT FAT <1 g (5% of total calories) / CARB 11 g / PROTEIN 1 g / CHOL 0 mg / SODIUM 70 mg

CHEESY POTATOES

1½ cups lowfat cottage cheese
1 cup nonfat sour cream alternative
¼ cup finely minced green onions
½ teaspoon salt

¼ teaspoon garlic salt
5 cups diced, cooked potatoes
½ cup shredded low fat sharp Cheddar cheese
Paprika

1. Heat oven to 325°. Grease 1½-quart casserole.
2. Combine cottage cheese, "sour cream", onion, salt, and garlic salt in large bowl. Fold in potatoes. Spoon into casserole. Top with cheese and sprinkle with paprika.
3. Bake at 325° for 45 minutes.

6 Servings

245 CALORIES / FAT 4 g (32 CAL or 14% of total calories) / SAT FAT 2 g (8% of total calories) / CARB 30 g / PROTEIN 18 g / CHOL 20 mg / SODIUM 635 mg

OLD STYLE SCALLOPED POTATOES

3 tablespoons Crisco Oil
½ cup chopped onion
¼ cup all-purpose flour
¾ teaspoon salt
¼ teaspoon pepper
⅛ teaspoon paprika

2 cups skim milk
2 pounds all-purpose potatoes, peeled and thinly sliced (8 cups)
Paprika
2 tablespoons chopped fresh parsley

1. Heat oven to 350°. Oil 2-quart casserole lightly.
2. Heat Crisco Oil in medium saucepan on medium-high heat. Add onion. Cook and stir until tender. Stir in flour, salt, pepper and ⅛ teaspoon paprika. Blend in milk. Cook and stir on medium-high heat until sauce comes to a boil and is thickened.
3. Layer one-third of potatoes in bottom of casserole. Top with one-third of the sauce. Repeat twice. Cover.
4. Bake at 350° for one hour 15 minutes. Uncover. Bake 15 minutes longer or until potatoes are tender. Sprinkle with paprika and parsley.

8 Servings

175 CALORIES / FAT 6 g (50 CAL or 28% of total calories) / SAT FAT <1 g (<5% of total calories) / CARB 27 g / PROTEIN 5 g / CHOL 0 mg / SODIUM 240 mg

POTATOES, POTATOES

2 pounds tiny new potatoes	1 teaspoon dried vegetable
2 tablespoons vegetable oil	seasoning
3 tablespoons low fat margarine	¼ teaspoon pepper
1 large onion, minced	1 tablespoon Parmesan cheese
2 garlic cloves, minced	3 tomatoes, sliced
6 sprigs parsley, minced	

1. Boil potatoes until almost done. Cool slightly. Peel.
2. Heat oil and margarine in large skillet on low heat. Add potatoes, onion, garlic, parsley, seasoning and pepper. Cook, shaking skillet occasionally, until onion is tender and potatoes are lightly browned.
3. Spoon into serving dish. Sprinkle with Parmesan cheese. Serve with chilled sliced tomatoes on the side.

6 Servings.

205 CALORIES / FAT 7 g (65 CAL or 32% of total calories) / SAT FAT 1 g (<5% of total calories) / CARB 33 g / PROTEIN 4 g / CHOL 0 mg / SODIUM 80 mg

Adaptation from Recipe
Juanita Wilkinson
NCNW Fund Committee

TROPICAL YAM BAKE

2 cans (18 ounces each) yams or sweet potatoes, mashed, or 2¼ pounds fresh, cooked, drained, mashed	¼ cup orange juice
	3 tablespoons Crisco Oil
	1½ teaspoons grated lime peel
	2 tablespoons lime juice
2 eggs	½ teaspoon nutmeg
½ cup firmly packed light brown sugar	2 bananas, peeled, diced
	Grated lime peel

1. Heat oven to 350°. Oil 11¾ X 7½-inch baking dish.
2. Combine yams, eggs, brown sugar, orange juice, Crisco Oil, 1½ teaspoons lime peel, lime juice and nutmeg in large bowl. Beat at low speed of electric mixer until just blended. Increase speed to medium. Beat until well blended.
3. Fold in bananas with spoon. Transfer to baking dish. Cover dish with foil.
4. Bake at 350° for 20 minutes. Remove foil. Bake 10 minutes. Sprinkle with additional lime peel.

8 Servings

315 CALORIES / FAT 7 g (63 CAL or 20% of total calories) / SAT FAT 1 g (<5% of total calories) / CARB 60 g / PROTEIN 4 g / CHOL 55 mg / SODIUM 30 mg

(continued)

I Leave You Faith

A friend asked me to deliver a pound cake she had baked for Dr. Height. When I arrived, Dr. Height invited me to join her for a slice of cake and a cup of tea. As we talked, she learned I was a seminarian who worked with the youth at my church. She talked about her involvement with the World Conference on Life and Work of the Churches as a youth delegate. I listened to her describe her involvement with ministers, clergy people and lay students of all denominations who gathered in the 1930's to investigate the social and economic causes of world strife. Dr. Height told me that Abyssinian Baptist Church in New York had helped with her expenses for the trip. Adam Clayton Powell, Sr. was the pastor then and Dr. Height said when he introduced her to the congregation he said, "Dorothy is a smart girl and we're proud that she's going to England, but she can't walk on water, so let's see how we can help her get there." An appropriate outpouring of love for such a deserving spirit.

Her memory is phenomenal... she told me the advice the custodian at the church, Mr. Dixon, gave her about how much to tip

ORANGE APRICOT DRESSING

1 cup water
2 tablespoons margarine
1 (8 ounce) package herb seasoned stuffing crumbs
½ cup chopped celery
¼ cup chopped green onions and tops (2 or 3 onions)
½ cup orange marmalade
½ cup finely chopped fresh apricots or canned drained juice pack apricots
¼ cup chopped pecans
⅛ teaspoon pepper

1. Combine water and margarine in large saucepan. Place on medium heat. Stir to melt. Remove from heat.
2. Stir in stuffing crumbs, celery, onions, marmalade, apricots, nuts, and pepper. Serve immediately as side dish with poultry or pork.

10 Servings

165 CALORIES / FAT 5 g (45 CAL or 27% of total calories) / SAT FAT 1 g (5% of total calories) / CARB 28 g / PROTEIN 4 g / CHOL 0 mg / SODIUM 600 mg

DEVILED BEETS

2 cups sliced, cooked beets
1 tablespoon margarine
2 tablespoons prepared mustard
3 tablespoons honey
1 teaspoon Worcestershire sauce
½ teaspoon salt
¼ teaspoon paprika

1. Heat oven to 350°.
2. Place beets in small shallow baking dish.
3. Melt margarine in small saucepan. Add mustard, honey, and Worcestershire sauce. Season with salt and paprika. Stir in well. Heat. Pour over beets.
4. Bake at 350° for 15 minutes.

8 Servings

100 CALORIES / FAT 2 g (20 CAL or 20% of total calories) / SAT FAT <1 g (<5% of total calories) / CARB 17 g / PROTEIN 4 g / CHOL 5 mg / SODIUM 306 mg

HOPPIN' JOHN

6	cups water
1	pound dried black-eyed peas
¼	cup Crisco Shortening or Crisco Oil
1	large green bell pepper, chopped
1	large onion chopped
6	cloves garlic, minced
1	teaspoon ground cumin
1	teaspoon dried thyme leaves
1	can (6 ounces) tomato paste
1	teaspoon chili powder
2	pounds brown rice
8	slices cooked bacon, crumbled
¼	teaspoon salt
¼	teaspoon pepper

1. Combine water and black-eyed peas in large saucepan. Cook until almost tender, about one hour. Add more water, if needed.
2. Heat Crisco Shortening or Crisco Oil in medium skillet on medium heat. Add green pepper, onion, garlic, cumin and thyme. Cook and stir until browned. Add tomato paste and chili powder. Stir. Add a little water. Stir. Pour into beans. Add rice, bacon, salt and pepper. Stir. Add enough water to cover by 1½-inches. Cover. Bring to a boil. Reduce heat. Simmer 30 minutes.

6 to 8 Servings

740 CALORIES / FAT 15 g (131 CAL or 18% of total calories) / SAT FAT 3 g (<5% of total calories) / CARB 129 g / PROTEIN 26 g / CHOL 5 mg / SODIUM 365 mg

HERITAGE RECIPE

(continued)

the porters on an ocean liner and how to avoid seasickness. Her trip to Oxford with other young Christian men and women fascinated me. She traveled to England with Dr. and Mrs. Benjamin Mays and visited cathedrals and villages all over the countryside. Dr. Height said that like all the conference participants, she felt as if she had been called by God to build a new world of faith and good works.

Rev. Courtenay Miller

HOT 'N SPICY BLACK-EYED PEAS & RICE

6 cups water
1 pound dried black-eye peas
1 cup turkey ham, diced (8 ounces)
1 cup celery, chopped
1 large onion, chopped
1 teaspoon garlic powder

1 teaspoon chili powder
½ teaspoon cayenne pepper
½ teaspoon black pepper
4 cups cooked rice (without salt or fat)
1 can (6 ounces) tomato paste

1. Place water, peas, ham, celery, onion, garlic powder, chili powder, cayenne and black pepper in large, deep cooking pot. Cover. Simmer about 1 hour 30 minutes or until peas are tender. Add more water as needed.
2. Stir in rice and tomato paste. Cover. Let stand to heat thoroughly before serving.

8 Servings

390 CALORIES / FAT 3 g (25 CAL or 6% of total calories) / SAT FAT 1g (<5% of total calories) / CARB 69 g / PROTEIN 23 g / CHOL 15 mg / SODIUM 465 mg

TANGY BLACK BEANS 'N RICE

Tangy Sauce

1 can (14½ ounces) tomatoes, undrained, chopped
¾ cup chopped onion

½ teaspoon garlic powder
½ teaspoon salt
1 teaspoon red pepper sauce

Beans

1¼ cups dried black beans
1 onion peeled
½ teaspoon salt
1¾ cups chopped onion
1 green bell pepper, chopped

1 clove garlic, minced
1 tablespoon Crisco Shortening or Crisco Oil
2⅔ cups hot cooked rice (without salt or fat)

1. For sauce, combine tomatoes, chopped onion, garlic powder, salt and red pepper sauce. Cover. Refrigerate overnight.
2. For beans, cover beans with water. Cover. Soak overnight. Drain.
3. Place beans in large saucepan. Cover with water. Add whole onion and salt. Bring to a boil. Cover pan. Reduce heat. Simmer 60 minutes or until tender.
4. Heat Crisco Shortening or Crisco Oil in small skillet on medium heat. Sauté onion, green pepper, and garlic. Add to beans.
5. Simmer a few minutes to blend flavors. Remove whole onion. Serve beans over rice. Top with Tangy Sauce.

6 Servings

305 CALORIES / FAT 3 g (31 CAL or 10% of total calories) / SAT FAT <1 g (<5% of total calories) / CARB 58 g / PROTEIN 12 g / CHOL 0 mg / SODIUM 470 mg

STUFFED BELL PEPPERS WITH COLLARD GREENS

3 bunches collard greens, stems removed (about 3 pounds)
Salt and pepper
2 tablespoons salad oil
4 yellow or red bell peppers

2 medium carrots, diced and blanched
2 medium turnips, diced and blanched

1. Wash and julienne collard greens. Place in large saucepan. Season with salt and pepper. Add oil. Stir. Cook on low heat one hour or until tender. Add water if needed.
2. Cut peppers in half. Remove seeds. Blanch in hot water about 10 minutes.
3. Remove from water. Rinse with cold water. Drain well.
4. Stuff peppers with collard greens. Garnish with diced carrots and turnips.

8 Servings

85 CALORIES / FAT 3 g (27 CAL or 31% of total calories) / SAT FAT <1 g (<5% of total calories) / CARB 13 g / PROTEIN 4 g / CHOL 0 mg / SODIUM 130 mg

**Adaptation from Recipe
Chef B. E. Lowder,
Los Angeles, CA**

CONFETTI SCALLOPED CORN

1 cup skim milk
1 egg, beaten
1 cup coarsely crushed saltine crackers (21 or 22 2-inch square crackers), divided
¼ teaspoon salt
⅛ teaspoon pepper

1 can (16½ ounces) yellow cream style corn
¼ cup finely chopped onion
1 jar (2 ounces) diced pimiento, drained
1 tablespoon Crisco Oil
1 tablespoon snipped fresh parsley

1. Heat oven to 350°.
2. Combine milk, egg, ⅔ cup cracker crumbs, salt and pepper in medium bowl. Stir in corn, onion and pimiento. Pour into ungreased one-quart casserole or baking dish.
3. Toss remaining ⅓ cup cracker crumbs with Crisco Oil. Sprinkle over top of corn mixture.
4. Bake at 350° for one hour or until knife inserted in center comes out clean. Sprinkle with parsley. Let stand 5 to 15 minutes before serving.

6 Servings

155 CALORIES / FAT 5 g (42 CAL or 27% of total calories) / SAT FAT 1 g (6% of total calories) / CARB 25 g / PROTEIN 4 g / CHOL 40 mg / SODIUM 485 mg

OKRA & CORN PILAF

1 tablespoon Crisco Shortening or Crisco Oil
2 cups sliced okra, fresh or frozen
1 cup chopped onion
¼ cup chopped green bell pepper
2 cups low sodium chicken broth
1 package (10 ounces) frozen corn
1 cup uncooked long grain rice
1 teaspoon salt
1 can (14½ ounces) no salt added tomatoes, drained and chopped
3 slices bacon cooked and crumbled

1. Heat Crisco Shortening or Crisco Oil in Dutch oven on medium heat. Add okra, onion and green pepper. Cook until tender. Add broth, corn, rice and salt. Bring to a boil. Stir once.
2. Simmer, uncovered, 20 minutes or until rice is done. Stir in tomatoes and bacon. Heat through. Serve immediately.

8 Servings

175 CALORIES / FAT 3 g (25 CAL or 15% of total calories) / SAT FAT <1 g (<5% of total calories) / CARB 34 g / PROTEIN 6 g / CHOL 3mg / SODIUM 410 mg

OKRA TOMATO OVEN BAKE

1 tablespoon Crisco Shortening or Crisco Oil
1 medium onion, finely chopped
2 packages (10 ounces each) frozen okra or 3 to 4 cups cut fresh okra
2 tablespoons uncooked instant rice
1 small green bell pepper, finely chopped
4 slices turkey bacon, cooked and crumbled
1 can (14½ ounces) tomatoes
1 tablespoon sugar
¼ teaspoon salt
⅛ teaspoon garlic salt
⅛ teaspoon pepper
¼ cup Parmesan cheese
¼ cup fine dry bread crumbs

1. Heat oven to 350°. Grease 11¾ X 7½-inch casserole.
2. Heat Crisco Shortening or Crisco Oil in large skillet on medium heat. Add onion and okra. Cook until softened. Place in casserole. Add rice, green pepper an crumbled bacon. Mix well.
3. Combine undrained tomatoes, sugar, salt, garlic salt and pepper in food processor. Process on low speed 1 minute. Pour mixture over okra. Sprinkle with Parmesan cheese and bread crumbs.
4. Bake at 350° for 30 to 45 minutes or until hot and bubbly.

10 Servings

95 CALORIES / FAT 3 g (28 CAL or 30% of total calories) / SAT FAT 1 g (8% of total calories) / CARB 14 g / PROTEIN 5 g / CHOL 5 mg / SODIUM 320 mg

CREAMY MACARONI & CHEESE

1½ cups uncooked small elbow macaroni, cooked without salt or fat, well drained
2 tablespoons Crisco Oil
½ cup chopped green onions
1 clove garlic, minced
2 tablespoons all-purpose flour
¼ teaspoon dried basil leaves
¼ teaspoon dry mustard
⅛ teaspoon pepper

2 cups skim milk
½ cup nonfat sour cream alternative
4 ounces sharp, reduced (⅓ less) fat Cheddar cheese, shredded
1 teaspoon Worcestershire sauce
Dash hot pepper sauce
1 tablespoon unseasoned fine dry bread crumbs

1. Heat oven to 350°. Oil 2-quart casserole. Set aside.
2. Heat Crisco Oil in large skillet on medium heat. Add onions and garlic. Sauté until tender.
3. Stir in flour, basil, dry mustard, pepper, Worcestershire, and hot pepper sauce. Stir until well blended . Stir in milk. Cook and stir on medium heat until mixture thickens and gradually bubbles. Add "sour cream", cheese, Worcestershire sauce and hot pepper sauce. Stir until smooth.
4. Add sauce to macaroni. Toss to mix. Pour into casserole. Sprinkle with bread crumbs.
5. Bake at 350° for 25 minutes.

6 Servings

260 CALORIES / FAT 9 g (78 CAL or 30% of total calories) / SAT FAT 3 g (9% of total calories) / CARB 29 g / PROTEIN 13 g / CHOL 15 mg / SODIUM 215 mg

Mexican Variation: Omit bread crumbs. Crumble enough corn chips to measure ¼ cup. Add 1 can (4 ounces) chopped green chilies, drained, 1 jar (2 ounces) diced pimento, drained, and 1 teaspoon chili powder to sauce in step 3. Top casserole with crumbled corn chips.

290 CALORIES / FAT 10 g (90 CAL or 31% of total calories) / SAT FAT 3 g (9% of total calories) / CARB 34 g / PROTEIN 14 g / CHOL 15 mg / SODIUM 240 mg

To microwave:
1. Combine Crisco Oil, onion and garlic in large microwave-safe dish. Cover with plastic wrap. Microwave at HIGH for 2 minutes.
2. Follow step 3, above, through addition of milk. Cover. Microwave at HIGH about 6 minutes, stirring every 2 minutes, until mixture boils. Add "sour cream" and cheese. Stir until cheese melts. Stir in cooked macaroni. Cover. Microwave at HIGH for 4 minutes, stirring after 2 minutes. Uncover. Microwave at HIGH for 2 minutes. Sprinkle with crumbs.

Harlem

While I have had many conversations with Dorothy Height over the years, the one that stands out most in my mind took place in the late seventies. We were at a dinner in New York and she shared with me her ongoing love affair with Harlem. She told me that when she came to NYU for college, she lived in Harlem and for many years thereafter, Harlem was her "neighborhood". I think she must have known everyone there! She talked about the churches in Harlem and how important a vehicle those churches were for community organizing and sharing information. But her interest in Harlem transcended the purely political. She loved the culture and the people of Harlem. She mentioned legendary names like W. C. Handy, Langston Hughes, Dr. Dubois, Fats Waller, Eubie Blake, James Weldon Johnson, all of whom she knew personally. She spoke with delight about the American Negro Theatre where she heard Harry Belafonte and Sidney Poitier reading plays long before they were famous.

She told me that coming from the little town of Rankin, Pennsylvania, Harlem was a totally new

(continued)

LIBERIAN COLLARD GREENS

4	bunches collard greens (about 4 pounds)
4	bunches mustard greens (about 4 pounds)
3	tablespoons baking soda
2	tablespoons margarine
3	tablespoons minced garlic
2	onions, chopped
2	green bell peppers, julienned
2	red bell peppers, julienned
1	tablespoon crushed dried red pepper
3	cups water
1½	pounds smoked turkey wings and/or turkey drumsticks
3	low sodium bouillon cubes
⅓	cup distilled vinegar
24	medium shrimp (about ½ pound), peeled and deveined

1. Remove stems from greens. Wash until water is clear. Fill sink with water. Add baking soda. Dissolve. Soak greens several minutes. (Baking soda keeps greens green during cooking). Rinse greens in fresh water.
2. Melt margarine in 2-gallon pot or spaghetti cooker on medium heat. Add garlic. Cook until lightly colored. Add onions, green peppers, red peppers and dried red pepper. Add drained greens mixture a portion at a time. Stir well. Add 3 cups of water. Cook on high heat until greens are limp. Add more greens until all are cooked and limp.
3. Add smoked turkey parts and additional water to cover. Add bouillon cubes after water comes to a boil. Stir well. Reduce heat to low. Add vinegar. Cook 2 to 3 hours on low heat.
4. Add shrimp about 20 minutes before cooking is finished.

8 Servings

320 CALORIES / FAT 10 g (90 CAL or 28% of total calories) / SAT FAT 3 g (8% of total calories) / CARB 27 g / PROTEIN 36 g / CHOL 100 mg / SODIUM 1075 mg

**Adaptation from Recipe
Chef Eric L. Robertson, Sr.**

BAKED STUFFED TOMATOES

8	medium size firm tomatoes
1	tablespoon Crisco Shortening or Crisco Oil
⅓	cup chopped celery
2	tablespoons chopped onion
2	cups cooked brown rice (cooked without salt or fat)
¼	cup grated Parmesan cheese
1	tablespoon snipped fresh parsley
1¼	teaspoons dried basil leaves
¼	teaspoon salt
⅛	teaspoon pepper
⅛	teaspoon garlic powder
	Additional snipped fresh parsley (optional)

1. Cut thin slice from each tomato top. Reserve slices. Scoop out centers of tomatoes. Chop pulp and reserve. Drain shells upside down on paper towels.
2. Heat oven to 350°. Oil 11¾ X 7½ rectangular glass baking dish lightly.
3. Heat Crisco Shortening or Crisco Oil in medium saucepan. Add celery and onion. Sauté on medium heat until celery is tender. Remove from heat. Add reserved tomato pulp, rice, Parmesan cheese, parsley, basil, salt, pepper and garlic powder. Mix well. Spoon into tomato shells. Replace tops if desired. Place in baking dish. Cover with foil.
4. Bake at 350° for 35 to 40 minutes, or until tomatoes are tender. Season with additional salt and pepper and garnish with additional parsley, if desired.

8 Servings
Note: Bake tomatoes in individual oiled custard cups instead of pie plate or dish, if desired.

110 CALORIES / FAT 3 g (30 CAL or 27% of total calories) / SAT FAT 1 g (7% of total calories) / CARB 18 g / PROTEIN 3 g / CHOL 0 mg / SODIUM 130 mg

(continued)
experience. She thrived on the energy and the diversity of Harlem. I am convinced that Harlem was an incubator for her in a way nowhere else in America could have been.

Julian Bond

GRAND'S COLLARD GREENS & OKRA

The Meal Is to Listen and Enjoy

Any meal occasion with Dr. Dorothy Irene Height is a memorable experience. She is one of the truly great mealtime conversationalists still among us. Soft spoken, gentle dignity, profound recall, subtle wit and grand scale action plans… that is how I have known her. She effortlessly draws upon vast experiences of being in the leadership vanguard of the most significant national and international movements of the century. Like Dr. Mary McLeod Bethune, her predecessor and 1935 founder of the National Council of Negro Women, she has been a formidable moral, political and cultural force through her personal and organizational demonstrations of women's leadership in civil rights, human dignity, family strength and organizational effectiveness. Moreover, she has never permitted the vitality and impact of the NCNW to wane through all the years of her leadership. I am fortunate to have witnessed personally and been a beneficiary of the greatness of Dr. Bethune and to have been in nearby Talladega College when Dr. Bethune and Mrs. Eleanor Roosevelt (continued)

3 pounds collard greens
1 pound fresh okra
1 large red onion, sliced
5 cloves garlic, crushed
2 tablespoons Crisco Oil
1 tablespoon ground coriander
½ teaspoon cayenne pepper
½ cup coarsely chopped cilantro leaves

1. Wash collard leaves thoroughly. Stack approximately 15 leaves evenly. Roll from long side in cigar fashion. Cut into ⅛ inch ribbons. Continue until all leaves are cut. Drop into boiling water just to cover. Blanche 4 minutes. Reserve one cup cooking liquid. Drain.
2. Cut off tops of okra. Slice diagonally into about 4 to 5 slices per stem.
3. Heat Crisco Oil in large skillet on medium heat. Add okra, onion and garlic. Sauté 8 minutes. Add drained collards, coriander and cayenne. Stir-fry on medium high heat 5 minutes. Serve immediately with cilantro as garnish. Add a little pot juices, if desired.

8 Servings

105 CALORIES / FAT 4 g (37 CAL or 35% of total calories) / SAT FAT <1 g (<5% of total calories) / CARB 15 g / PROTEIN 6 g / CHOL 0 mg / SODIUM 45 mg

HERITAGE RECIPE

MELBA'S COLLARD GREENS & TURKEY WINGS

3   pounds fresh collard greens
    About 2 cups water
1   medium onion, chopped
1   pound smoked turkey wings
    Sugar
    Pepper
    Garlic powder
    Salt substitute seasoning

1. Soak and wash collard greens. Remove all grit. Remove hard stems. Place greens together in small bunches. Roll together. Cut crosswise into wide strips.
2. Place greens, water, onion and turkey wings in large pan. Season with sugar, pepper, garlic and salt substitute seasoning. Cook until greens are soft and tender.

6 Servings

Adaptation from Recipe
Melba Moore
Entertainer

170 CALORIES / FAT 6 g (53 CAL or 31% of total calories) / SAT FAT 2 g (9% of total calories) / CARB 7 g / PROTEIN 24 g / CHOL 60 mg / SODIUM 855 mg

(continued)
organized the Southern Interracial Conference in Birmingham, Alabama in 1938. I was in the same setting when Mrs. Rosa L. Parks of the NAACP and Mrs. Mary Fair Burks and Mrs. Jo Ann Robinson of the Women's Political Action Council of Dexter Avenue Baptist Church in Montgomery, Alabama actually initiated the Montgomery Bus Boycott in 1955 which was galvanized into the Montgomery Improvement Association and set the stage for the emergence of the eloquent clarity and moral rectitude of Dr. Martin Luther King, Jr., whose high ideals and courageous actions prodded this nation into the passage of the 1964 Civil Rights Act and the 1965 Voting Rights Act. I have a deep respect for the role that African-American women have played in setting right actions into motion and making it impossible for men not to respond to them.

At both family meals and as a speaker at major dinner occasions, those influences are articulated by Dr. Height in the African-American women's oral tradition like no historian has been capable of writing them. It is awe-inspiring just to listen as she eats graciously and (continued)

MUSTARD GREENS WITH PEANUT SAUCE

(continued from previous page)

talks with such casual profundity. I listen to Dr. Height because I know that from her early YWCA service background through her NCNW leadership in the years of the segregationist death threats and the racist taunts from Mississippi, Alabama and Louisiana to Michigan, Illinois and New York to the triumphant 1963 Freedom March on Washington, Dr. Height was there at every turn in the planning, the orchestration and the leadership... and she knows whereof she speaks.

I love and deeply respect her because, whether on an NCNW dinner occasion, a Black Family Reunion or in the Washington, DC apartment of my niece, Ms. Alexis M. Herman... a formidable national leader in her own right of which I am so proud... three things always are common when Dr. Height is present. There will be inspiring recollections out of her own experience, clearly articulated visions of plans for the future and the sure confidence that within a short time those plans will be translated into realities.

Immediately comes to mind how she achieved the Bethune statue in Lincoln Park in the (continued)

2	pounds fresh mustard greens
	Water
¼	teaspoon salt
1	bunch green onions, chopped
½	pound cherry tomatoes
⅛	teaspoon black pepper
½	cup creamy peanut butter
¼	cup water
3⅓	cups hot cooked rice (without salt or fat)

1. Wash greens carefully. Trim off tough stems. Hold three or four leaves together. Tear into small, even pieces.
2. Bring small amount of water to a boil in large saucepan. Add salt and greens. Cook until greens are tender. Stir occasionally.
3. Add onions, whole cherry tomatoes and pepper. Cook until slightly limp.
4. Combine peanut butter and water. Stir until well blended. Pour over surface of greens. Simmer 10 minutes, stirring continually to blend. Cook until moist, not runny. Serve with rice.

4 Servings

490 CALORIES / FAT 17 g (156 CAL or 32% of total calories) / SAT FAT 3 g (6% of total calories) / CARB 70 g / PROTEIN 20 g / CHOL 0 mg / SODIUM 360 mg

HERITAGE RECIPE

JOE WEAVER'S SEASONED GREENS

3 pounds mustard greens
1 ham hock
8 cups water
2 teaspoons Crisco Shortening or Crisco Oil
2 large onions, chopped
3 cloves garlic, minced
1 can (14½ ounces) whole tomatoes, drained, coarsely chopped
½ teaspoon red pepper flakes
¼ teaspoon salt
Freshly ground pepper, to taste

1. Clean greens. Remove thick stalks. Roll leaves. Slice.
2. Combine ham hock and water in Dutch oven. Place on medium high heat. Bring to a boil. Reduce heat. Simmer about 1½ hours or until liquid has been reduced to about 3 cups. Add greens to Dutch oven. Cover. Simmer for 15 minutes. Remove cover. Simmer 30 minutes.
3. Heat Crisco Shortening or Crisco Oil in large skillet on medium heat. Add onion and garlic. Sauté 10 minutes or until onion is softened. Stir in tomatoes, red pepper flakes, salt and pepper. Simmer 10 to 15 minutes.
4. Stir tomato mixture into greens when almost done and most of the liquid has evaporated. Simmer, uncovered, 15 minutes or until greens are tender and most of the liquid has evaporated.

6 to 8 Servings

130 CALORIES / FAT 5 g (43 CAL or 33% of total calories) / SAT FAT 1 g (9% of total calories) / CARB 14 g / PROTEIN 11 g / CHOL 10 mg / SODIUM 570 mg

(continued)
nation's capital, the conversion of the Bethune Council House into an international museum and research center dedicated to the achievements of African and African-American women and the initiation of the Black Family Reunions on the Federal Mall and around the nation. (While all others were doing all they could to stigmatize rather than appreciate the great strength of the African-American family, she went about demonstrating both the historicity and the strength of that foundation and pillar of black culture and resiliency.) Presently, she imbues you with the vision of the NCNW National Headquarters and Women's Resource Center Project which shortly will be another landmark in her legacy. It, too, will come to reality. Moreover, even as others were engaging in rhetoric, but doing little to strengthen African and African-American bonds of kinship and common cause, she organized chapters of the NCNW from Senegal to Zimbabwe and from Nigeria to Egypt to assure an effective African-American-African women's organizational network throughout the African continent. How well we all also should remember her perceptive characterization (continued)

SQUASH WITH APPLES

2 acorn squash, cut in half, lengthwise
2 medium tart cooking apples, peeled and chopped (about ⅔ pound or 2 cups)
1½ teaspoons grated lemon peel
1 tablespoon lemon juice
3 tablespoons Crisco Shortening or Crisco Oil, melted, divided
½ cup firmly packed light brown sugar
½ teaspoon salt
⅛ teaspoon cinnamon
Apple slices (optional)
Lemon slices (optional)

1. Heat oven to 400°.
2. Remove seeds from squash halves. Place cut-side-down in baking dish. Add ½ inch boiling water.
3. Bake at 400° for 20 minutes.
4. Combine apples, lemon peel, lemon juice, 2 tablespoons melted Crisco Shortening or Crisco Oil and brown sugar.
5. Turn squash halves cut-side-up. Brush with remaining 1 tablespoon Crisco Shortening or Crisco oil. Sprinkle salt and cinnamon over halves. Fill hollow centers with apple mixture.
6. Add boiling water to ½-inch level in baking dish. Cover with foil.
7 Bake 30 minutes. Garnish with apple slices or lemon wedges, if desired.

4 Servings

295 CALORIES / FAT 12 g (104 CAL or 35% of total calories) / SAT FAT 1 g (<5% of total calories) / CARB 52 g / PROTEIN 4 g / CHOL 0 mg / SODIUM 85 mg

(continued from previous page)

that "Africans were not slaves, they were villagers, griots, kings and queens... noble people rich in culture and tradition... who were made slaves."
Her example to all of us, and possibly the secret of her and Mrs. Rosa Parks longevity, is that they still are the inspirers, doers and exemplars of the real human virtues that our whole nation so desperately needs. I learned years ago that the best and most enjoyable way to dine with Dr. Height or Mrs. Parks and those rare others of their gifts of larger than life longevity is to attune your minds and hearts to theirs and vicariously become their persona. In Dr. Height's presence, the meal is not so much to eat as to listen very carefully. She will enlarge your very being and encourage your own best effort like only she can do.

Dr. Broadus N. Butler
Silver Spring, Maryland

HOT & SPICY CABBAGE MEDLEY

1   teaspoon Crisco Shortening or
Crisco Oil
⅛   pound center cut smoked ham
chopped
½   cup chopped onion
½   cup chopped green bell pepper

1   can (10 ounces) tomatoes with
green chilies, chopped
½   teaspoon sugar
4   cups cabbage, sliced
⅛   teaspoon pepper
⅛   teaspoon hot pepper sauce

Heat Crisco Shortening or Crisco Oil in large skillet on medium heat. Add ham, onion, and green pepper. Stir-fry until crisp-tender. Add undrained tomatoes and sugar. Simmer 2 to 3 minutes. Add cabbage, pepper and hot pepper sauce. Simmer 15 minutes.

8 Servings

35 CALORIES / FAT 1 g (10 CAL or 28% of total calories) / SAT FAT <1 g (5% of total calories) / CARB 5 g / PROTEIN 2 g / CHOL 5 mg / SODIUM 165 mg

HONEY GLAZED CARROTS

4   cups carrots, diagonally sliced
1   cup water
¼   teaspoon salt
2   teaspoons cornstarch
½   teaspoon grated orange peel

½   cup orange juice
2   tablespoons margarine
2   tablespoons honey
Parsley (optional)

1.   Combine carrots, water and salt in medium saucepan. Heat to boiling. Cook, covered, on medium heat until just tender.
2.   Combine cornstarch, orange peel, and orange juice in small pan. Stir well. Place on medium heat. Add margarine and honey. Stir constantly until thickened and clear.
3.   Drain carrots. Add honey glaze. Mix well. Sprinkle with parsley, if desired.

6 Servings

135 CALORIES / FAT 4 g (37 CAL or 27% of total calories) / SAT FAT 1 g (5% of total calories) / CARB 25 g / PROTEIN 2 g / CHOL 0 mg / SODIUM 235 mg

CAULIFLOWER CASSEROLE

1 package (10 ounces) frozen cauliflower, cooked, well drained
2 packages (10 ounces) frozen peas and carrots, cooked, well drained
1 cup nonfat sour cream alternative

1 can (10¾ ounces) cream of celery soup
1 tablespoon instant minced onion
Pepper
1 tomato, peeled and sliced
½ cup lowfat American cheese, grated

1. Heat oven to 325°. Grease 2-quart casserole.
2. Combine cauliflower and peas and carrots. Place in casserole.
3. Combine "sour cream", celery soup, and minced onion. Stir well. Season with pepper. Pour over vegetables. Top with tomato slices. Sprinkle with grated cheese.
4. Bake at 325° for 25 minutes or until bubbly.

6 Servings

155 CALORIES / FAT 4 g (37 CAL or 24% of total calories) / SAT FAT 2 g (10% of total calories) / CARB 22 g / PROTEIN 10 g / CHOL 10 mg / SODIUM 610 mg

CREAMED GREEN BEANS & POTATOES

1½ quarts water
4 cups fresh green beans
1½ cups new red potatoes, diced
2 cups skim milk

2 tablespoons cornstarch
2 tablespoons margarine
Pepper to taste

1. Combine water, green beans and potatoes in large saucepan. Cook on medium heat until green beans and potatoes are tender. Drain. Return to pan.
2. Combine ¼ cup skim milk and 2 tablespoons cornstarch. Stir until dissolved. Add remaining 1¾ cups skim milk. Pour into green beans and potatoes. Add margarine. Cook until thickened. Add pepper to taste.

8 Servings

90 CALORIES / FAT 3 g (27 CAL or 30% of total calories) / SAT FAT 1 g (6% of total calories) / CARB 13 g / PROTEIN 4 g / CHOL 0 mg / SODIUM 70 mg

HARVEST VEGETABLE MEDLEY

2 tablespoons Crisco Shortening
  or Crisco Oil
4 onions, thinly sliced
3 green bell peppers, cut into
  ¼-inch strips
2 cloves garlic, chopped
4 medium zucchini, cut into
  ½-inch cubes
1 eggplant, cut into ½-inch cubes
4 or 5 fresh tomatoes, peeled and
  quartered or 1 can (14½
  ounces)

1 teaspoon dill weed
¾ teaspoon dried basil leaves
½ teaspoon pepper
½ teaspoon dried oregano leaves
¼ teaspoon salt
¼ cup lemon juice
1 package (9 ounces) frozen peas
2 tablespoons fresh minced or 2
  teaspoon dried parsley

1. Heat Crisco Shortening or Crisco Oil in Dutch oven (non-reactive or non-cast iron) on medium heat. Add onions, green peppers and garlic. Sauté until tender.
2. Add zucchini and eggplant. Cook 5 minutes, stirring occasionally. Add tomatoes, dill weed, basil, pepper, oregano and salt. Reduce heat. Cover. Simmer 20 minutes.
3. Add peas. Simmer 3 to 5 minutes or until peas are thawed and heated. Stir in lemon juice. Serve hot or chilled sprinkled with parsley.

12 Servings

80 CALORIES / FAT 3 g (25 CAL or 32% of total calories) / SAT FAT <1 g (<5% of total calories) / CARB 12 g / PROTEIN 3 g / CHOL 0 mg / SODIUM 75 mg

JULIE'S GREEN BEAN & CORN CASSEROLE

1 can (11 ounces) whole kernel
  corn, drained
1 can (13 to 17 ounces) French
  style green beans, drained
½ cup chopped celery
½ cup chopped onions

1 carton (8 ounces) nonfat sour
  cream alternative
1 can (10¾ ounces) cream of
  celery soup
½ cup snack crackers or cheese
  cracker, crushed
2 tablespoons margarine, melted

1. Heat oven to 350°. Grease 1½-quart casserole.
2. Combine corn, green beans, celery, onions, "sour cream", and celery soup. Pour into casserole. Sprinkle with crackers. Drizzle with margarine.
3. Bake at 350° for 40 to 50 minutes or until hot and bubbly.

8 Servings

160 CALORIES / FAT 5 g (41 CAL or 26% of total calories) / SAT FAT 1 g (6% of total calories) / CARB 23 g / PROTEIN 8 g / CHOL 10 mg / SODIUM 840 mg

BETTER TASTIN' GREEN BEANS

1 pound green beans, trimmed	1 tablespoon salt-free vegetable
1 whole Spanish onion, chopped	seasoning blend
2 slices turkey bacon, cut into ½-inch pieces	1 tablespoon lemon pepper seasoning

1. Fill large saucepan one-fourth full with water.
2. Add green beans, onion, bacon, vegetable seasoning blend and lemon pepper. Cover. Cook on medium low heat until tender. Serve hot.

6 Servings

40 CALORIES / FAT 1 g (6 CAL or 15% of total calories) / SAT FAT <1 g (5% of total calories) / CARB 8 g / PROTEIN 3 g / CHOL 0 mg / SODIUM 70 mg

SUMMER GREEN TOMATO CRISPS

4 very firm green tomatoes	⅛ teaspoon pepper
½ cup yellow cornmeal	1 tablespoon Crisco Shortening or
1¼ teaspoons salt	Crisco Oil
½ teaspoon sugar	

1. Cut out stem ends of tomatoes. Cut into ½-inch slices.
2. Combine cornmeal, salt, sugar and pepper on waxed paper. Coat both sides of tomato slices with mixture.
3. Heat Crisco Shortening or Crisco Oil on medium-high heat in large non-stick skillet. Place single layer of tomato slices in skillet. Brown each side lightly. Cook only until tender. Serve immediately.

4 Servings

115 CALORIES / FAT 4 g (39 CAL or 33% of total calories) / SAT FAT <1 g (<5% of total calories) / CARB 19 g / PROTEIN 3 g / CHOL 0 mg / SODIUM 690 mg

HERITAGE RECIPE

COLORFUL SQUASH CASSEROLE

1 can (10¾ ounces) condensed cream of celery soup
1 cup nonfat sour cream alterative
5 slices (¾ ounce each) fat free process cheese product, diced
1 cup shredded carrot
¼ cup chopped onion
1 tablespoon all-purpose flour

2 medium yellow summer squash, cut in ¼-inch slices
2 medium zucchini, cut in ¼-inch slices
2 cups herb seasoned stuffing mix
2 tablespoons Butter Flavor Crisco, melted

1. Heat oven to 350°. Grease 3-quart casserole or baking dish.
2. Combine soup, "sour cream", cheese, carrot, onion and flour in large bowl. Add squash slices. Toss to coat. Spoon into casserole.
3. Combine dry stuffing mix and melted Butter Flavor Crisco. Spoon over squash.
4. Bake, uncovered, at 350° for 40 minutes or until hot and bubbly.

8 to 10 Servings

120 CALORIES / FAT 4 g (38 CAL or 31% of total calories) / SAT FAT 1 g (8% of total calories) / CARB 15 g / PROTEIN 6 g / CHOL 5 mg / SODIUM 460 mg

SMOTHERED SUMMER SQUASH

6 medium summer squash, cut in ¼-inch slices
1 large onion, chopped

1 tablespoon Butter Flavor Crisco
1 tablespoon sugar

1. Place squash in large saucepan. Cover with water. Cook on medium heat, covered, until squash is tender. Drain.
2. Heat Butter Flavor Crisco in large skillet on medium heat. Add onion. Cook until tender. Add squash and sugar. Cook on medium high heat, stirring frequently. Cook most of the moisture out of squash. Remove from heat. Cover. Serve in 10 to 15 minutes.

6 Servings

65 CALORIES / FAT 2 g (21 CAL or 32% of total calories) / SAT FAT 1 g (8% of total calories) / CARB 11 g / PROTEIN 2 g / CHOL 0 mg / SODIUM 5 mg

SHIRLEY'S EGGPLANT CASSEROLE

1 large eggplant, peeled and cubed	¼ cup green bell pepper, chopped
1 tablespoon olive oil	1½ cups fine, dry bread crumbs, divided
1 large fresh tomato, chopped and seeded	¼ cup grated ⅓ less fat mild Cheddar cheese
¼ cup green onions, chopped	

1. Heat oven to 350°. Grease 1-quart casserole.
2. Place eggplant in medium saucepan. Cover with water. Simmer until softened. Drain well.
3. Heat olive oil in medium skillet on medium heat. Add tomatoes, onions and green pepper. Sauté until tender. Stir in 1¼ cups bread crumbs, cheese and eggplant. Spoon into casserole. Sprinkle with remaining ¼ cup bread crumbs.
4. Bake at 350° for 25 minutes.

4 Servings

270 CALORIES / FAT 8 g (72 CAL or 27% of total calories) / SAT FAT 3 g (9% of total calories) / CARB 41 g / PROTEIN 11 g / CHOL 10 mg / SODIUM 390 mg

HOROSSES

4 medium red apples	⅓ cup blackberry wine
⅓ cup honey	⅓ cup chopped walnuts

Core apples. Do not peel. Place apples in food processor. Process on and off until chopped medium. Transfer to large bowl. Add honey, wine and nuts. Mix well. Serve as side dish.

6 Servings

175 CALORIES / FAT 6 g (57 CAL or 33% of total calories) / SAT FAT <1 g (<5% of total calories) / CARB 27 g / PROTEIN 3 g / CHOL 0 mg / SODIUM 0 mg

**Adaptation from Recipe
Chef B. E. Lowder
Los Angeles, California**

"Refuge of Self" by Francelise Dawkins (Glens Falls, NY)

In the cold month of February 1992, in upstate New York, I made this piece after visiting a greenhouse. The faces of three women and a child prodigy emerge out of tropical plants. Equally alive are plants and expressive looks which can travel deep in our subconscious. This quilted piece made of silk, velvet and African cotton prints, symbolizes the child within the three women inside me: seductive, contemplative or paradoxical. The one in the middle resembles my French Caribbean grandmother as she appeared to me in a dream long ago, planting in me the seed of patience. I found the title of the piece after reading the book "The Teachings of the Compassionate Buddha", from which I understood that in the heart of our nature, the self is always safe.

Francelise Dawkins

While story quilts have their roots in Africa, they came to fruition in America. African-American quilters created story quilts that depict the role of black people in American history. Bible stories, family histories and womanist themes have all been lovingly stitched in cloth.

For example, some quilts sent messages for those traveling the Underground Railroad. Quilts containing black fabric or made in the Rob Peter to Pay Paul patchwork pattern were hung on clothes lines as a way to signal a refuge for escaping bondsmen. Southern burial traditions also figure into quilting since enslaved African-Americans used quilts to wrap the bodies of their loved ones for their "final journey".

COUNTRY BAKING POWDER BISCUITS

1¾ cups all-purpose flour
2 tablespoons + 2 teaspoons
  granulated sugar
1 tablespoon baking powder

½ teaspoon salt
⅔ cup skim milk
¼ cup Crisco Oil

1. Heat oven to 425°.
2. Combine flour, sugar, baking powder and salt in medium bowl.
3. Combine milk and Crisco Oil. Add to flour mixture. Stir with fork just until
   dough forms. Place on well floured surface. Pat into circle about one-half
   inch thick. Cut with floured 2½-inch round cutter (Press dough scraps
   together to form some biscuits to make total of 8). Place on ungreased
   baking sheet.
4. Bake at 425° for 10 to 12 minutes or until golden brown.

8 Biscuits

190 CALORIES / FAT 7 g (66 CAL or 35% of total calories) / SAT FAT <1 g (<5% of total calories) / CARB 26 g /
PROTEIN 4 g / CHOL 0 mg / SODIUM 270 mg

MOLASSES MUFFINS

1⅔ cups all-purpose flour
3 tablespoons sugar
2 teaspoons baking powder
1 teaspoon ginger
½ teaspoon salt

½ cup dark molasses
1 whole egg and 2 whites, lightly
  beaten
¼ cup vegetable oil
¼ cup skim milk

1. Heat oven to 400°. Place paper liners in twelve medium (about 2½-inch)
   muffin cups.
2. Combine flour, sugar, baking powder, ginger and salt in medium bowl. Make
   a well in center.
3. Blend molasses, egg whites, oil and milk in small bowl. Pour into well in dry
   ingredients. Stir just until ingredients are moistened. Spoon into lined muffin
   cups, filling each about ⅔ full.
4. Bake at 400°, about 15 minutes, or until centers spring back when touched
   lightly.

Variation: Orange Raisin Muffins -
Follow recipe above, omitting ginger. Add ½ cup raisins and 2 teaspoons grated
orange peel to dry ingredients.

12 muffins

155 CALORIES / FAT 5 g (47 CAL or 30% of total calories) / SAT FAT <1 g (<5% of total calories) / CARB 24 g /
PROTEIN 3 g / CHOL 20 mg / SODIUM 165 mg

CLASSIC MUFFINS

Even An Ordinary Staff Meeting is Inspirational

One of the unique experiences I have had as an educational consultant to NCNW involves staff meetings. These are held regularly to keep staff up to date but there is an additional purpose to the meetings... inspiring everyone involved with NCNW to work towards making the legacy of Mrs. Mary McLeod Bethune a reality.

Dr. Height typically begins the meeting with prayer or silent meditation. Whatever the agenda may cover, Dr. Height always recounts at least one inspirational anecdote about Mary McLeod Bethune. Dr. Height also draws from her own experiences at the YWCA and her work with her sorority to help the NCNW national staff understand that it sets the tone for the sections and the affiliates all over the country.

She forever keeps in front of her staff the Bethune legacy and our responsibility in keeping the legacy alive. I have been mesmerized listening to Dr. Height evaluate and refine what comes up as a "new" program. Her aura as a person combines with her extensive experience to bring us all together to

(continued)

1   egg
½   cup skim milk
¼   cup Crisco Oil
1½ cups all-purpose flour
½   cup sugar
2   teaspoons baking powder
½   teaspoon salt

1. Heat oven to 400°. Place paper liners in twelve medium (about 2½-inch) muffin cups.
2. Combine egg, milk and Crisco Oil in large bowl.
3. Combine flour, sugar, baking powder and salt. Stir into egg mixture. Mix just until dry ingredients are moistened. Spoon into muffins cups, filling each about two-thirds full.
4. Bake at 400° for 18 to 20 minutes or until lightly browned.

12 Muffins

140 CALORIES / FAT 5 g (47 CAL or 34% of total calories) / SAT FAT <1 g (<5% of total calories) / CARB 21 g / PROTEIN 3 g / CHOL 20 mg / SODIUM 155 mg

Variations:
Preserve-Filled Muffins -
Fill muffin cups. Remove one teaspoon batter from each. Fill holes with ½ teaspoon preserves. Cover preserves with reserved batter.

150 CALORIES / FAT 5 g (47 CAL or 32% of total calories) / SAT FAT <1 g (<5% of total calories) / CARB 23 g / PROTEIN 3 g / CHOL 20 mg / SODIUM 155 mg

Corn and Peppers Muffin -
Fold in ½ cup thawed frozen corn and 2 tablespoons each chopped red and green bell pepper. Serve with red or green sweet pepper jelly.

145 CALORIES / FAT 5 g (47 CAL or 33% of total calories) / SAT FAT <1 g (<5% of total calories) / CARB 23 g / PROTEIN 3 g / CHOL 20 mg / SODIUM 155 mg

FILLIN' FRUIT BAKERY STYLE MUFFINS

1   cup dry oat bran high fiber hot cereal
1   cup whole wheat flour
¾   cup all-purpose flour
½   cup quick-cooking oats (not instant or old fashioned)
1   tablespoon baking powder
½   teaspoon cinnamon
¼   teaspoon salt
2   eggs, lightly beaten
2   teaspoons grated orange peel
1   cup orange juice
½   cup honey
⅓   cup Crisco Oil
¼   cup skim milk

1. Heat oven to 400°. Oil 12 large (2¾-inch) muffin cups lightly.
2. Combine oat bran, whole wheat and all-purpose flour, oats, baking powder, cinnamon and salt in large bowl. Mix well.
3. Combine eggs, orange peel, orange juice, honey, Crisco Oil and milk in medium bowl. Mix until well blended. Add to flour mixture. Stir just until dry ingredients are moistened.
4. Spoon batter into muffin cups, filling almost full.
5. Bake at 400° for 16 to 18 minutes or until lightly browned and firm to the touch. Cool in pan on cooling rack about 5 minutes before removing.

One Dozen Muffins

Variation: Bake in 15 medium (about 2½-inch) muffin cups at 400° for 16 minutes.

220 CALORIES / FAT 8 g (72 CAL or 33% of total calories) / SAT FAT 1 g (<5% of total calories) / CARB 34 g / PROTEIN 5 g / CHOL 35 mg / SODIUM 140 mg

(continued)
focus on a single issue. She can analyze a project and take you back to when the idea may have first surfaced. Dr. Height encourages her staff to do research on projects that have already been tried and look for ways to refine and develop and improve upon those ideas rather than constantly trying to reinvent the wheel.

The other striking part of the staff meeting is that it always takes place over a meal. It may be take out Chinese food, deli sandwiches or a soul food feast. When you meet at NCNW you know there will always be sweet potato pie in honor of Mrs. Bethune who baked and sold pies to finance her school which became Bethune Cookman College. The meetings often end with all of us singing "We are Climbing Jacob's Ladder."

As an elected school board official and consultant to a non-profit organization, I am always struck by the skill Dr. Height uses in making her staff feel the global connection to women everywhere. The needs of African-American women may be unique, but the needs of women and families all over the world have a universal quality to them which Dr. Height understands and stresses.

(continued)

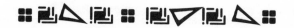

ORANGE BLUEBERRY COUNTRY MUFFINS

1¾ cups all-purpose flour
1 tablespoon baking powder
½ teaspoon cinnamon
¼ teaspoon nutmeg
¼ teaspoon salt
1 cup fresh or frozen dry pack blueberries
2 eggs
¾ cup orange juice
¼ cup Crisco Oil

1. Heat oven to 400°. Oil 18 medium (about 2½-inch) muffin cups or use paper or foil liners.
2. Combine flour, baking powder, cinnamon, nutmeg and salt in medium bowl. Remove one tablespoon. Toss with blueberries.
3. Combine eggs, orange juice and Crisco Oil in small bowl. Beat with fork until blended. Add all at once to flour mixture, stirring with fork just until dry ingredients are moistened. Fold in berries. Spoon evenly into muffin cups, filling about half full.
4. Bake at 400° for 20 minutes or until tops are very lightly browned. Cool 5 minutes before removing. Serve warm.

1½ Dozen Muffins

103 CALORIES / FAT 4 g (34 CAL or 33% of total calories) / SAT FAT <1 g (<5% of total calories) / CARB 15 g / PROTEIN 2 g / CHOL 25 mg / SODIUM 90 mg

(continued from previous page)

I leave every staff meeting re-energized and re-dedicated to the organization, to Dr. Height and to solving the problems of women and children.

**Wilma Harvey
Ward 1 School Board
Member
Washington, DC**

HOE CAKES

2 tablespoons Crisco Shortening or Crisco Oil, divided	¼ teaspoon baking soda
1½ cups self-rising cornmeal	1¼ cups low fat buttermilk
	1 egg, lightly beaten

1. Combine cornmeal and baking soda in medium bowl. Add buttermilk, egg and one tablespoon melted shortening. Stir just until dry ingredients are moistened.
2. Heat 1 tablespoon Crisco Shortening or Crisco Oil on medium-high heat in heavy large non-stick skillet.
3. Pour ¼ cup batter into skillet for each hoe cake. Fry 1 to 2 minutes or until golden brown on each side. Drain on paper towels. Serve immediately.

6 Servings

185 CALORIES / FAT 7 g (63 CAL or 34% of total calories) / SAT FAT 1 g (<5% of total calories) / CARB 27 g / PROTEIN 6 g / CHOL 35 mg / SODIUM 125 mg

HERITAGE RECIPE

JOHNNY CAKES

1 egg	1 cup all-purpose flour
⅓ cup sugar	¾ cup cornmeal
¼ cup Butter Flavor Crisco, melted, divided	½ teaspoon salt
1 cup sour milk	18 teaspoons maple syrup, jam or honey
1 teaspoon baking soda	

1. Combine egg, sugar and 1 tablespoon plus 1 teaspoon Butter Flavor Crisco in medium bowl. Stir in sour milk and baking soda. Add flour, cornmeal and salt. Stir just until dry ingredients are moistened. Cover. Let stand in cool place for 30 minutes.
2. Pour remaining shortening on griddle or in large skillet. Heat on medium heat. Spoon tablespoonfuls of batter onto griddle. Brown on one side. Turn. Brown on other side. Serve with syrup, jam or honey.

18 Johnny Cakes

115 CALORIES / FAT 4 g (32 CAL or 28% of total calories) / SAT FAT 1 g (8% of total calories) / CARB 19 g / PROTEIN 2 g / CHOL 15 mg / SODIUM 175 mg

ERNESTINE'S BAKED GRITS

1 tablespoon Butter Flavor Crisco	1½ cups skim evaporated milk
½ pound fresh mushrooms, chopped	1 cup grated Parmesan cheese
5 cups cooked grits	2 dashes cayenne pepper
4 eggs, beaten	Paprika

1. Heat oven to 375°. Grease large baking dish with Butter Flavor Crisco.
2. Melt Butter Flavor Crisco in large skillet. Add mushrooms. Sauté until mushrooms give up their liquid, about 5 minutes.
3. Place grits in large bowl. Mash if they are leftovers. Add mushrooms, eggs, evaporated milk, cheese, and cayenne. Stir gently to mix. Pour into casserole.
4. Bake at 375° for 25 to 30 minutes. Sprinkle with paprika.

8 Servings

230 CALORIES / FAT 8 g (68 CAL or 29% of total calories) / SAT FAT 3 g (12% of total calories) / CARB 27 g / PROTEIN 14 g / CHOL 115 mg / SODIUM 275 mg

HERITAGE
RECIPE

BUTTERMILK CORNSTICKS OR MUFFINS

1¼ cups yellow cornmeal	1¼ cups low fat buttermilk
¾ cup all-purpose flour	1 egg, lightly beaten
1 tablespoon sugar	2 tablespoons Butter Flavor
2½ teaspoons baking powder	Crisco, melted

1. Heat oven to 425°. Grease well 2 cornstick pans or 12 medium (about 2½ inches) muffin cups. Place in oven to heat.
2. Combine cornmeal, flour, sugar and baking powder in medium bowl.
3. Combine buttermilk, egg and Butter Flavor Crisco. Add to dry ingredients. Stir just until dry ingredients are moistened. Spoon batter into cornstick pans or muffin cups, filling almost full.
4. Bake at 425°. Cornsticks 15 to 18 minutes. Muffins 16 to 19 minutes.

14 Cornsticks (about 5 inches or 12 muffins)
Variations
Bacon Cornbread: Add 4 slices cooked and crumbled bacon in step #3.
Hot Jalapeño Cornbread: Add ¼ cup finely chopped jalapeño peppers and 1 cup grated ⅓ less fat sharp Cheddar cheese in step #3.

120 CALORIES / FAT 3 g (26 CAL or 22% of total calories) / SAT FAT 1 g (5% of total calories) / CARB 20 g / PROTEIN 4 g / CHOL 20 mg / SODIUM 110 mg

MR. TIM'S BAKED HUSH PUPPIES

¼ cup yellow cornmeal
¼ cup all-purpose flour
¾ teaspoon baking powder
¼ teaspoon salt
¼ teaspoon sugar
¼ teaspoon garlic powder
¼ teaspoon celery flakes
⅛ teaspoon cayenne pepper
1 egg white, beaten
2 tablespoons milk
2 teaspoons Crisco Oil
2 tablespoons chopped green onions
1 tablespoon minced fresh parsley

1. Heat oven to 425°. Grease 8 miniature (1¾-inch) muffin pans.
2. Combine cornmeal, flour, baking powder, salt, sugar, garlic powder, celery flakes and cayenne pepper in medium bowl. Stir until well blended.
3. Combine egg white, milk and oil in small bowl. Stir well. Add to dry ingredients. Stir just until blended. Stir in green onions and parsley. Spoon one tablespoon batter into each muffin cup.
4. Bake at 425° for 15 to 20 minutes or until hush puppies are golden brown. Remove immediately. Serve warm.

8 Servings

45 CALORIES / FAT 1 g (13 CAL or 28% of total calories) / SAT FAT <1 g (<5% of total calories) / CARB 7 g / PROTEIN 1 g / CHOL 0 mg / SODIUM 110 mg

Friendship

Dr. Height visited my home one summer afternoon to celebrate the birthday of a mutual friend. There were several children at the party and they gravitated to Dr. Height who sent them to find a story book. In the midst of the party, she sat down with the children and read to them. They were delighted. As we ate lunch, Dr. Height talked to the children about the meal, telling them stories about George Washington Carver and the sweet potato because, of course, we had sweet potato pie in her honor. She talked to them about the mango ice cream, telling them about tropical countries where there were people of African descent just like them. As Dr. Height talked, I could see the friendship she professes for children all over the world is truly genuine and extends to every child she meets. I hope as the children at the party grow up, they will understand what a remarkable experience they had one summer afternoon with Dr. Height.

Margo Briggs
President/CEO ESI
Security Company

TEX-MEX CORNBREAD

1 cup self-rising cornmeal
¼ teaspoon cayenne pepper
½ cup chopped onion
½ cup chopped green bell pepper
½ cup (2 ounces) shredded ⅓ less
    fat Cheddar cheese

½ cup skim milk
2 eggs, beaten
1 can (8½ ounces) cream style
    corn

1. Heat oven to 450°. Grease 8-inch square casserole.
2. Combine cornmeal and cayenne pepper in large bowl. Add onion, green
   pepper, cheese, milk, eggs and corn. Mix well. Spoon batter into casserole.
3. Bake at 450° for 25 minutes or until golden. Cut into 2-inch squares.

16 Servings

80 CALORIES / FAT 2 g (21 CAL or 27% of total calories) / SAT FAT 1 g (8% of total calories) / CARB 11 g /
PROTEIN 3 g / CHOL 30 mg / SODIUM 85 mg

CHILI-CHEESE CORNBREAD

1 cup yellow cornmeal
⅔ cup all-purpose flour
2 teaspoons baking powder
½ teaspoon salt
¾ cup nonfat sour cream
    alternative
2 egg whites
1 egg

¼ cup Crisco Oil
1½ cups finely diced fat free
    process cheese product slices
    (about 6 ounces)
1 can (8¾ ounces) whole kernel
    corn, drained
1 can (4 ounces) chopped green
    chilies, drained

1. Heat oven to 400°. Grease 9-inch square pan.
2. Combine cornmeal, flour, baking powder and salt in small bowl.
3. Combine "sour cream", egg whites, egg and Crisco Oil in medium bowl. Stir
   well. Add cornmeal mixture, cheese, corn and chilies. Mix well. Pour into
   pan.
4. Bake at 400° for 30 to 35 minutes, or until toothpick inserted in center comes
   out clean. Cool 10 to 15 minutes. Cut into squares. Serve warm.

One 9-Inch Pan (Eight Servings)

255 CALORIES / FAT 8 g (76 CAL or 30% of total calories) / SAT FAT 1 g (<5% of total calories) / CARB 33 g /
PROTEIN 11 g / CHOL 30 mg / SODIUM 860 mg

CRACKLIN' OAT CORNBREAD

¼ cup peanut oil
3 cups 2% milk
2 egg whites
2 cups white corn meal
1 cup oatmeal, quick or old fashioned, divided, uncooked
1 bunch green onions, chopped
2 teaspoons baking powder
1 tablespoon sage or poultry seasoning
1 teaspoon salt
½ teaspoon pepper

1. Heat oven to 350°.
2. Place peanut oil in 8-inch square pan. Place in oven.
3. Combine milk and egg whites in large bowl. Whip until smooth.
4. Add (while still whipping) corn meal, green onions, baking powder, sage, salt, pepper and ½ cup oatmeal flakes slowly. Mix until smooth.
5. Remove hot oiled pan from oven. Pour cornbread mixture in pan. Sprinkle with remaining ½ cup oatmeal. Return to oven for about 20 minutes or until golden brown.

8 Servings

**Adaptation from Recipe
Johnny Rivers, Executive Chef
Walt Disney World**

280 CALORIES / FAT 10 g (88 CAL or 31% of total calories) / SAT FAT 2 g (8% of total calories) / CARB 39 g / PROTEIN 9 g / CHOL 10 mg / SODIUM 410 mg

Teach Them What You Know

When I first met Dr. Height, I had just started a new job teaching Spanish language and literature at the University of Delaware. The first quarter had ended and I talked to Dr. Height about the challenges of teaching. We talked all through dinner and at the end of the meal, she told me about her first teaching experience. When she was just a child, she decided she would teach music lessons. Like any smart entrepreneur, she advertised by putting up a sign in her front window saying, "Piano lessons 25 cents." Dr. Height told me when her mother came home one day and saw the sign, she wanted to know why her child had put it there. Dr. Height told her "I want to give music lessons." Her mother reminded her she didn't know all that much herself, to which Dr. Height replied, "But I can teach them what I know." She told me even though she was only a few lessons ahead of what she was teaching, she was still able to get other children interested in playing the piano and that several of them actually became musicians.

Millicent Bolden

It was Like Watching a Field Commander in Action

Like many people, the meal I shared with Dr. Dorothy Height was in a public gathering. It was fitting that it be this way because so much of her life has been lived in the public arena.

Dr. Height called to ask if I could be the luncheon speaker at the annual NCNW convention. Although I wanted to forego the opportunity because I was leaving the country later that day, I knew no one turns Dr. Height down. When she asks you to do something, you do it. This selfless, dedicated woman has given her life to others, so I felt I had no right to refuse her.

Being seated at Dr. Height's table gave me a chance to see her in action. Like a field commander, with a group of dedicated followers, she orchestrated the event with a deft touch. Dr. Height smoothed ruffled feathers, gave out doses of praise, entertained her special guests and corporate supporters, and took care of minor emergencies while not skipping a beat. I was truly amazed at how she

(continued)

APPLESAUCE STREUSEL LOAF

Loaf
2	cups all-purpose flour
¾	cup oats (quick or old fashioned)
2	teaspoons baking powder
1½	teaspoons pumpkin pie spice
½	teaspoon salt (optional)
¼	teaspoon baking soda
½	cup raisins
1	cup chunky applesauce
2	eggs, lightly beaten
½	cup granulated sugar
½	cup vegetable oil
2	tablespoons milk

Streusel
¼	cup oats (quick or old fashioned)
1	tablespoon margarine
2	teaspoons firmly packed brown sugar

Icing
½	cup confectioners sugar
1½	teaspoons skim milk
¼	teaspoon vanilla

Topping
1½	cups chunky applesauce

1. Heat oven to 350°. Grease and flour 8 X 4-inch loaf pan.
2. For loaf, combine flour, oats, baking powder, pumpkin pie spice, salt and baking soda in medium bowl. Mix well. Stir in raisins.
3. Combine applesauce, eggs, granulated sugar, oil and milk in large bowl. Mix well. Add flour mixture. Stir just until moistened. Pour into pan.
4. For streusel, mix oats, margarine and brown sugar until crumbly. Sprinkle over loaf, pressing gently.
5. Bake at 350° for 60 to 70 minutes or until toothpick inserted in center comes out clean. Cool 10 minutes. Cover top with foil to hold streusel in place. Remove from pan. Remove foil. Cool on wire rack.
6. For icing, mix confectioners sugar, milk and vanilla until smooth. Drizzle over top. Serve with 1 to 2 tablespoons of chunky applesauce used as a spread instead of butter or margarine.

12 servings

310 CALORIES / FAT 12 g (107 CAL or 35% of total calories) / SAT FAT 1g (<5% of total calories) / CARB 48 g / PROTEIN 5 g / CHOL 36 mg / SODIUM 185 mg

SUNRISE BLUEBERRY COFFEE CAKE

Batter
1¼ cups all-purpose flour
½ cup sugar
2 teaspoons baking powder
½ teaspoon cinnamon
¼ teaspoon salt
½ cup skim milk
3 tablespoons Crisco Oil
1 egg, well beaten
½ teaspoon vanilla

Topping
1½ cups fresh or frozen blueberries
2 tablespoons sugar
½ teaspoon cinnamon
2 tablespoons chopped pecans

1. Heat oven to 350°. Oil 8-inch square pan lightly.
2. For batter, combine flour, sugar, baking powder, cinnamon and salt in medium bowl. Make a well in center.
3. Combine milk, Crisco Oil, egg and vanilla. Add all at once to flour mixture. Stir just until dry ingredients are moistened. Pour batter into pan.
4. For topping, spread blueberries over top of batter. Combine sugar and cinnamon. Spoon over blueberries. Sprinkle with nuts.
5. Bake at 350° for 40 minutes or until toothpick inserted in center comes out clean.

One 8-Inch Cake (9 Servings)

195 CALORIES / FAT 7 g (60 CAL or 31% of total calories) / SAT FAT 1g (<5% of total calories) / CARB 32 g / PROTEIN 3 g / CHOL 25 mg / SODIUM 150 mg

(continued)
had her gentle but firm hand on everything that was going on at the luncheon without neglecting anyone. It occurred to me that this venerable lady is a "do-er". She comes from a long line of resourceful African-American women who have acquired the important skill of accomplishing a multitude of tasks simultaneously while making it look so ordinary and natural. Dorothy Height has earned her place alongside her mentors, Dr. Mary McLeod Bethune, Ida B. Wells Barnett, Fannie Lou Hamer and countless other great African-American women leaders who were all "do-ers".

What I learned is that sharing a meal with Dr. Height is more like an exciting adventure that one savors with each remembrance. Surely, one never forgets the experience.

Dr. Joyce A. Ladner
Vice President for
Academic Affairs
Howard University

TINA'S SOUR CREAM COFFEE CAKE

Cake

3	cups all-purpose flour	2	teaspoons cinnamon
1½	teaspoons baking powder	¾	cup Crisco Shortening
1½	teaspoons baking soda	1	teaspoon vanilla
1	teaspoon salt	2	eggs
2	cups granulated sugar, divided	2	egg whites
¾	cup raisins	1½	cups nonfat sour cream
½	cup finely chopped walnuts		alternative

Icing

1	cup confectioners sugar	¼	teaspoon vanilla
1	tablespoon skim milk		

1. Heat oven to 350°. Grease 10-inch tube pan.
2. For cake, combine flour, baking powder, baking soda and salt in medium bowl.
3. Combine ¾ cup granulated sugar, raisins, nuts and cinnamon in small bowl.
4. Place remaining 1¼ cups sugar, Crisco and vanilla in large bowl. Beat at medium speed of electric mixer until well blended. Add eggs and egg whites, one at a time, beating well after each. Add flour mixture alternately with "sour cream", mixing until blended after each addition. (Batter will be thick.)
5. Spread half of the batter in pan. Sprinkle with half of nut mixture (about ¾ cup). Repeat.
6. Bake at 350° for 50 to 55 minutes or until toothpick inserted in center comes out clean. Cool 20 minutes on cooling rack. Remove from pan. Invert on rack.
7. For icing, combine confectioners sugar, milk and vanilla in small bowl. Add more milk, if necessary, until of drizzling consistency. Drizzle over cake. Serve warm or at room temperature.

12 Servings

475 CALORIES / FAT 16 g (144 CAL or 30% of total calories) / SAT FAT 4 g (7% of total calories) / CARB 75 g / PROTEIN 8 g / CHOL 35 mg / SODIUM 365 mg

"Counting Thy Blessings" by Anita H. Knox (Fort Worth, TX)

"Counting Thy Blessings" is a blend of traditional and African fabrics just as we are a blend of and are able to embrace the best of both worlds. The Acacia trees are symbolic of our roots, the green of the leaves represent our love of nature and living things, and the buttons symbolize the handing down or passing on of something small but significant "to remember me".

Anita Knox

Quilts were a way for people who had been stripped of all their possessions, dragged from their homelands and denied access to education to have "something"... a prized possession. Through quilting, the most impoverished enslaved person was able to take scraps of cloth, a bit of beautiful fabric, a piece of lace or an idea and turn it into a tangible product that was not only beautiful but also practical.

CLASSIC SHORTENING 9-INCH SINGLE CRUST*

1¼ cups all-purpose flour	⅓ cup Crisco Shortening
½ teaspoon salt (optional)	¼ cup orange juice

1. Combine flour and salt (if used) in medium bowl. Cut in Crisco using pastry blender (or 2 knives) until all flour is blended in to form pea-size chunks.
2. Sprinkle orange juice over flour mixture, one tablespoon at a time. Toss lightly with fork until dough forms. (May seem slightly dry and crumbly.) Press into ball. Press between hands to form 5 to 6-inch "pancake".
3. Roll "pancake" between unfloured sheets of waxed paper. Peel off top sheet. Trim one inch larger than upside-down 9-inch pie plate. Flip into pie plate. Remove other sheet. Press to fit. Fold edge under. Flute.
4. For unbaked pie shell, follow individual recipe for baking temperature and time.
5. For baked pie shell, prick bottom and sides with fork (50 times) to prevent shrinkage. Bake at 425° for 10 to 15 minutes or until lightly browned. Cool before filling.

Note: For double crust, double ingredients above. Follow individual recipe for procedure.

CLASSIC OIL 9-INCH SINGLE CRUST*

1⅓ cups all-purpose flour	⅓ cup Crisco Oil
½ teaspoon salt (optional)	3 tablespoons skim milk

1. Combine flour and salt (if used) in medium bowl.
2. Blend Crisco Oil and milk in small bowl. Add to flour mixture. Stir with fork until mixture forms large clumps. Press into ball. Press between hands to form 5 to 6-inch "pancake".
3. Roll "pancake" between unfloured sheets of waxed paper. Peel off top sheet. Trim one inch larger than upside-down 9-inch pie plate. Flip into pie plate. Remove other sheet. Press to fit. Fold edge under. Flute.
4. For unbaked pie shell, follow individual recipe for baking temperature and time.
5. For baked pie shell, prick bottom and sides with fork (50 times) to prevent shrinkage. Bake at 375° for 12 to 15 minutes or until lightly browned. Cool before filling.

Note: For double crust, double ingredients above. Follow individual recipe for procedure.

APPLE-CRANBERRY STREUSEL PIE

Crust

Unbaked 9-inch Crisco Shortening or Crisco Oil Single Crust

Apple-Cranberry Filling

4   cups peeled, thinly sliced cooking apples (about 1⅓ pounds or 4 to 5 medium apples)
1   tablespoon lemon juice
1   container (12 ounces) cranberry apple or cranberry orange fruit sauce

3   tablespoons cornstarch
3   tablespoons firmly packed light brown sugar
1   teaspoon grated orange peel
½   teaspoon cinnamon
¼   teaspoon nutmeg

Topping

¼   cup all-purpose flour
¼   cup firmly packed light brown sugar

1   tablespoon plus 1½ teaspoons Crisco Oil

1.   Heat oven to 400°.
2.   For crust, combine flour and salt in medium bowl. Combine Crisco Oil and milk in small bowl. Add to flour mixture. Stir with fork until mixture forms large clumps. Press with fingers to form ball. Flatten between hands to form 5 to 6-inch "pancake". Roll "pancake" between unfloured sheets of waxed paper (or plastic wrap) on dampened countertop. Peel off top sheet. Trim one inch larger than upside-down 9-inch pie plate, flip into pie plate. Remove other sheet. Press into place. Fold edge under. Flute.
3.   For filling, combine apples, lemon juice, cranberry fruit sauce, cornstarch, brown sugar, orange peel, cinnamon and nutmeg. Toss to mix well. Spoon into unbaked pie shell.
4.   For topping, mix flour and brown sugar in small bowl. Add Crisco Oil. Blend until mixture forms fine crumbs. Sprinkle over apple-cranberry filling.
5.   Place foil lightly on top. Bake at 400° for 15 minutes. Remove foil. Bake 25 to 30 minutes or until apples are tender. Cover edge with foil, if necessary, to prevent overbrowning. Cool until barely warm or to room temperature before serving.

One 9-Inch Pie (8 Servings)

355 CALORIES / FAT 12 g (112 CAL or 31% of total calories) / SAT FAT 1 g (<5% of total calories) / CARB 61 g / PROTEIN 3 g / CHOL 0 mg / SODIUM 155 mg

OLD FASHIONED DUTCH APPLE PIE

Crust

Unbaked 9-inch Crisco
Shortening or Crisco Oil Single
Crust

Filling

½ cup granulated sugar
2 tablespoons all-purpose flour
¾ teaspoon cinnamon
¼ teaspoon nutmeg

5 cups peeled, thinly sliced
Granny Smith apples (about 1¾
pounds or 5 to 6 medium)
1 tablespoon lemon juice

Topping

⅓ cup all-purpose flour
⅓ cup firmly packed brown sugar

2 tablespoons Crisco Oil

1. Heat oven to 400°.
2. For crust, combine flour and salt in medium bowl. Combine Crisco Oil and milk in small bowl. Add to flour mixture. Stir with fork until mixture forms large clumps. Press with fingers to form ball. Flatten between hands to form 5- to 6-inch "pancake". Roll "pancake" between unfloured sheets of waxed paper (or plastic wrap) on dampened countertop. Peel off top sheet. Trim one inch larger than upside-down 9-inch pie plate. Flip into pie plate. Remove other sheet. Press into place. Fold edge under. Flute.
3. For filling, combine granulated sugar, flour, cinnamon, and nutmeg in small bowl. Toss apples with lemon juice in large bowl. Add sugar mixture. Toss to mix well. Spoon into unbaked pie crust.
4. For topping, mix flour and brown sugar in small bowl. Add Crisco Oil. Stir until mixture forms fine crumbs. Sprinkle over apples. Place foil lightly over top of pie.
5. Bake at 400° for 15 minutes. Remove foil. Bake 25 to 30 minutes or until apples are tender. Cool until barely warm or to room temperature before serving.

One 9-Inch Pie (8 Servings)

To Microwave:
1. Follow step 2, above, using microwave-safe pie plate. Microwave crust at HIGH for 3 minutes, turn ¼ turn, microwave at HIGH for 3 minutes, turn ¼ turn, microwave at HIGH for 30 seconds or until crust is dry and puffed, and light brown spots begin to appear.
2. Follow steps 3 and 4, above. Microwave at HIGH for 7 minutes, turn ¼ turn, microwave at HIGH for one minute.

350 CALORIES / FAT 13 g (121 CAL or 34% of total calories) / SAT FAT 1 g (<5% of total calories) / CARB 57 g / PROTEIN 3 g / CHOL 0 mg / SODIUM 140 mg

LIGHT LEMON MERINGUE PIE

Crust
Unbaked 9-inch Crisco
Shortening or Crisco Oil Single
Crust

Filling

1	cup sugar	1	egg yolk, lightly beaten
⅓	cup cornstarch	1	teaspoon finely grated fresh
⅛	teaspoon salt (optional)		lemon peel
1½	cups cold water	⅓	cup fresh lemon juice

Meringue

3	egg whites	¼	cup sugar
⅛	teaspoon salt (optional)	½	teaspoon vanilla

1. Heat oven to 375°.
2. For crust, combine flour and salt in medium bowl.
3. Combine Crisco Oil and milk in small bowl. Add to flour mixture. Stir with fork until mixture forms large clumps. Press with fingers to form ball. Flatten between hands to form 5-to 6-inch "pancake". Roll "pancake" between unfloured sheets of waxed paper (or plastic wrap) on dampened countertop. Peel off top sheet. Trim one inch larger than upside-down 9-inch pie plate. Flip into pie plate. Remove other sheet. Press into place. Fold edges under. Flute. Prick bottom and sides thoroughly with fork (50 times) to prevent shrinkage.
4. Bake at 375° for 12 to 15 minutes or until lightly browned.
5. Reduce oven temperature to 350°.
6. For filling, combine sugar, cornstarch and salt (if used) in medium saucepan. Stir in water, gradually. Stir until smooth. Cook and stir on medium-high heat until filling comes to a boil. Reduce heat to medium. Cook and stir 5 minutes. Remove from heat.
7. Stir small amount of hot mixture into egg yolk. Return mixture to saucepan. Cook and stir one minute. Remove from heat. Stir in lemon peel and juice.
8. For meringue, beat egg whites and salt (if used) until frothy. Add sugar gradually, beating well after each addition. Beat until stiff, but not dry. Add vanilla.
9. Spoon filling into baked pie shell. Spread meringue over filling, sealing meringue to edge of pie shell.
10. Bake at 350° for 15 minutes or until golden brown. Cool completely on rack. Cut with sharp knife dipped in hot water.

One 9-Inch Pie (8 Servings)
Note: Substitute bottled lemon peel and bottled lemon juice, if desired.

305 CALORIES / FAT 10 g (90 CAL or 30% of total calories) / SAT FAT 1 g (<5% of total calories) / CARB 52 g / PROTEIN 4 g / CHOL 25 mg / SODIUM 225 mg

ALVA'S CHERRY CREAM PIE

Crust

Unbaked 9-inch Crisco Shortening or Crisco Oil Single Crust

Filling

¾ cup skim milk
1 envelope (about 1 tablespoon) unflavored gelatin
⅓ cup sugar
1 container (16 ounces) 2% lowfat cottage cheese
1 teaspoon vanilla

Topping

1 can (21 ounces) light cherry pie filling
½ teaspoon almond extract

1. Heat oven to 375°.
2. For crust, combine flour and salt in medium bowl. Blend Crisco Oil and milk in small bowl. Add to flour mixture. Stir with fork until mixture forms large clumps. Press with fingers to form ball. Flatten between hands to form 5- to 6-inch "pancake". Roll "pancake" into circle between unfloured sheets of waxed paper (or plastic wrap) on dampened countertop. Peel off top sheet. Trim one inch larger than upside-down 9-inch pie plate. Flip into pie plate. Remove other sheet. Press into place. Fold edge under. Flute Prick bottom and sides thoroughly with fork (50 times) to prevent shrinkage.
3. Bake at 375° for 12 to 15 minutes or until lightly browned. Cool completely.
4. For filling, pour milk into small saucepan. Sprinkle with gelatin. Let stand 5 minutes to soften. Heat until almost at a boil. Stir to dissolve gelatin. Pour into blender container. Add sugar. Blend at high speed 30 seconds.
5. Add cheese and vanilla. Blend one minute 30 seconds or until smooth. Pour into cooled baked crust. Refrigerate 1½ hours or until firm.
6. For topping, combine pie filling and almond extract. Spoon over cream layer. Refrigerate one hour or longer.
7. Cut in wedges to serve. Refrigerate leftovers.

One 9-Inch Pie (8 Servings)

315 CALORIES / FAT 10g (95 CAL or 30% of total calories) / SAT FAT 1 g (<5% of total calories) / CARB 43 g / PROTEIN 12 g / CHOL 5 mg / SODIUM 395 mg

A Meal With a King

I was home on break from Morehouse when my parents and I had dinner with Dr. Height. She told wonderful stories about her life all through the meal and when I told her I was a freshman at Morehouse, she told me about having dinner many years ago with another Morehouse freshman.

Dr. Height told me that when she was in Atlanta working for the YWCA all the hotels were segregated so she lived "in residence" as the houseguest of Dr. and Mrs. Mays. Dr. Benjamin Mays was president of Morehouse at the time and he and Mrs. Mays told her to come home from work earlier than usual because they wanted her to have dinner with a promising young student. They wanted her to meet a student who was only 15 but who already exhibited all the qualities which Morehouse works to instill in us. She told me that the student talked to her about what he wanted to do with his life... whether he wanted to go into law or the ministry. Dr. Height said the young man was incredibly impressive and a delightful dinner companion. When I asked her his name, she told me that it was Martin Luther King, Jr.

Jason Crump
Morehouse College

The Godmother

I call Dr. Dorothy Height "the Godmother" because for decades she has been a central leader and guardian of everything that is important and memorable in the African-American community. "Grandmother" certainly would not describe this lady who leaves me breathing heavily simply by trying to keep up with her catalytic acts of leadership, globe trotting and invention of much that is most needed. The Black Family Reunion that she started and has taken throughout the country is an obvious recent example.

When I think of Dorothy, I think of the frontier. She has led black women and men into uncharted territory to let them know that everything was fine. On reproductive choice and on feminism itself, she has been there all along, coaxing others along, including her counterparts in the black male leadership. She has never shrunk from her full identity and that of the National Council of Negro Women as both black and female. A wonderfully effective coalitionist, Dorothy is proud to be called an African-American and she is a proud feminist as well. Just as no man

(continued)

UNCLE ED'S FAVORITE BANANA CREAM PIE

Crust

Baked 9-inch Crisco Shortening or Crisco Oil Single Crust

Filling

3	tablespoons cornstarch
¼	teaspoon salt
1⅔	cups water
1	can (14 ounces) sweetened condensed milk (not evaporated)
2	eggs, beaten
1	tablespoon margarine
1	teaspoon vanilla
4	medium bananas, divided
	Lemon juice

Topping

1	cup whipped topping (made from dry mix)

1. For filling, dissolve cornstarch and salt in water in medium saucepan. Stir in sweetened condensed milk and eggs. Cook and stir until thickened and bubbly. Remove from heat. Add butter and vanilla. Cool slightly.
2. Slice 3 bananas. Dip in lemon juice. Drain. Arrange on bottom of baked pastry shell. Pour filling over bananas. Cover. Chill 4 hours or until set.
3. Slice remaining banana. Dip in lemon juice. Drain. Garnish top of pie with whipped topping and bananas. Refrigerate leftover pie.

One 9-Inch Pie

425 CALORIES / FAT 17 g (150 CAL or 35% of total calories) / SAT FAT 4 g (9% of total calories) / CARB 60 g / PROTEIN 8 g / CHOL 70 mg / SODIUM 300 mg

OLD SOUTH MOLASSES CRUMB PIE

Crust

Unbaked 9-inch Crisco Shortening or Crisco Oil Single Crust

Filling

2 tablespoons Crisco Shortening
¾ cup all-purpose flour
½ cup firmly packed light brown sugar
¼ teaspoon salt
½ teaspoon cinnamon
¼ teaspoon nutmeg
¼ teaspoon ginger
¼ teaspoon cloves
¼ teaspoon baking soda
¾ cup boiling water
½ cup molasses
2 egg whites

1. Heat oven to 425°.
2. For filling, place Crisco in medium bowl. Add flour, brown sugar, salt, cinnamon, nutmeg, ginger and cloves. Beat at low speed of electric mixer until crumbs form.
3. Add baking soda to boiling water. Stir in molasses and egg whites.
4. Sprinkle bottom of unbaked pie shell generously with crumb mixture. Cover with molasses mixture. Repeat, finishing with crumbs on top.
5. Bake at 425° for 10 minutes. Reduce temperature to 350°. Bake for 25 minutes. Serve at room temperature.

One 9-Inch Pie

330 CALORIES / FAT 13 g (117 CAL or 35% of total calories) / SAT FAT 2 g (<5% of total calories) / CARB 49 g / PROTEIN 4 g / CHOL 25 mg / SODIUM 235 mg

(continued)
would submerge any vital part of his identity, his blackness or his maleness, Dorothy has taught us that integrity lies in being whole. She has taught us to be proud African-American women.
The Godmother continues to watch over us. We know that we are safe.

Honorable Eleanor Holmes Norton Congress of the United States House of Representatives

BETHUNE SWEET POTATO PIE

The Living Link

When meeting or eating with Dr. Height, one is always impressed with her gentle nature and with her rich sense of history. She is the living link in this century to our most prominent leaders. Dr. Height is not merely a survivor but a contributor of great scope. She has a sense of things as private as a mother's struggle to get prenatal care or, against all odds, to get that child through college. The scope of her life's work extends to a tremendous sense of world history and world diplomacy.

So when I'm with Dr. Height, sharing a meal, I always get a peek of history by asking her what Adam Clayton Powell, senior and junior were really like or Paul Robeson or A. Phillip Randolph or Mrs. Bethune at the height of his or her career. She literally observed leaders like Whitney Young, Malcolm X and Dr. King emerge in the struggle because she knew their parents and predecessors. So when you eat with Dr. Height you can be assured of several things; you'll be full of food, joy, esteem and a sense of history.

**Rev. Jesse L. Jackson
President and Founder
National Rainbow
Coalition, Inc.**

Crust

3   unbaked 9-inch Crisco Shortening or Crisco Oil Single Crusts

Filling

9   medium sweet potatoes or yams (about 4 pounds)
¼   cup light margarine, softened
½   cup granulated sugar
½   cup firmly packed light brown sugar
½   teaspoon salt
¼   teaspoon nutmeg
2   eggs, well beaten
2   egg whites
2   cups skim milk
1   tablespoon vanilla

1.   For filling, boil sweet potatoes until tender. Peel and mash.
2.   Heat oven to 350°.
3.   Combine margarine, granulated sugar, brown sugar, salt and nutmeg in large bowl. Beat at medium speed of electric mixer until creamy. Beat in sweet potatoes, until well mixed. Beat in eggs and egg whites. Beat in milk and vanilla slowly. Spoon into 3 unbaked pie shells, using about 4 cups filling per shell.
4.   Bake at 350° for 50 to 60 minutes or until set. Cool to room temperature before serving. Refrigerate leftover pie.

Three 9-Inch Pies

295 CALORIES / FAT 12 g (104 CAL or 35% of total calories) / SAT FAT 1 g (<5% of total calories) / CARB 43 g / PROTEIN 5 g / CHOL 20 mg / SODIUM 285 mg

**HERITAGE
RECIPE**

BLACKBERRY ICE CREAM PIE

Crust

Baked 9-inch Crisco Shortening or Crisco Oil Single Crust

Filling

1   package (4-serving size) peach or berry flavor gelatin (not sugar free)
1   cup boiling water
1   pint frozen vanilla nonfat yogurt, softened
1¾ cups fresh or frozen dry pack blackberries, partially thawed

Topping

1   cup whipped topping (made from dry mix)
2   cups fresh berries

1.   For filling, combine gelatin and water in large bowl. Stir until dissolved. Cut yogurt into small chunks. Add to gelatin mixture, a spoonful at a time. Blend with wire whisk after each addition.
2.   Dry blackberries between paper towels. Fold into gelatin mixture. Spoon into cooled baked pie crust. Refrigerate or freeze several hours before serving. Top with whipped topping and fresh berries.

One 9-Inch Pie

295 CALORIES / FAT 11 g (98 CAL or 33% of total calories) / SAT FAT 2 g (5% of total calories) / CARB 41 g / PROTEIN 5 g / CHOL 5 mg / SODIUM 175 mg

Food for the Spirit

My most impressive memory of breaking bread with Dr. Dorothy Height occurred at one of the National Board meetings of the NCNW. It was at that time I understood why she is such an exemplary leader. The comfort of everyone assembled was her first priority. Attention to details necessary for an enlightening exchange of information was also her utmost concern, so much so that she never ate her own dinner. I would gently remind her that she had not touched her dinner, to which she would acknowledgingly nod. She certainly is a role model for the kind of unselfish spirit that bespeaks a true leader. Her love for her work and the people who are a part of her mission is demonstrated by her unselfish concern for others. Even though Dr. Height did not eat, I certainly did and I enjoyed the physical and spiritual nourishment shared that evening.

**Gwendolyn E. Boyd
Eastern Regional
Director, Delta Sigma
Theta Sorority, Inc.**

PINTO BEAN PIE

Crust

Unbaked 9-inch Crisco Shortening or Crisco Oil
Single Crust

Filling

2 eggs, lightly beaten
1 cup skim milk
2 cups mashed pinto beans, home cooked* or canned
⅔ cup sugar
¾ teaspoon cinnamon
¼ teaspoon salt
¼ teaspoon ginger
¼ teaspoon nutmeg
¼ teaspoon cloves

1. Heat oven to 425°.
2. Combine eggs and evaporated milk in large bowl. Stir until well blended. Add pinto beans, sugar, cinnamon, salt, ginger, nutmeg and cloves. Beat at low speed of electric mixer until well blended. Pour into pie shell.
3. Bake at 425° for 15 minutes. Reduce oven temperature to 350°. Bake 35 minutes, or until knife inserted in center comes out clean. Serve warm or at room temperature.

One 9-Inch Pie

Note: Home preparation of beans. Rinse pinto beans. Place in large saucepan. Cover with cold water. Cook 3 to 5 minutes, covered, or until water is hot. Remove from heat. Set aside for 1 hour 30 minutes or until soft enough to mash. Drain. Mash.

315 CALORIES / FAT 12 g (104 CAL or 33% of total calories) / SAT FAT 2 g (<5% of total calories) / CARB 45 g / PROTEIN 8 g / CHOL 55 mg / SODIUM 235 mg

HERITAGE
RECIPE

Keep the Pulse Beating

Dorothy I. Height is a legendary role model for all women. Her dedication and commitment to the National Council of Negro Women is continuously demonstrated over and over throughout the years. Whenever she and I share a meal together, whether in California at the Chi Eta Phi Sorority Confab, in Atlanta at the Black Family Reunion or in Baltimore at a national convention, her constant refrain has been "the survival of NCNW". While we are eating, we exchange ideas about women's issues and how to keep the pulse of the NCNW beating.

Verdelle B. Bellamy
Atlanta, Georgia

APPLE-CRANBERRY CRISP

Topping
- 1½ cups oats (quick or old fashioned)
- ½ cup firmly packed brown sugar
- ⅓ cup all-purpose flour
- ½ teaspoon cinnamon
- ⅓ cup margarine, melted
- 1 tablespoon water

Filling
- 1 can (16 ounces) whole berry cranberry sauce
- 2 tablespoons cornstarch
- 5 cups thinly sliced peeled apples (about 5 medium)

1. Heat oven to 375°.
2. For topping, combine oats, brown sugar, flour and cinnamon. Mix well. Stir in melted margarine and water. Mix until crumbly.
3. For filling, combine cranberry sauce and cornstarch in large saucepan. Mix well. Heat on medium-high heat, stirring occasionally, 2 minutes or until sauce bubbles. Add apples, tossing to coat. Spoon into 8-inch square glass baking dish. Crumble topping over fruit.
4. Bake at 375° for 25 to 35 minutes or until apples are tender. Serve warm.

9 servings

290 CALORIES / FAT 8 g (71 CAL or 24% of total calories) / SAT FAT 2 g (<5% of total calories) / CARB 54 g / PROTEIN 3 g / CHOL 0 mg / SODIUM 100 mg

ARKANSAS BEST PUMPKIN PIE

Crust
Unbaked 9-inch Crisco Shortening or Crisco Oil Single Crust

Filling
1¾ cups canned solid pack pumpkin (not pumpkin pie filling)
1¼ cups evaporated skim milk
2 eggs, beaten
¾ cup granulated sugar
1 teaspoon cinnamon
¼ teaspoon salt

Topping
½ cup all-purpose flour
⅓ cup firmly packed brown sugar
2 tablespoons Butter Flavor Crisco
½ teaspoon cinnamon
⅛ teaspoon salt
¼ cup chopped pecans

Garnish
1 cup whipped topping (made from dry mix)

1. Heat oven to 350°.
2. For filling, combine pumpkin, evaporated milk, eggs, granulated sugar, cinnamon and salt in large bowl. Stir until smooth and creamy. Pour into unbaked pie shell.
3. For topping, combine flour, brown sugar, shortening, cinnamon and salt. Mix with fork or pastry blender until coarse crumbs form. Stir in chopped nuts. Sprinkle evenly over filling.
4. Bake at 350° for 45 to 55 minutes or until knife inserted in center comes out clean. Garnish pie with whipped topping when cool. Serve at room temperature. Refrigerate leftover pie.

One 9-Inch Pie

425 CALORIES / FAT 17 g (149 CAL or 35% of total calories) / SAT FAT 2 g (5% of total calories) / CARB 60 g / PROTEIN 10 g / CHOL 55 mg / SODIUM 315 mg

A Tribute
Being the articulate and profound speaker that she is, I had never seen Dr. Height at a loss for words until March, 1991 when the NCNW gave her a surprise birthday party. She was speechless, totally surprised and had no idea about the party where a good time was had by all. The birthday celebration, held at the NCNW office, was a warm, informal gathering attended by her staff, colleagues and friends. We dined sufficiently, enjoying the refreshments served: chicken, collard greens, potato salad, sweet potatoes and several other soul food dishes. Jesse Jackson gave a very moving tribute to Dr. Height and I was truly inspired hearing his and the many other testimonies given on her behalf. I join them in saying she is a very important black woman who has accomplished much.

**Madeline Young Lawson
Olney, Maryland**

PANDOWDY

Filling
- 5 cups sliced, peeled cooking apples, pears or peaches
- ½ cup pure maple syrup or maple-flavored pancake syrup
- 2 tablespoons lemon juice
- ½ teaspoon cinnamon
- ¼ teaspoon nutmeg
- 1 tablespoon Butter Flavor Crisco

Crust
- 9-inch Classic Crisco Shortening or Crisco Oil Single Crust dough

Glaze
- 2 teaspoons skim milk
- 1 teaspoon sugar

Topping
- 12 tablespoons whipped topping (made from dry mix)

1. For filling, toss apples with maple syrup, lemon juice, cinnamon and nutmeg in large bowl. Spoon into 8-inch square glass baking dish. Dot with Butter Flavor Crisco.
2. Heat oven to 400°.
3. For crust, roll dough into 8½ to 9-inch square between lightly floured sheets of waxed paper on dampened countertop. Peel off top sheet of waxed paper. Flip dough over on top of apples. Remove other sheet of waxed paper. Press dough down along insides of dish. Trim pastry along inside edge. Cut large vents to allow steam to escape.
4. For glaze, brush with milk. Sprinkle with sugar. Bake at 400° for 25 to 30 minutes or until crust is light golden brown. Remove from oven.
5. Cut pastry into 2-inch squares. Spoon juice from bottom of dish over entire top of pastry. Return to oven. Bake 20 to 25 minutes or until top is deep golden brown. Serve warm with whipped topping.

8 Servings

285 CALORIES / FAT 11 g (101 CAL or 35% of total calories) /
SAT FAT 1 g (<5% of total calories) / CARB 45 g /
PROTEIN 3 g / CHOL 0 mg / SODIUM 145 mg

HERITAGE RECIPE

A Legacy to Remember

The ballroom was elegant, glittering chandeliers, immaculate table settings and enthusiastic guests who wore their finest evening wear. We were in New York city at the Waldorf Astoria Hotel for a spectacular birthday celebration for Dr. Dorothy Height. It was a grand dinner party for a grand lady. Bill Cosby was the master of ceremonies, First Lady Barbara Bush was honorary chairperson; many chief executives from the corporate sector were in attendance. Chartered buses arrived from DC, Maryland and Virginia and other cities had transported Delta Sigma Theta sorority sisters, NCNW members and friends to the affair. It was a night to remember, unforgettable — just as the work and leadership of Dr. Height is unforgettable... a legacy to remember.

Beulah Sutherland

SEASONAL FRUIT COBBLER

Apple
      5   cups sliced, peeled cooking apples (about 1⅔ pounds or 5 medium)
      1   cup sugar
      ⅓   cup water or apple juice
      2   tablespoons margarine
      2   tablespoons all-purpose flour
      ½   teaspoon cinnamon
      ¼   teaspoon nutmeg

Blueberry
      4   cups blueberries
      ½   cup sugar
      1   tablespoon cornstarch
      1   teaspoon lemon juice
      1   teaspoon grated lemon peel

Cherry
      4   cups pitted fresh or thawed frozen dry pack red tart cherries
      1¼ cups sugar
      3   tablespoons cornstarch
      ¼   teaspoon cinnamon
      ¼   teaspoon almond extract

Peach
      4   cups sliced, peeled peaches or 1 bag (20 ounces) thawed frozen dry pack peach slices
      ½   cup sugar
      ⅓   cup water
      1   tablespoon cornstarch
      ¼   teaspoon cinnamon
          Dash of nutmeg

Cobbler Crust
      1   cup all-purpose flour
      2   tablespoons sugar
      1½ teaspoons baking powder
      ¼   teaspoon salt
      ¼   cup Crisco Shortening
      1   egg, slightly beaten
      ¼   cup milk
      ½   teaspoon vanilla

(continued on facing page)

Seasonal Fruit Cobbler *(continued from facing page)*

1. Select fruit recipe. Heat oven to 400°. Combine fruit ingredients in large saucepan. Cook and stir on medium heat until mixture comes to a boil and thickens. Simmer and stir 1 minute. Pour into 8-inch square glass baking dish or 2-quart baking dish. Place in oven.
2. For cobbler crust, combine flour, sugar, baking powder and salt. Cut in Crisco until coarse crumbs form. Combine egg, milk and vanilla. Add all at once to flour mixture. Stir just until moistened. Remove baking dish from oven. Drop dough in 8 mounds on top of hot fruit.
3. Bake at 400° for 15 to 20 minutes or until golden brown. Serve warm.

8 Servings

Apple

330 CALORIES / FAT 10 g (92 CAL or 28% of total calories) / SAT FAT 2 g (7% of total calories) / CARB 57 g / PROTEIN 3 g / CHOL 30 mg / SODIUM 175 mg

Blueberry

230 CALORIES / FAT 7 g (66 CAL or 28% of total calories) / SAT FAT 2 g (7% of total calories) / CARB 39 g / PROTEIN 3 g / CHOL 30 mg / SODIUM 145 mg

Cherry

305 CALORIES / FAT 7 g (66 CAL or 22% of total calories) / SAT FAT 2 g (6% of total calories) / CARB 57 g / PROTEIN 3 g / CHOL 30 mg / SODIUM 140 mg

Peach

220 CALORIES / FAT 7 g (64 CAL or 29% of total calories) / SAT FAT 2 g (8% of total calories) / CARB 37 g / PROTEIN 3 g / CHOL 30 mg / SODIUM 140 mg

Stormy Weather

It has been my pleasure to share many meals with Dr. Height at special events, meetings, conventions, etc., sponsored by Delta Sigma Sorority, the National Council of Negro Women and other organizations throughout the country. When I recollect those occasions, I remember her traveling to my hometown, Charlotte, North Carolina several years ago for a meeting with several civil rights strategists including attorney Julius Chambers and others.

With Dr. Height one of the few women in attendance, I was quite proud to know that this extraordinary female civil and human rights leader was among the "kitchen cabinet" meeting in Charlotte. I wanted to make her comfortable in my city and support her in any way needed. When I asked her how I could be of assistance, she said that since a sudden downpour of rain had occurred she really needed a rain scarf. I obligingly went to purchase a rain scarf for this great lady.

Dr. Bertha Maxwell Roddey
National President, Delta Sigma Theta Sorority, Inc.

Troubled Times

One of the things I remember most vividly about Dr. Height involves a meeting that my friend Juanita Poitier and I arranged in the sixties. We held the meeting at the Poitier home because they lived in a secluded area, the times were frightening and there was a lot of anxiety in the black leadership. (It was the time of McCarthy and the witch-hunts.) Martin was in jail and we all felt we were under siege. Of course, since we met all day, there were several meals. The initial small tensions soon gave way as we shared food and fellowship. We decided to hold the meeting, which was actually like a summit, to bring together people like Dorothy Height, Roy Wilkins, my husband, Ossie Davis, Lorraine Hansberry, Malcolm X... Sidney came later, and several others that I can't recall now to develop a Declaration of Human Rights for Black Americans. You have no idea of how troubled the times were. We took no photographs because so many dastardly things had been done with photographs. We held no press conference, we just wanted sincere, thinking people to get together in

(continued)

GEORGIA APPLE BROWN BETTY

1¼ cups firmly packed brown sugar, divided
1   cup water
¼   cup light corn syrup
1   tablespoon lemon juice
1   teaspoon cinnamon
4   cups diced, peeled apples (about 1⅓ pounds or 4 medium)
4   cups toast cubes
¼   cup Butter Flavor Crisco, melted

1. Heat oven to 450°. Grease 1-quart casserole with Butter Flavor Crisco.
2. Combine 1 cup brown sugar, water, corn syrup, lemon juice and cinnamon in large saucepan. Bring to a boil. Add apples. Boil 5 minutes. Add toast cubes. Mix lightly until liquid is absorbed. Spoon into casserole. Press lightly. Sprinkle with remaining ¼ cup brown sugar. Drizzle with Butter Flavor Crisco. Bake at 450° for 10 to 15 minutes or until top is crisp.

8 Servings

285 CALORIES / FAT 7 g (61 CAL or 21% of total calories) / SAT FAT 2 g (5% of total calories) / CARB 56 g / PROTEIN 1 g / CHOL 0 mg / SODIUM 95 mg

HERITAGE
RECIPE

CLASSIC POUND CAKE

1	cup Butter Flavor Crisco
2½	cups sugar
4	eggs
1	teaspoon grated lemon peel
2	tablespoons lemon juice
2	teaspoons vanilla
3½	cups all-purpose flour
1	teaspoon baking powder
½	teaspoon salt
1⅓	cups skim milk

1. Heat oven to 350°. Grease two 9 X 5 X 2¾-inch loaf pans with Butter Flavor Crisco. Flour lightly.
2. Combine Butter Flavor Crisco, sugar, eggs, grated lemon peel, lemon juice and vanilla in large bowl. Beat at low speed of electric mixer until blended, scraping bowl constantly. Beat at high speed 5 minutes, scraping bowl occasionally.
3. Combine flour, baking powder and salt in medium bowl. Add to batter alternately with milk at low speed. Beat until batter is smooth after each addition. Pour into pans.
4. Bake at 350° for 58 to 62 minutes, or until deep golden brown and toothpick inserted in center comes out clean. Cool on cooling rack 20 minutes. Turn out of pan onto rack. Cool completely.

Two Loaves (24 Servings)

235 CALORIES / FAT 9 g (81 CAL or 34% of total calories) / SAT FAT 2 g (9% of total calories) / CARB 36 g / PROTEIN 3 g / CHOL 35 mg / SODIUM 75 mg

(continued)
an informal setting so that we could talk about what was happening to the Movement and where we needed to go. We had to formulate an agenda to which we could all subscribe.

Our plan was to find out if Malcolm would take the Declaration to heads of African states to find out if such a declaration were presented in the United Nations, would they support it. I remember Dorothy participated a great deal in all the discussions and helped move us to consensus on the need to continue meeting on a regular basis. She told a story that Mary McLeod Bethune had told her about the fingers in a hand: it was that a single finger could make no impact, but all five fingers balled up into a fist could deliver a mighty blow. We were to be that fist.

Since that time, I have counted Dorothy among my dearest friends. I have tried to do whatever she has asked of me. My husband says Dorothy has never gotten all the credit she deserves for her role in being at the very forefront of the struggle. She was remarkable then and she remains so to this day.

Ruby Dee
Actor

(continued)

LEMON POPPY SEED CAKE

Cake

1 package (18.25 ounces) Duncan Hines Moist Deluxe Lemon Cake Mix
1¼ cups water
3 egg whites
3 tablespoons poppy seed
⅓ cup Crisco Oil

Glaze

1 cup confectioners sugar
3 to 4 teaspoons lemon juice

1. Heat oven to 350°. Grease and flour 12-cup Bundt pan.
2. For cake, empty cake mix into large bowl. Add water, egg whites, poppy seed and Crisco Oil. Prepare, bake and cool following package directions.
3. For glaze, combine sugar and lemon juice. Stir until well blended. Drizzle over top of cake.

One Bundt Cake (16 Servings)

205 CALORIES / FAT 8 g (72 CAL or 35% of total calories) / SAT FAT 1 g (<5% of total calories) / CARB 32 g / PROTEIN 2 g / CHOL 0 mg / SODIUM 220 mg

CARROT RAISIN CAKE WITH CREAM CHEESE GLAZE

Cake

1½	cups granulated sugar
½	cup Crisco Oil
2	eggs
1	egg white
2⅓	cups all-purpose flour
¼	cup skim milk
2	teaspoons baking soda
1	teaspoon cinnamon
½	teaspoon baking powder
½	teaspoon salt (optional)
2	cups finely shredded carrots (about 4 medium)
⅔	cup raisins

Glaze

1	ounce cream cheese, softened
½	cup confectioners sugar
1	to 1½ teaspoons skim milk

1. Heat oven to 350°. Grease and flour 12-cup Bundt pan.
2. For cake, combine sugar, Crisco Oil, eggs and egg white in large bowl. Beat at medium speed of electric mixer until light and fluffy. Add flour, milk, baking soda, cinnamon, baking powder and salt (if used). Beat at low speed until blended, scraping bowl constantly. Beat at medium speed 2 minutes, scraping bowl occasionally. Stir in carrots and raisins with spoon. Spoon into pan.
3. Bake at 350° for 50 to 55 minutes or until toothpick inserted in center comes out clean. Cool in pan 5 minutes. Invert on wire rack. Cool completely.
4. For glaze, combine cream cheese and sugar in small bowl. Stir to blend. Add milk gradually. Stir until well blended and smooth. Drizzle over cake.

One Bundt Cake (16 Slices)

240 CALORIES / FAT 8 g (74 CAL or 31% of total calories) / SAT FAT 1 g (<5% of total calories) / CARB 39 g / PROTEIN 3 g / CHOL 30 mg / SODIUM 210 mg

(continued)

Dr. Height's request, we made four stops for her to get out and give greetings at the pavilions along our route. We were all hungry and tired. When we finally arrived at the dining room, we were all relieved that home cooked food had been saved for us. We were most appreciative when the plates were brought out and set before us. Each contained fried chicken, baked ham, string beans, macaroni and cheese, lettuce and tomato salad with pound cake and ice cream for dessert. I am always so amazed at the energy Dr. Height expends and the way she is able to delay eating until all bases have been touched and her mission has been accomplished. Once settled at the table she was generous in her praise of how delicious the home cooked dishes were with a special emphasis on the pound cake.

**Carrie Ayers Haynes
National Director, Self-
Enhancing Literacy
Fundamentals
Los Angeles, California**

PINEAPPLE UPSIDE DOWN RUM CAKE

Cake

¾ cup margarine, divided
⅔ cup granulated sugar
1 egg plus 2 egg whites, beaten
½ cup skim milk
2½ cups all-purpose flour

4 teaspoons baking powder
1 teaspoon salt
¼ cup firmly packed brown sugar
6 canned pineapple slices

Glaze

¼ cup water
¼ cup granulated sugar

3 tablespoons rum

1. Heat oven to 350°.
2. For cake, cream ¼ cup margarine in large bowl at medium speed of electric mixer. Add granulated sugar gradually. Add beaten egg and egg whites. Beat until well blended. Add milk gradually.
3. Sift flour, baking powder and salt together. Add slowly to creamed mixture.
4. Melt remaining ½ cup margarine. Pour into 9-inch square cake pan. Sprinkle brown sugar over margarine. Place pineapple slices on top of brown sugar.
5. Pour cake batter carefully over pineapple.
6. Bake at 350° for 50 minutes or until toothpick inserted in cake comes out clean.
7. For glaze, heat water to boiling in small saucepan. Add sugar. Stir until dissolved. Add rum. Cool.
8. Pour glaze over top of hot cake. Cool slightly. Turn onto serving platter.

8 servings.

475 CALORIES / FAT 18 g (164CAL or 34% of total calories) / SAT FAT 4 g (7% of total calories) / CARB 70 g / PROTEIN 7 g / CHOL 25 mg / SODIUM 665 mg

**Adaptation from Recipe
Chef Mark Cornish
Forest Club, Houston, Texas**

SPICY PUMPKIN TORTE

Cake

1 package (18.25 ounces) Duncan Hines Moist Deluxe Yellow Cake Mix
1 teaspoon cinnamon
½ teaspoon nutmeg

¼ teaspoon cloves
3 egg whites
1¼ cups water
⅓ cup Crisco Oil

Filling

1 package (4-serving size) butterscotch flavor pudding and pie filling mix
½ teaspoon cinnamon
¼ teaspoon ginger
⅛ teaspoon cloves

⅛ teaspoon nutmeg
2 cups skim milk, divided
½ cup solid pack pumpkin (not pumpkin pie filling)
1 envelope whipped topping mix
½ teaspoon vanilla

Garnish

2 tablespoons reserved filling

1. Heat oven to 350°. Grease and flour two 8- or 9-inch round cake pans.
2. For cake, combine cake mix, cinnamon, nutmeg and cloves in large bowl. Stir well. Add egg whites and Crisco Oil. Bake and cool cake following package directions. Chill cooled layers for ease in splitting.
3. For filling, combine pudding mix, cinnamon, ginger, cloves and nutmeg in medium saucepan. Stir in 1½ cups skim milk. Cook following package directions. Add pumpkin. Stir until well blended. Cover surface with plastic wrap. Cool.
4. Prepare whipped topping using remaining ½ cup milk and vanilla. Follow package directions for mixing. Remove 2 tablespoons filling. Fold whipped topping into remaining filling.
5. To assemble torte, split each cake layer in half horizontally. Spread one-fourth pumpkin whipped topping mixture on one cake layer. Place second layer on top of filling. Repeat with remaining layers. Spread last fourth of mixture on top.
6. For garnish, dot top with reserved filling. Swirl with tip of knife. Refrigerate until ready to serve.

One 8 or 9 Inch Cake (12 Servings)

260 CALORIES / FAT 10 g (87 CAL or 33% of total calories) / SAT FAT 1 g (<5% of total calories) / CARB 40 g / PROTEIN 4 g / CHOL 0 mg / SODIUM 325 mg

BANANA FUDGE MARBLE CAKE

Cake

1   package (18.25 ounces) Duncan Hines Moist Deluxe Fudge Marble Cake Mix
3   egg whites
1   cup ripe mashed banana
½   cup water
⅓   cup Crisco Oil

Frosting

1   package (4-serving size) banana flavor instant pudding and pie filling mix
2   envelopes whipped topping mix
1¼   cups lowfat milk

Topping

1   sliced banana
½   cup frozen whipped topping, thawed
      Lemon Juice

1. Heat oven to 350°. Grease and flour two 9-inch round cake pans.
2. For cake, combine cake mix, egg whites, mashed banana, water and Crisco Oil in large bowl. Prepare, bake and cool following package directions.
3. For frosting, combine pudding mix, whipped topping mix and milk in large bowl. Beat at high speed of electric mixer 2 to 3 minutes or until light and fluffy. Fill and frost cake. Refrigerate for several hours before serving.
4. For topping, dip banana slices in lemon juice. Blot dry on paper towel. Garnish cake with whipped topping and banana slices.

Tip: For a wonderful flavor variation, serve cake slices with one or 2 tablespoons Fudge Sauce.

One 9-Inch Cake (12 Servings)

290 CALORIES / FAT 11 g (101 CAL or 35% of total calories) / SAT FAT 2 g (8% of total calories) / CARB 45 g / PROTEIN 4 g / CHOL 5 mg / SODIUM 315 mg

BUTTERY CHOCOLATE SNACKING CAKE

1   package (18.5 ounces) Duncan Hines Butter Recipe
     Fudge Cake Mix
6   egg whites
1   cup water
¼   cup Crisco Oil
     Confectioners sugar (optional)

1.   Heat oven to 375°. Oil 13 X 9 X 2-inch pan. Flour
     lightly.
2.   Combine cake mix, egg whites, water and Crisco Oil
     in large bowl.
3.   Beat at low speed of electric mixer until moistened.
     Beat at medium speed 4 minutes. Pour batter into
     pan.
4.   Bake at 375° for 28 to 32 minutes or until toothpick
     inserted in center comes out clean. Cool.

One 13 X 9-Inch Cake (12 Servings)
Note: Sprinkle confectioners sugar lightly over top of cooled cake, if desired.

240 CALORIES / FAT 9 g (78 CAL or 33% of total calories) / SAT FAT 2 g (9% of total calories) / CARB 35 g / PROTEIN 4 g / CHOL 0 mg / SODIUM 270 mg

A Forty Year Friendship

I have been privileged to know Dorothy Irene Height for more than 40 years and she has been mentor, role model, soror, employer and close family friend.

While in school at New York University, I was a frequent visitor and diner (usually eating lunch or dinner) at her apartment in Harlem on 152nd Street between Amsterdam and St. Nicholas Avenues, long before she moved downtown to Waterside Plaza... and she could cook! REALLY! I remember her tuna casserole, a special rutabaga (yellow turnips) dish and corn pudding (the very best and a secret recipe) and sweet potato pie. What Dorothy Height IS and what she DOES make her a Very Special Person.

Frances Morton Flippen

PLANTATION GINGER CAKES

A Sounding Board

Many years ago when I was working in Atlanta with the Minority Women's Employment Program (MWEP) I shared a meal with Dr. Height that included a conversation which changed the course of my life. We had fried chicken at Pascal's Restaurant as Dr. Height and I discussed whether or not I should accept a position as head of the Women's Bureau in the Department of Labor in the Carter Administration. I was really struggling with the decision because I didn't want to leave Atlanta or MWEP. Dr. Height was in Atlanta working on Dr. King's Birthday celebration and as we talked, she told me about meeting Dr. King when he was just a boy and a student at Morehouse. She talked about the many career choices he considered early in his life. Through that discussion Dr. Height helped put the Women's Bureau in context for me. Dr. Height let me talk about my reservations. As we talked, she began to review the history of the Women's Bureau... she described its early days, its significance and how important it would be for me to begin working on women's issues on the

(continued)

1²⁄₃ cups all-purpose flour
¼ cup sugar
2 tablespoons baking powder
½ teaspoon cinnamon
½ teaspoon ginger
½ teaspoon nutmeg
½ teaspoon salt
½ cup raisins
2 eggs, lightly beaten
¼ cup Crisco Oil
⅓ cup 2% lowfat milk
½ teaspoon vanilla
½ cup dark molasses

Spiced Sugar Topping* (optional)
2 tablespoons sugar
⅛ teaspoon cinnamon
⅛ teaspoon ginger
⅛ teaspoon nutmeg

1. Heat oven to 375°. Place paper or foil liners in twelve medium (about 2½-inch) muffin cups.
2. Combine flour, sugar, baking powder, cinnamon, ginger, nutmeg and salt in medium bowl. Stir well. Stir in raisins.
3. Combine eggs and Crisco Oil in small bowl. Mix well. Stir in milk and vanilla. Add molasses. Mix well. Stir into flour mixture with spoon. Mix just until moistened. Spoon evenly into muffin cups.
4. For spiced sugar topping, blend sugar, cinnamon, ginger and nutmeg. Sprinkle over batter.
5. Bake at 375° for 16 to 20 minutes or until toothpick inserted in center comes out clean. Cool.

*Note: Sift confectioners sugar over top of cooled, baked muffins if spiced sugar topping is omitted.

One Dozen Muffin Cakes

195 CALORIES / FAT 6 g (53 CAL or 27% of total calories) / SAT FAT 1 g (<5% of total calories) / CARB 33 g / PROTEIN 3 g / CHOL 35 mg / SODIUM 280 mg

HONEY CAKE WITH ICE CREAM

2½ cups all-purpose flour
2½ teaspoons baking powder
½ teaspoon cinnamon
¼ teaspoon salt
¼ teaspoon baking soda
⅛ teaspoon cloves
¾ cup Crisco Shortening
½ cup sugar
1 teaspoon vanilla
¾ cup honey
1 beaten egg
1 cup hot water
1 cup raisins
⅓ cup chopped walnuts, divided
1 quart lowfat vanilla ice cream

1. Heat oven to 350°. Grease 13 X 9 X 2-inch baking pan.
2. Combine flour, baking powder, cinnamon, salt, baking soda and cloves in medium bowl.
3. Combine Crisco, sugar and vanilla in large bowl. Beat at medium speed of electric mixer until creamy. Add honey and egg. Beat well. Add flour mixture alternately with hot water. Beat well after each addition. Stir in raisins and ¼ cup nuts. Spread in prepared pan. Sprinkle with remaining 1 tablespoon plus 1 teaspoon nuts.
4. Bake at 350° for 30 to 35 minutes or until toothpick inserted in center comes out clean. Cool on wire rack.
5. Serve warm or at room temperature with lowfat vanilla ice cream.

12 Servings

445 CALORIES / FAT 16 g (144 CAL or 32% of total calories) / SAT FAT 4 g (8% of total calories) / CARB 70 g / PROTEIN 7 g / CHOL 20 mg / SODIUM 180 mg

(continued)

national level. She told me I could make a difference if I would accept the position. I remember her asking me how many people, let alone a young African-American woman under 30, would be offered such an opportunity. Seeing the position through her eyes made me realize what my decision had to be.

**Alexis Herman
Deputy Chair, Democratic National Committee
Former Head/Women's Bureau**

STRAWBERRY TEA CAKE WITH ICE CREAM

Tea Cake

1 package (10 ounces) frozen sliced strawberries, thawed
1 tablespoon cornstarch
2 cups all-purpose flour
¾ cup granulated sugar
½ teaspoon baking powder
½ teaspoon baking soda

¼ teaspoon salt
⅔ cup Crisco Shortening
1 beaten egg
¾ cup lowfat buttermilk or sour milk
1 teaspoon vanilla

Icing

1 cup confectioners sugar
4 teaspoons milk

¼ teaspoon vanilla
1 quart lowfat vanilla ice cream

1. Heat oven to 350°. Grease and flour 10 X 2-inch round tart pan with removable bottom or 11 X 7 X 1½-inch baking pan.
2. For cake, combine undrained strawberries and cornstarch in small saucepan. Cook and stir on medium heat until thickened and bubbly. Sieve mixture. Discard seeds. Cool.
3. Combine flour, sugar, baking powder, baking soda and salt in large bowl. Cut in Crisco until crumbly. Make well in center.
4. Combine egg, buttermilk and vanilla in small bowl. Add to flour mixture. Stir just until moistened. Spread two-thirds of batter over bottom and one inch up sides of prepared pan. Spread strawberry mixture carefully over batter in pan. Spoon remaining batter in small mounds on top of strawberry mixture.
5. Bake at 350° for 30 minutes or until toothpick inserted in center comes out clean. Cool 15 minutes. Remove from pan (leave in 11 X 7-inch pan).
6. For icing, place confectioners sugar in small bowl. Stir in milk 1 teaspoon at a time until of drizzling consistency. Stir in vanilla. Drizzle over cake. Serve warm with lowfat ice cream.

8 to 10 Servings

445 CALORIES / FAT 15 g (135 CAL or 31% of total calories) / SAT FAT 4 g (9% of total calories) / CARB 70 g / PROTEIN 7 g / CHOL 25 mg / SODIUM 195 mg

CREAMY LEMON CHEESECAKE

Crust

1 cup graham cracker crumbs	3 tablespoons Crisco Oil
¼ cup sugar	

Filling

3 ounces Neufchâtel cheese
2 cups lowfat (1%) cottage cheese
2 egg whites
½ cup sugar

1 teaspoon freshly grated lemon peel
3 tablespoons fresh lemon juice
1 teaspoon vanilla

1. Heat oven to 350°.
2. For crust, combine graham cracker crumbs, sugar and Crisco Oil in 9-inch pie plate. Mix well with fork. Press firmly against bottom and halfway up sides of pie plate.
3. For filling, blend Neufchâtel and cottage cheeses in food processor or blender*, until completely smooth.
4. Add egg whites, sugar, lemon peel, lemon juice and vanilla. Blend well. Pour mixture into crust.
5. Bake at 350° for 30 minutes. Turn oven off and allow cheesecake to remain in oven for 5 minutes. Cool. Refrigerate until cold.
6. Cut in wedges. Garnish with fresh fruit, if desired.

8 Servings
*Note: If blender is used, place egg whites, sugar, lemon peel, lemon juice and vanilla in blender container before adding Neufchâtel and cottage cheeses. Blend until completely smooth, stopping blender and scraping as necessary.

To Microwave:

1. Spoon 2 to 3 tablespoons crumb mixture into 8 small custard cups. Press firmly against bottoms of cups. Pour about ⅓ cup filling into each cup.
2. Arrange cups in circle on large microwave-safe platter or directly on floor of microwave oven. Microwave at MEDIUM for 9 to 10 minutes, or until filling begins to set around edges, turning platter or rearranging cups after each 3 minutes.
3. Let stand on countertop or board 10 minutes. Refrigerate one hour or longer.

255 CALORIES / FAT 10 g (90 CAL or 35% of total calories) / SAT FAT 3 g (10% of total calories) / CARB 33 g / PROTEIN 10 g / CHOL 10 mg / SODIUM 380 mg

New Year's Eve

When my husband passed away in 1974, I received Dr. Height's gracious invitation to join her and a few special friends in her lovely New York apartment overlooking the East River for New Year's Eve dinner and conversation. I'll never forget the year my son, who was visiting from Los Angeles, joined us for one of these memorable get togethers. After a great traditional "meal for luck" which included baked ham, turkey, candied sweet potatoes, corn pudding, fresh string beans, greens, homemade rolls and a vegetable salad, we all gathered around Dr. Height to listen to her marvelous stories of Harlem in the 40's, her experiences as a social worker and teacher in India and as a delegate to the United Nations Decade for Women.
Among those sharing in this enlightening and lively conversation was an international travel writer, a retired professor who was just completing a novel about his experiences in India and Georgette, a fantastic gourmet cook. As we chatted, we raved over Dr. Height's famous sweet potato pie. I can still hear the laughter and joy of the

(continued)

PEAR UPSIDE-DOWN CAKE

2	tablespoons firmly packed brown sugar
2	tablespoons Butter Flavor Crisco, melted
2	medium pears, peeled, cored and sliced
3	eggs, separated
½	cup granulated sugar
1	cup all-purpose flour
1	teaspoon baking powder
1	teaspoon cinnamon
¼	teaspoon mace
⅛	teaspoon nutmeg
⅓	cup milk
1	teaspoon grated lemon peel
1	teaspoon vanilla

1. Heat oven to 350°. Brush 9-inch square pan lightly with Crisco Oil. Line with waxed paper.
2. Combine brown sugar and Butter Flavor Crisco. Spread in bottom of pan. Arrange pear slices in single layer over brown sugar mixture.
3. Beat egg yolks until thick and lemon colored. Add sugar gradually, beating well.
4. Combine flour, baking powder, cinnamon, mace and nutmeg. Add to egg mixture. Stir in milk, lemon peel and vanilla.
5. Beat egg whites until stiff peaks form. Fold into flour mixture. Spread over pear slices.
6. Bake at 350° for 30 minutes or until toothpick inserted in center comes our clean. Cool one minute. Invert cake onto plate.

One 9-Inch Square Cake (9 Servings)

180 CALORIES / FAT 5 g (44 CAL or 24% of total calories) / SAT FAT 1 g (7% of total calories) / CARB 31 g / PROTEIN 4 g / CHOL 70 mg / SODIUM 65 mg

HERMIT COOKIE BARS

Cookies

½ cup Crisco Oil
¾ cup firmly packed brown sugar
1 egg and 1 egg white
3 tablespoons skim milk
1½ cups all-purpose flour
¾ teaspoon cinnamon
½ teaspoon nutmeg
½ teaspoon baking soda
¼ teaspoon salt
¼ teaspoon ground cloves
1⅓ cups raisins
1 tablespoon chopped walnuts

Topping

2 tablespoons confectioners sugar

1. Heat oven to 350°. Oil 13 X 9 X 2-inch pan.
2. Combine Crisco Oil and brown sugar in large bowl. Beat at medium speed of electric mixer until well blended. Add egg. Beat well. Add egg white. Beat well. Mix in milk.
3. Combine flour, cinnamon, nutmeg, baking soda, salt and cloves. Add to creamed mixture slowly. Stir in raisins. Spread in pan. Sprinkle with nuts. Press lightly.
4. Bake at 350° for 22 to 25 minutes, or until wooden toothpick inserted in center comes out clean. Cool in pan. Cut into bars, about 2 X 1½ inches. Sift confectioners sugar over bars.

3 Dozen Bars

Drop Cookie Variation: Drop batter by level measuring tablespoonfuls 2 inches apart on oiled baking sheets. Bake at 350° for 8 or 9 minutes. Remove to cooling rack. Cool. Sift confectioners sugar over cookies.

85 CALORIES / FAT 3 g (31 CAL or 36% of total calories) / SAT FAT <1 g (<5% of total calories) / CARB 13 g / PROTEIN 1 g / CHOL 5 mg / SODIUM 35 mg

(continued)
guests and feel the warmth of that memorable occasion of wonderful food, good friends and stimulating conversation as we brought in the New Year.

Patricia P. Gibson (Mrs. D. Parke Gibson)

COCOA BROWNIE COOKIE BARS

Bars

4	egg whites
⅓	cup Crisco Oil
¼	cup nonfat vanilla yogurt
1	teaspoon vanilla
1⅓	cups granulated sugar
½	cup unsweetened cocoa powder
1¼	cups all-purpose flour
¼	teaspoon salt

Topping

1 tablespoon confectioners sugar

1. Heat oven to 350°. Oil bottom of 9-inch square pan.
2. For bars, place egg whites in large bowl. Beat with spoon until slightly frothy. Add Crisco Oil, yogurt and vanilla. Mix well. Add sugar and cocoa. Mix well. Add flour and salt. Mix until blended. Pour into pan.
3. Bake at 350° for 26 to 28 minutes. Avoid overbaking.
4. For topping, dust with confectioners sugar. Cut into 2¼ X 1½-inch bars.

2 Dozen Bars

105 CALORIES / FAT 3 g (31 CAL or 30% of total calories) / SAT FAT <1 g (<5% of total calories) / CARB 17 g / PROTEIN 1 g / CHOL 0 mg / SODIUM 35 mg

OATMEAL RAISIN COOKIES

⅔ cup Crisco Oil
1½ cups firmly packed light brown sugar
  2 eggs
  2 tablespoons skim milk
  2 teaspoons vanilla
1¾ cups all purpose flour
  ¾ teaspoon salt
  ½ teaspoon cinnamon
2¼ cups quick oats (not instant or old fashioned)
  ¼ cup dry oat bran high-fiber hot cereal
  1 cup raisins

1. Heat oven to 350°. Oil baking sheet lightly.
2. Combine Crisco Oil and brown sugar in large bowl.
    Stir until well blended. Add eggs, milk and vanilla. Stir
    until well blended.
3. Combine flour, salt, baking soda and cinnamon. Add
    to sugar mixture. Mix well. Stir in oats, oat bran cereal
    and raisins. Drop by slightly rounded measuring
    tablespoonfuls 2 inches apart onto baking sheet.
4. Bake at 350° for 9 to 10 minutes or until bottoms are
    lightly browned (tops will not brown). Cool on
    baking sheet 2 minutes before removing to cooling
    rack.

3½ Dozen Cookies

110 CALORIES / FAT 4 g (37 CAL or 34% of total calories) / SAT FAT <1 g (<5%
of total calories) / CARB 18 g / PROTEIN 2 g / CHOL 10 mg / SODIUM 55 mg

(continued)

was the true trait of black
Americans as other traits
have been developed by
other racial groups.

**Vincent Warren
Henderson
Washington, DC**

Coloring My Sensibilities

During the past decade, I have had at least fifty meals together with Dr. Height. A take-away meal at her desk, room service at a hotel suite, a catered lunch at a Black Family Reunion tent and a restaurant nearby to a meeting site are among the venues where these have taken place.

I cannot think of anyone in my life who has had greater influence in coloring my sensibilities. My collective experience of listening to Dr. Height and watching how she deals with situations has greatly impacted how I speak, how I act and how I view the world. Dr. Height truly usurped the pantheon of high school and college teachers who had inspired me and given me purpose. But during all our time together, I think the most important and meaningful moments have been when we have broken for a meal.

It is at that time when matters of business and urgency are shunted aside for a moment. It becomes more personal, up-close and revealing. Sometimes I have been moved to take out my notebook and write down a comment of Dr. Height's because it has been so classic and I knew (continued)

CHOCOLATE CHIP COOKIES

2   cups all-purpose flour
1   teaspoon baking soda
½   teaspoon salt
1   egg
3   tablespoons water
1   teaspoon vanilla
1   cup firmly packed light brown sugar
¼   cup Crisco Oil
½   cup semi-sweet chocolate chips

1. Heat oven to 375°. Grease baking sheets well.
2. Combine flour, soda and salt in small bowl.
3. Combine egg, water and vanilla in another small bowl.
4. Combine brown sugar and Crisco Oil in large bowl. Beat at low speed of electric mixer until blended. Add egg mixture. Beat until smooth. Add flour mixture in three parts at lowest speed. Scrape bowl well after each addition. Stir in chocolate chips.
5. Drop dough by rounded teaspoonfuls 2 inches apart onto baking sheet.
6. Bake at 375° for 7 or 8 minutes or until lightly browned. Cool on baking sheet one minute before removing to cooling rack.

3 Dozen Cookies

75 CALORIES / FAT 3 g (23 CAL or 31% of total calories) / SAT FAT 1 g (8% of total calories) / CARB 13 g / PROTEIN 1 g / CHOL 5 mg / SODIUM 55 mg

FORGOTTEN TEA CAKES

Dough

- ⅓ cup Butter Flavor Crisco
- ½ cup sugar
- 1 egg
- 1 teaspoon vanilla
- 2 cups all-purpose flour
- 2 teaspoons baking powder
- ¼ teaspoon baking soda
- ¼ teaspoon salt
- ¼ cup buttermilk

Topping

- 1 teaspoon sugar
- ¼ teaspoon nutmeg

1. Heat oven to 375°. Grease baking sheet with Butter Flavor Crisco.
2. For dough, combine Butter Flavor Crisco and sugar in large bowl. Beat at medium speed of electric mixer until blended. Beat in egg and vanilla.
3. Combine flour, baking powder, baking soda and salt. Add alternately with buttermilk to creamed mixture at low speed. Mix well after each addition.
4. Roll dough to ½-inch thickness on lightly floured surface. Cut with floured 2½-inch round cutter. Place on baking sheet.
5. For topping, combine sugar and nutmeg. Sprinkle over tops of tea cakes.
6. Bake at 375° for 7 to 9 minutes or until set. Remove to cooling rack. Serve warm or at room temperature.

16 Tea Cakes

115 CALORIES / FAT 4 g (38 CAL or 32% of total calories) / SAT FAT 1 g (8% of total calories) / CARB 18 g / PROTEIN 2 g / CHOL 15 mg / SODIUM 90 mg

HERITAGE RECIPE

(continued)

I would soon forget it. A good example: "Even the flea has a purpose — it keeps the dog moving." But even more importantly, mealtime unleashes Dorothy Height the storyteller: her childhood in Rankin, her social work in India and Harlem, her trips to England and Nazi Germany in the 1930's, her travels through segregated America, her work in forging the civil rights movement and so on. True to the test of the best storytellers, it is equally enjoyable to hear the same story for the first or tenth time. Above all, Dr. Height does not waste words. Every story she has ever told is for a purpose. There is a moral, a value, a quality that the listener takes away, one that is transmitted in the most subtle yet powerful way.

Joel Brokaw

BANANA OATMEAL COOKIES

"Reel Food"

I had seen Dorothy Height many times over the years contributing where outstanding leaders in every field gathered. This time she had entered my world in Memphis, Tennessee, when we held our luncheon at the Peabody "Ducks" Hotel announcing our first Black Family Reunion Celebration. Now Dr. Height probably enjoyed lunch, but she had much on her mind about fundraising and the importance of making the right remarks to energize the audience for all kinds of support. She persevered graciously through lunch, another meeting and reception, but about 6:30 p.m. she expressed her real sentiments about wanting "reel food." Dr. Height was ready for some serious seafood! We hauled her to Catfish Cabin where she nearly fainted at the proportions then proceeded to dig in. Once we knew of her love of catfish, we saved the deluxe meal until her return to the next Black Family Reunion Celebration and rewarded her with a trip to the Four Way Grill for catfish and cobbler, blackberry of course. Eating simple food in folksy places with a gourmet's appreciation

(continued)

1½ cups all-purpose flour
1   cup sugar
½   teaspoon baking soda
1   teaspoon salt
¼   teaspoon nutmeg
¾   teaspoon cinnamon
½   cup Butter Flavor Crisco
1   egg
1   tablespoon skim milk
1   cup mashed bananas
1¾   cups quick oats (not instant or old fashioned)
½   cup raisins
¼   cup chopped walnuts

1. Heat oven to 375°.
2. Combine flour, sugar, baking soda, salt, nutmeg and cinnamon in large bowl. Add Butter Flavor Crisco, egg, milk and bananas. Beat well.
3. Stir in oatmeal, raisins and nuts until thoroughly blended.
4. Drop by teaspoonfuls onto ungreased baking sheet.
5. Bake at 375° for 10 minutes or until lightly browned around edges. Cool 2 minutes before removing to cooling rack.

4½ Dozen Cookies

65 CALORIES / FAT 2 g (22 CAL or 34% of total calories) / SAT FAT 1 g (8% of total calories) / CARB 10 g / PROTEIN 1 g / CHOL <5 mg / SODIUM 50 mg

PEARL'S PECAN DROPS

1½ cups sugar
½ cup Butter Flavor Crisco
2 teaspoons vanilla
3 cups all-purpose flour
1 teaspoon baking soda
1 teaspoon cream of tartar
¾ cup low fat buttermilk
½ cup finely chopped pecans

1. Heat oven to 375°. Grease baking sheet with Butter Flavor Crisco.
2. Combine sugar, Butter Flavor Crisco and vanilla in large bowl. Beat at medium speed of electric mixer until blended and crumbly.
3. Combine flour, baking soda and cream of tartar. Add to creamed mixture alternately with buttermilk in three additions, mixing thoroughly after each addition, at low speed. Stir in nuts with spoon. Drop by teaspoonfuls onto baking sheet 2 inches apart.
4. Bake at 375° for 9 to 11 minutes or until lightly browned. Cool 2 minutes on baking sheet before removing to cooling rack.

5 Dozen

65 CALORIES / FAT 2 g (21 CAL or 33% of total calories) / SAT FAT <1 g (7% of total calories) / CARB 10 g / PROTEIN 1 g / CHOL 0 mg / SODIUM 20 mg

(continued)

speaks to Dr. Height's special gift of walking with kings and queens without losing the common touch.

Sonia Walker

GINGERBREAD APPLE BARS

1 cup applesauce	¼ cup Crisco Oil
½ cup raisins	1½ cups all-purpose flour
⅓ cup unsulfured light molasses	1½ teaspoons ginger
1 teaspoon baking soda	1 teaspoon cinnamon
2 eggs	¼ teaspoon cloves
¼ cup sugar	⅛ teaspoon salt

1. Heat oven to 350°. Oil 8-inch square pan lightly.
2. Place applesauce and raisins in small saucepan. Cook and stir on low heat until mixture comes to a boil. Remove from heat. Stir in molasses and baking soda. Cool slightly.
3. Combine eggs and sugar in large bowl. Beat in Crisco Oil gradually.
4. Combine flour, ginger, cinnamon, cloves and salt. Add to creamed mixture alternately with applesauce mixture, beginning and ending with flour. Spoon into pan.
5. Bake at 350° for 30 minutes or until toothpick inserted in center comes out clean. Cool in pan on cooling rack. Cut into bars. Serve warm or at room temperature.

12 Servings

170 CALORIES / FAT 6 g (51 CAL or 30% of total calories) / SAT FAT 1 g (<5% of total calories) / CARB 28 g / PROTEIN 3 g / CHOL 35 mg / SODIUM 105 mg

BLACK RASPBERRY PATCH BARS

1 cup firmly packed light brown sugar	½ teaspoon baking soda
½ cup Butter Flavor Crisco	1½ cups quick oats (not instant or old fashioned)
⅓ cup skim milk	1 jar (12 ounces) seedless black raspberry jam
1¾ cups all-purpose flour	
1 teaspoon salt	

1. Heat oven to 400°. Grease 13 X 9 X 2-inch pan with Butter Flavor Crisco.
2. Combine brown sugar, Butter Flavor Crisco, and milk in large bowl. Mix with spoon until well blended.
3. Mix in flour, salt and baking soda until well blended. Stir in oats.
4. Press half of mixture in bottom of pan. Spread with jam. Sprinkle with remaining oat mixture. Press lightly.
5. Bake at 400° for 25 minutes or until golden brown. Loosen from sides of pan while still warm. Cool before cutting into bars.

24 Servings

165 CALORIES / FAT 4 g (40 CAL or 24% of total calories) / SAT FAT 1 g (6% of total calories) / CARB 29 g / PROTEIN 2 g / CHOL 0 mg / SODIUM 105 mg

LUSCIOUS LEMON BARS

Crust
¼ cup Crisco Oil
¼ cup granulated sugar
¼ teaspoon salt (optional)

1 cup all-purpose flour
1½ teaspoons skim milk

Filling
1 egg
1 egg white
1 cup granulated sugar
2 teaspoons grated lemon peel

3 tablespoons fresh lemon juice
2 tablespoons all-purpose flour
½ teaspoon baking powder

Drizzle
¾ cup confectioners sugar
1 tablespoon skim milk

½ teaspoon vanilla
¼ teaspoon grated lemon peel

1. Heat oven to 350°.
2. For crust, combine Crisco Oil, granulated sugar and salt in large bowl. Beat at medium speed of electric mixer until well blended. Add flour and milk. Stir with spoon until crumbly and well mixed. Turn into pan. Press evenly against bottom.
3. Bake at 350° for 15 minutes.
4. For filling, combine egg, egg white, granulated sugar, lemon peel, lemon juice, flour and baking powder. Beat at high speed 3 minutes. Pour over hot, baked crust.
5. Bake at 350° for 25 minutes or until light golden brown. Loosen from edge while still warm. Cool.
6. For drizzle, combine confectioners sugar, milk, vanilla and lemon peel. Drizzle over top. Allow to stand before cutting into bars.

2 Dozen Bars

100 CALORIES / FAT 3 g (24 CAL or 24% of total calories) / SAT FAT <1 g (<5% of total calories) / CARB 18 g / PROTEIN 1 g / CHOL 10 mg / SODIUM 30 mg

FANCY WALNUT GLAZED BROWNIES

In Conclusion...

"Nobody Can Speak For Me Better Than I Can Speak For Myself"

Each person tells a story colored by his or her own experience. When the stories are quilted together by the thread of one person's remarkable life they form a quilt of unsurpassed beauty. But a quilt is more than just a colorful covering. It is a substantial item filled with cotton batting that gives it warmth... it is a work of art made with love that carries into the future. The stories that people tell about Dorothy Irene Height reflect her vision... a vision that today includes the dream of an African-American Women's Resource Center. "At 80, you look another way than you do at 18 and what you see is not the past, not what you should have done, but the future, what remains undone. From childhood, I have had a driving interest in being part of helping to shape things... reaching out.... Never in my lifetime did I not know what to do; basketball, glee club, Latin, oratorical club, studying, working wherever I was. I knew if I was in it, I had to be involved." The philosophy of always (continued)

Brownies

1	package (18.25 ounces) Duncan Hines Brownies Plus Walnuts Mix
1	egg
⅓	cup water
⅓	cup Crisco Oil

Glaze

4½	cups confectioners sugar
½	cup lowfat milk or water
24	walnut halves, for garnish

Chocolate Drizzle

| ⅓ | cup semi-sweet chocolate chips |
| 1 | tablespoon Crisco Shortening |

1. Heat oven to 350°. Place 24 two-inch foil muffin cup liners on baking sheet.
2. For brownies, combine brownie mix, egg, water and Crisco Oil in large bowl. Stir with spoon until well blended, about 50 strokes. Stir in contents of walnut packet from Mix. Fill each liner with 2 generous tablespoons batter.
3. Bake at 350° for 20 to 25 minutes or until set. Cool completely. Remove cupcake liners. Place cooling rack over waxed paper. Turn brownies upside down on rack.
4. For glaze, combine confectioners sugar and milk. Stir until smooth. Spoon glaze over first brownie to completely cover. Top immediately with walnut half. Repeat for remaining brownies. Allow glaze to set.
5. For chocolate drizzle, place chocolate chips and shortening in resealable sandwich bag. Seal. Microwave at MEDIUM power. Knead bag after one minute. Repeat until smooth (or melt by placing in bowl of hot water). Cut off pinpoint corner of bag. Drizzle chocolate over brownies.

2 Dozen Brownies

255 CALORIES / FAT 10 g (90 CAL or 35% of total calories) / SAT FAT 2 g (7% of total calories) / CARB 40 g / PROTEIN 2 g / CHOL 10 mg / SODIUM 105 mg

CHOCOLATE FILLED DREAM PUFFS

Cream Puffs
¾ cup water
3 tablespoons Crisco Oil
1 cup all-purpose flour
¼ teaspoon salt
3 eggs
1 egg white

Filling
1 package (4-serving size) chocolate flavor instant pudding and pie filling mix
2 cups skim milk

1. Heat oven to 400°. Line baking sheet with foil. Oil foil lightly.
2. For cream puffs, combine water and Crisco Oil in medium saucepan. Bring to a boil on high heat. Reduce heat to low. Stir in flour and salt. Cook and stir until mixture leaves sides of pan and forms ball. Remove from heat.
3. Stir in eggs, one at a time, beating well after each addition. Stir in egg white, beating until mixture is smooth and glossy. Drop batter into 8 mounds on baking sheet, spacing 3 inches apart.
4. Bake at 400° for 25 to 30 minutes or until puffed, golden and crisp. Remove to cooling rack. Cool completely.
5. For filling, combine pudding mix and skim milk in medium bowl. Prepare according to package directions. Let stand 5 minutes.
6. Slice off top of each puff. Remove any soft dough inside and discard. Fill each puff with ¼ cup pudding. Replace tops. Serve immediately.

8 Filled Puffs

204 CALORIES / FAT 7 g (66 CAL or 33% of total calories) / SAT FAT 1 g (5% of total calories) / CARB 28 g / PROTEIN 6 g / CHOL 80 mg / SODIUM 370 mg

(continued)

being involved was illuminated one night at a sidewalk restaurant when a young boy on a bike rode up and started to talk to Dr. Height. "Aren't you somebody famous?" he asked with all the charm an 11 year old boy can bring to bear. "Well that depends on who you think I am. Do you know my name?" Dr. Height responded with a patience rarely displayed by "famous" people. "I think you are somebody who... wait, I know who you are. I wrote a report about Black history last year," he bragged. "What kind of grade did you get?" Dr. Height's query caused the child some consternation. "Well... my teacher lost the report and so I didn't get a grade," he replied. "That's a shame," Dr. Height commiserated with the boy. "Tell me your teacher's name and where you go to school so I can talk to her about losing important reports. When you go back to school, you tell your teacher that you met me. I'll give you my card so she'll know that we really did talk." The boy told her his teacher's name and the name of his school. As he pocketed Dr. Height's business card, he was clearly delighted to have a trophy to display.

(continued on following page)

PINEAPPLE RICE PUDDING

(continued from previous page)

He shouted as he rode off on his bike, "Your name is Dr. Height ain't it?" As her dinner companions marvelled at the exchange, Dr. Height said, "That little boy is the reason we need to have a Women's Resource Center... our children... all of us need a place where the history and contributions of African-American women are on display, where there is research material, photographs, and documents. African-American women have contributed to every facet of life in this nation and they... we... deserve a permanent home that displays those contribu-tions. We must tell our own stories because we cannot depend on anyone else to tell them for us. Mrs. Bethune used to say, 'Nobody can speak for me better than I can speak for myself.' That is still true." "When I think of the African-American Women's Resource Center I hear the voices of women all over America... women speaking for them-selves... women who have something important to say. Those women need a place to be heard. I can just see the exhibits where school children like our young friend on the (continued)

1¼	cups water
½	cup uncooked long grain rice
1	teaspoon Crisco Oil
¼	teaspoon salt
1	can (8 ounces) juice packed crushed pineapple, drained, juice reserved
1½	cups skim milk
½	cup raisins
⅓	cup firmly packed light brown sugar
½	teaspoon cinnamon
3	tablespoons all-purpose flour
1	tablespoon lemon juice
1¼	teaspoons vanilla
¼	cup slivered almonds, toasted

1. Bring water to a boil in medium saucepan. Add rice, Crisco Oil and salt. Reduce heat to low. Cover. Simmer 20 minutes.
2. Stir drained pineapple and milk into rice. Mix well. Cover. Simmer 15 minutes. Stir in raisins, brown sugar and cinnamon.
3. Combine reserved pineapple juice and flour. Stir until blended. Add to rice mixture gradually. Cook and stir on medium heat until bubbly and thickened. Remove from heat. Stir in lemon juice and vanilla. Spoon into individual dessert dishes. Sprinkle each with 1½ teaspoons nuts. Serve at room temperature or chilled.

8 Servings

180 CALORIES / FAT 3 g (30 CAL or 16% of total calories) / SAT FAT <1 g (<5% of total calories) / CARB 36 g / PROTEIN 4 g / CHOL 0 mg / SODIUM 100 mg

BANANA PUDDING

⅔ cup sugar
⅓ cup cornstarch
3 cups skim milk
½ teaspoon salt
2 eggs
3 tablespoons Butter Flavor Crisco
2 tablespoons vanilla
2 cups vanilla wafers
2 cups sliced ripe bananas

1. Heat oven to 350°.
2. Combine sugar, cornstarch, milk and salt in a large saucepan. Cook and stir on medium heat until thickened.
3. Beat eggs lightly with wire whisk. Add a little hot mixture to eggs and blend well. Pour eggs into mixture in saucepan.
4. Cook and stir for a few minutes. Add Butter Flavor Crisco and vanilla. Blend mixture well. Cover surface of pudding with plastic wrap. Cool slightly.
5. Place layer of vanilla wafers on bottom of 2-quart casserole. Alternate with layers of banana slices and pudding, ending with pudding on top.
6. Bake at 350° for 10 minutes.

6 Servings

395 CALORIES / FAT 13 g (114 CAL or 29% of total calories) / SAT FAT 4 g (8% of total calories) / CARB 64 g / PROTEIN 8 g / CHOL 90 mg / SODIUM 360 mg

HERITAGE RECIPE

(continued)

bicycle will come to learn about the history of this country. Tours, poster contests, oratorical contests... ways to get our children to become aware of their own rich and vital history... We have so much to share with each other... so many women who have faced insurmountable obstacles but who have overcome them all... the African-American Women's Resource Center right here in the nation's capitol is the perfect place to demonstrate what an effective presence women have had and continue to have... we must have a place to reach out... to showcase the lives and times of women... to bring people together."

Brenda Rhodes Cooper

INDIVIDUAL STRAWBERRY SHORTCAKES

Strawberry Mixture

4   cups fresh strawberries, sliced   2   tablespoons granulated sugar

Shortcake Biscuits

1¾   cups all-purpose flour   ½   teaspoon salt (optional)
  2   tablespoons plus 2 teaspoons   ⅔   cup skim milk
      granulated sugar   ¼   cup Crisco Oil
  1   tablespoon baking powder

Topping*

1   cup plain nonfat yogurt   ½   teaspoon vanilla
3   tablespoons brown sugar

1. For strawberry mixture, combine berries and sugar in medium bowl. Cover. Refrigerate.
2. Heat oven to 425°.
3. For biscuits, combine flour, sugar, baking powder and salt in medium bowl.
4. Combine milk and Crisco Oil. Add to flour mixture. Stir with fork just until dough forms. Place on well floured surface. Pat into circle about one-half inch thick. Cut with floured 2½-inch round cutter. (Press dough scraps together to form some biscuits to make total of 8.) Place on ungreased baking sheet.
5. Bake at 425° for 10 to 12 minutes or until golden brown.
6. For topping, combine yogurt, brown sugar and vanilla. Stir gently until smooth.
7. To assemble, split warm or cooled biscuits in half crosswise. Spoon about ¼ cup fruit over bottoms of biscuits. Add tops. Spoon yogurt sauce over tops. Add another spoonful of fruit.

8 Servings

*Alternate topping: Use lowfat vanilla yogurt. Omit brown sugar and vanilla.
Note: To save part of dessert for later use, wrap and freeze biscuits. Cover and refrigerate berries and yogurt mixture in separate containers. Use within a few days. Thaw biscuits before serving. Reheat if desired.

280 CALORIES / FAT 8 g (72 CAL or 26% of total calories) / SAT FAT 1 g (<5% of total calories) / CARB 49 g / PROTEIN 5 g / CHOL 0 mg / SODIUM 270 mg

SAUCY VANILLA RUM BREAD PUDDING

Pudding

1	pound loaf French bread (day old)
4	cups milk
2	cups sugar

3	eggs, beaten
1¼	cups raisins
1	cup chopped pecans
2	tablespoons vanilla

Vanilla Rum Sauce

¼	cup sugar
1	tablespoon cornstarch
1	cup water
⅛	teaspoon salt

1	tablespoon rum
1	teaspoon margarine
1	teaspoon vanilla

1. For pudding, heat oven to 350°. Grease 3-quart casserole.
2. Tear bread into 1-inch pieces. Place in large bowl. Add milk. Soak 20 minutes.
3. Combine sugar, eggs, raisins, nuts and vanilla. Mix well. Pour into casserole.
4. Bake at 350° for 40 minutes. Serve with Vanilla Rum Sauce. Serve warm or at room temperature. Refrigerate leftover pudding.
5. For Vanilla Rum Sauce, combine sugar and cornstarch in small saucepan. Stir to blend. Stir in water. Cook and stir on low heat until mixture comes to a boil and thickens. Remove from heat. Stir in rum, margarine and vanilla.

12 Servings

430 CALORIES / FAT 12 g (112 CAL or 26% of total calories) / SAT FAT 3 g (6% of total calories) / CARB 73 g / PROTEIN 9 g / CHOL 65 mg / SODIUM 290 mg

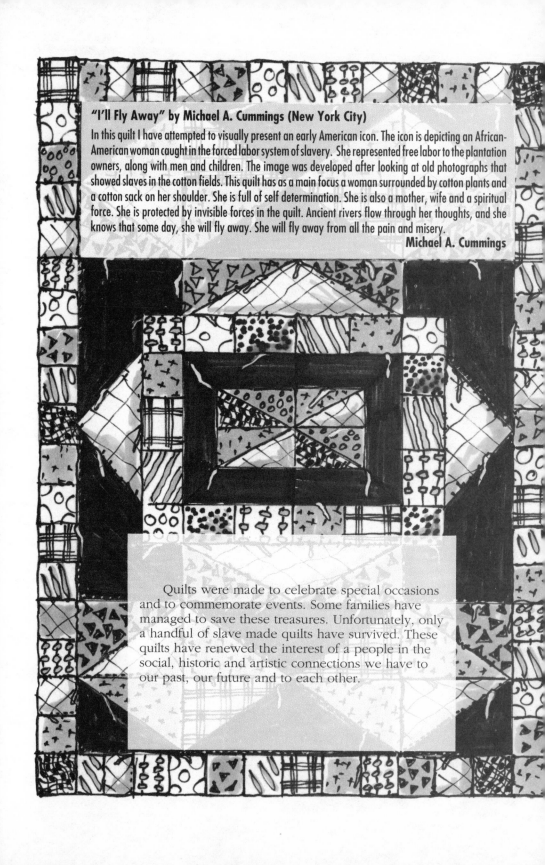

"I'll Fly Away" by Michael A. Cummings (New York City)

In this quilt I have attempted to visually present an early American icon. The icon is depicting an African-American woman caught in the forced labor system of slavery. She represented free labor to the plantation owners, along with men and children. The image was developed after looking at old photographs that showed slaves in the cotton fields. This quilt has as a main focus a woman surrounded by cotton plants and a cotton sack on her shoulder. She is full of self determination. She is also a mother, wife and a spiritual force. She is protected by invisible forces in the quilt. Ancient rivers flow through her thoughts, and she knows that some day, she will fly away. She will fly away from all the pain and misery.

Michael A. Cummings

Quilts were made to celebrate special occasions and to commemorate events. Some families have managed to save these treasures. Unfortunately, only a handful of slave made quilts have survived. These quilts have renewed the interest of a people in the social, historic and artistic connections we have to our past, our future and to each other.

HISTORY OF SOUL FOOD

by
Lauren Swann, M.S., R.D.

Introduction

The ***Black Family Dinner Quilt Cookbook*** is an important legacy of a very simple pleasure that cannot be underrated and is central to the fabric of African-American life. Good food shared among family and friends strengthens and nourishes. Food is often at the core of African-American family celebrations, festive holidays and commemorative gatherings.

This cookbook, with its health conscious recipes, will enable all people to recognize the role of nutrition in building strong families, drawing on the positive wealth of resources and diversity in African-American culture. Each meal is a time for physical and spiritual family nourishment.

The spirit which unifies all African-Americans in culture and heritage is part of soul food. 'Where family values are strong, the health of the community is likewise.' Just as mealtime strengthens the bond between family and friends, nutritious meals join the simple pleasure of food with the vitality of good health to strengthen our bodies and minds. During the past decades of public service leadership to improve the quality of African-American family life, medical evidence has revealed how healthful food practices can lower the risks of morbid diseases and strongly benefit a long enjoyable life.

In this cookbook, nutrient analysis is included. Recipes were selected to meet current Dietary Guidelines for Americans which include recommendations to avoid too much fat, saturated fat and cholesterol. The menu section emphasizes another dietary guideline: to eat a variety of foods. There are also tips for enjoying more indulgent favorites through balance and moderation of the total meal.

Nutritious healthful meals are at the roots of African-American cookery. This cuisine is proof that the taste appeal and satisfaction from traditional meals can be preserved while strengthening and nourishing our bodies. The scraps of food slaves survived on were heartily seasoned with good nutrition. These recipes are in the spirit of the same loving warmth that was lavished on shared meals for hundreds of years. They draw on the valuable resource of the healthful attributes of food preparation which have sustained African-Americans through life's challenges to this day.

HISTORICALLY HEALTHY

Soul food is fondly described as 'food made with feeling and care.' It evolved from the rich heritage of African customs, was shaped by Southern cookery practices, expanded by the similarly tribal habits of Native Americans, and regionally influenced by West Indian, Caribbean and French cooking.

As slaves, African-Americans were not permitted to learn how to read or write, so they cooked not from recipes but 'by knowing', giving strong credence to the essence of 'soul food'. Slaves had virtually no control or choice in life, so cooking became a way to express feeling, share love and nurture family and friends. Meals were a time for sharing common feelings of happiness and sorrow. Food was comfort while in bondage, and because they could control cooking, it was one of their few real pleasures, a way to feel free.

It is interesting that the roots of soul food, African diets, were very much in line with dietary recommendations today. Although they varied by continental region, the basic similarities included cereal from ground grains, rice, nuts, fish, wild fame, onions, yams, mangoes, melons, roots and leaves. Grains, rice, fruits, vegetables and plant parts are all major sources of complex carbohydrate which should make up most of the American diet. Additionally, wild game tends to be lower in fat than the domestic farm animals raised today for mass production.

Their involuntary journey away from the motherland removed Africans from their healthful roots. On ships enroute to America, slaves were fed a paste of boiled beans and lard, rice and yams. Peanuts were sometimes included but meat was rare. Nourishing meals to 'fatten slaves up' before sale were common. The survival of Africans on such a meager subsistence under severely stressful and abruptly different environmental conditions is evidence of a strong, hardy race of survivors.

With the slave trade came four major contributions to soul and southern cuisine. Sesame seeds, cowpeas or black-eyed peas, okra and watermelon seeds were originally brought to North America from Africa. The peanut, from which the term *goober* was derived from African pronunciation, originated in South America, but was introduced to North America by way of the slave trade. Except for watermelon, which was introduced from seeds, these new foods lasted during the slow ocean journey and adapted quickly to the Southern environment.

The birth of soul food began when the first African slaves arrived in the new land. Controlled by their owners, their diets were influenced by southern practices. It is ironic that pork is such a prominent part of soul food today, because most African tribal religious beliefs prohibited pork. Yet, it became the meat of choice in the South after the first settlers — who originally preferred mutton — discovered that pigs were easier to raise and quicker to fatten up.

Corn is another notable influence on soul food from the Americas. It was actually introduced to Africa from America. Because it could feed animals and slaves, and sow the land, corn was the plentiful grain of choice among Southerners.

It may also come as a surprise that pork and corn were actually the restricted foods in slave diets. Slaves were given a weekly ration of corn meal and meat scraps considered 'unfit' for the owners. They received as little as nine pints of corn and one pound of meat parts per person per week. Sometimes the basics were supplemented with rice, syrup and fruit.

So, the pigs feet, intestine or chitterlings, jowls and ribs; chicken feet, necks, backs, wings and organ meats; and cornmeal cereals and quick breads which created meals became known as soul food. The culinary skill which made such leftover odds and ends the nourishment for hard laborers is a unique distinction of soul food. Slaves cooked with their whole heart, doing their best with sparse ingredients. It was truly an expression of creativity with limited resources.

Slaves often grew vegetables near their quarters. During their rare free time, usually on Sundays, they could hunt and fish for wild game to supplement the limited meat in their diet. Since they prepared their own meals, the food and cooking methods they preferred were similar to native practices.

Sweet potatoes, for example, have always been popular among African-Americans. They originated in South America but to slaves who called them 'nyam' which means 'to eat', they appeared similar to African yams. Collard, mustard and turnip greens, cabbage and kale were like the leafy greens of their homeland. Grits, made from dried hulled corn kernels or hominy which originated from Native Americans, was similar to the cereal made from ground grain eaten in Africa. Beans, rice, squash and melons were also familiar foods.

With such a limited food supply, African-Americans found preparing food tastefully to be one of their rare creative outlets. The African tradition helped them to combine complementary ingredients. Small portions of meat were stretched to flavor vegetable dishes. Rice and corn were combined with beans and peas in dishes such as 'Hoppin' John'. Poke salad, a combination of greens

including dandelions and cresses was common. Stewing tenderized the meat while gravies from leftovers extended it.

The West Indian influence of full, rich tastes, hot spices and hearty seasoning such as garlic, peppers, bay leaves and hot pepper sauce resulted in regionally influenced meals. Soul food from the New Orleans region used Gulf shrimp in French-influenced Creole dishes like jambalya, and okra in dishes like gumbo. Red beans and rice were plentiful in Louisiana and cajun catfish popular along the Mississippi. Even the cooking utensils — cast iron skillets and large kettles over the fire — were a means of combining foods for hearty, satisfying one-pot meals.

African-Americans also shaped southern cuisine because slaves cooked for their owners. Deep fat frying, popular in the south, was a means of using high heat to cook meats quickly. The breaded coatings sealed in moisture during the process.

Barbecue, from a Spanish word meaning grate, originated from cooking over open fire or coals and was popular after big game catches. The young male slaves were responsible for roasting the meat or turning the whole carcass on a spit for their masters. Coating meats with sweetened sauce sealed in the juices, while the fats which dripped on the coals smoked a rich flavor back onto the meat.

The nutritional contributions of soul food are remarkable. Slaves had to be strong and hardy to survive on their meager diets under such physically demanding conditions. Once in America, male and female slaves labored all day, with a 30 minute break for breakfast in the morning and a two hour break at the hottest portion of the day when they often had to do lighter chores. They worked at least 12 hours in the fields, and five or six hours bringing in crops, carrying water from the well, caring for animals and cutting grass. At harvest time, some records show 18-hour workdays.

Back then, soul food was hearty nourishment that met intense labor needs. Corn, rice and beans met physical energy needs with carbohydrate and added fiber. The sparse but fatty meat scraps were sparing sources of protein and concentrated calories from fat, readily burned off with daily activity. Leafy green vegetables provided essential vitamins and minerals. Even the cooking water, which was full of nutrients and called 'pot likker', was drunk or used in soups and stews. Watermelon, which is more than 90% water, replenished fluid lost while toiling in the hot sun.

FREEDOM AND FOOD CHOICES

Since slave times, economic challenges have compounded somewhat elusive food choices. African-Americans were forced to make do economically in difficult times. So the foods known as soul foods continued after the Civil War. Resourcefulness and inventiveness became a distinctive culinary tradition as African-American women used their own style and flavor. Soul food continued as compassion food because the ability to cook and nourish children and friends has remained a real pleasure that bonds loved ones together.

NUTRITION IN TODAY'S TIMES

Soul food is as well known today as any other cuisine. Meal time is still time for family togetherness. A typical spread of deep fried chicken, collard greens with fatback, candied sweet potatoes, cornbread and fruit cobbler is a part of any family gathering just as grits and home fried potatoes are common for Sunday breakfast, black-eyed peas and ham hocks are a New Year's holiday tradition and barbecued spareribs and watermelon are a part of summer picnics.

All these foods are a powerhouse of nutrients. Greens and sweet potatoes are excellent sources of vitamin A and beta carotene which some health experts believe may protect against certain types of cancer. Beans, rice and corn, all good sources of fiber, provide complex carbohydrates, which the U.S. Dept. of Health and Human Services Dietary Guidelines recommend make up most of your diet. When combined these grains can also provide good sources of protein.

Along with freedom, however, energy needs have changed. Today's sedentary jobs require fewer calories. Yet, many African-Americans are choosing to indulge in overabundant portions of excessively fatty cuts of pork and beef, deep fried poultry and fish, heavily salted dishes and sugary desserts. A greater reliance on prepared snacks and fast foods is compromising the important balance of fruits and vegetables in the diet.

African-American men are more likely than Caucasian men to be hypertensive — a condition linked to excessive sodium and inadequate potassium that can lead to stroke. Obesity, which is directly related to a high calorie and high fat intake and can trigger diabetes, is more prevalent among African-American

women than white women. Heart and blood vessel diseases, linked to animal fats and colon-rectal cancer associated with high-fat, low-fiber diets, have all taken a serious toll on the quality of African-American health.

Besides overabundance, many African-American children and child-bearing females have low levels of iron which can cause anemia. Because diet can influence the prevention, treatment and control of all these health conditions, wise food selection is especially important today.

African-Americans need only to draw on the foods, habits and practices which sustained the race over the years to improve eating habits. Current guidelines recommend that whole grains, vegetables and fruits make up most of the diet. Corn, rice, dried beans and leafy greens are ethnically familiar food which meet these needs.

Although slaves were once forced to use meat sparingly, this very cooking technique is a valuable way to cut back on fat and cholesterol. The recom- mended three ounce serving of cooked meat may appear lacking. But, mixed with vegetables or rice, the portion is stretched, giving a flavorful meaty mouthful with every bite while remaining within healthful limits. Seasoning foods with garlic, onion, red and black pepper, hot sauce, bay leaf, lemon and vinegar bypasses salt with a Creole and Cajun flair. Even the old time cooking methods of cast iron skillets increase the content of iron in foods.

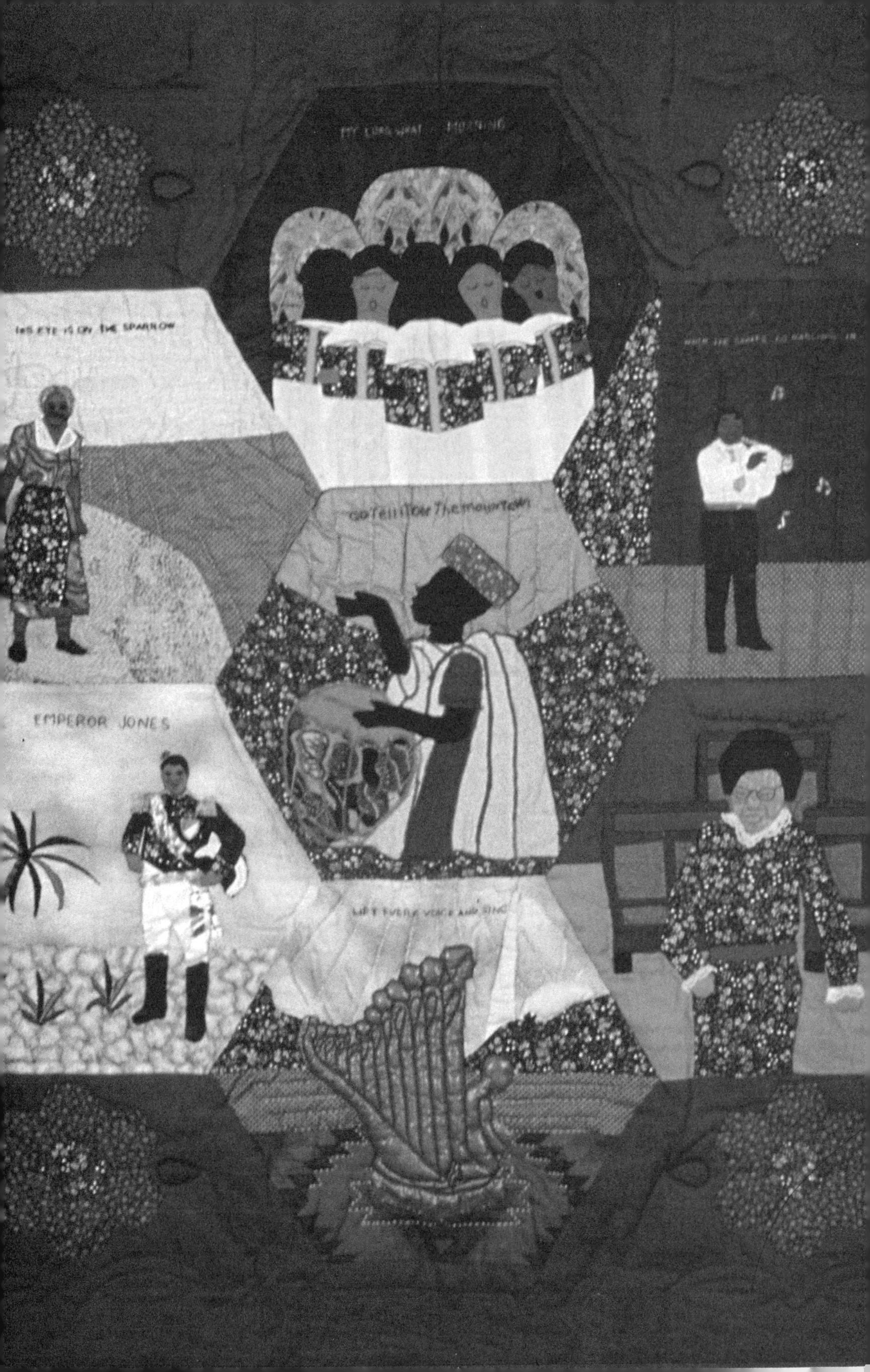

HIS EYE IS ON THE SPARROW
EMPEROR JONES

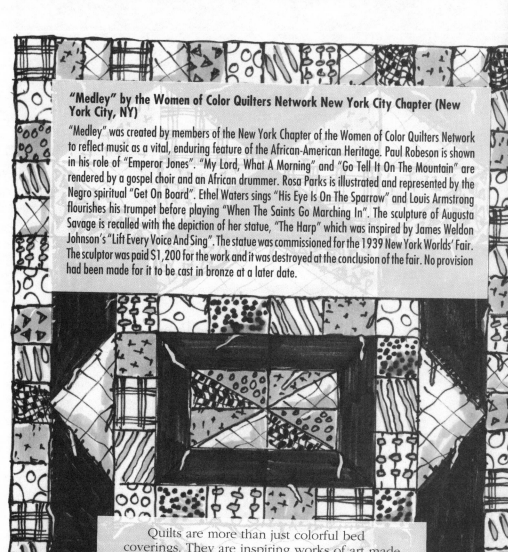

"Medley" by the Women of Color Quilters Network New York City Chapter (New York City, NY)

"Medley" was created by members of the New York Chapter of the Women of Color Quilters Network to reflect music as a vital, enduring feature of the African-American Heritage. Paul Robeson is shown in his role of "Emperor Jones". "My Lord, What A Morning" and "Go Tell It On The Mountain" are rendered by a gospel choir and an African drummer. Rosa Parks is illustrated and represented by the Negro spiritual "Get On Board". Ethel Waters sings "His Eye Is On The Sparrow" and Louis Armstrong flourishes his trumpet before playing "When The Saints Go Marching In". The sculpture of Augusta Savage is recalled with the depiction of her statue, "The Harp" which was inspired by James Weldon Johnson's "Lift Every Voice And Sing". The statue was commissioned for the 1939 New York Worlds' Fair. The sculptor was paid $1,200 for the work and it was destroyed at the conclusion of the fair. No provision had been made for it to be cast in bronze at a later date.

Quilts are more than just colorful bed coverings. They are inspiring works of art made with love that carries into the future, and they stand as a testament to creativity. They serve to inspire a resurgent interest in the social, historic, and artistic connection of a people to their past, future, and to each other. What started out as something to keep you warm has evolved into a legitimate and much appreciated art form as validated by the high demand for African-American quilts. These quilts provide a sense of permanence and will leave people in the future a diary of African-American life.

Carolyn Mazloomi

HOLIDAY MENUS

At holidays during slave times, food from the big house was more plentiful.

NEW YEAR'S EVE

Hoppin' John
Doc's Barbecue Pork Chops
Hot & Spicy Cabbage Medley
Country Baking Powder Biscuits
Pearl's Pecan Drops

EASTER

Molded Orange Pineapple Salad
Today's Poke Salad
Orange-Glazed Fresh Ham
Tropical Yam Bake
Classic Muffins
Light Lemon Meringue Pie

THANKSGIVING

Frozen Fruit Salad
Lemony Mushroom Turkey Breasts
Old Style Scalloped Potatoes
Better Tastin' Green Beans
Buttermilk Cornsticks
Arkansas Best Pumpkin Pie

KWANZAA

Mustard Greens & Potato Soup
Herbed Chicken & Rice
Confetti Scalloped Corn
Seasonal Fruit Cobbler

VALENTINE'S DAY

Turkey Vegetable Soup
West Indian Pork
Tangy Turnips 'n Taters
Squash with Apples
Alva's Cherry Cream Pie

MEMORIAL DAY

Chilled Shrimp Pasta Salad
Texas Barbecue Style Pork Chops
Three Bean Salad
Blackberry Ice Cream Pie

CELEBRATION MENUS

BIRTHDAY

Savory Fall Vegetable Soup

Celebration Chicken Buns

Grand's Collard Greens & Okra

Carrot Raisin Cake with Cream
Cheese Glaze

MARTIN LUTHER KING DAY

Mama's Catfish Chowder

Sunday Dinner Pot Roast

Mustard Greens with Peanut Sauce

Potatoes, Potatoes

Chocolate Filled Dream Puffs

GRADUATION

Jamaican Jerked Chicken

Okra & Corn Pilaf

Joe Weaver's Seasoned Greens

Individual Strawberry Shortcakes

JUNETEENTH DAY

Catfish with Vegetables

Creamy Macaroni & Cheese

Baked Stuffed Tomatoes

Black Raspberry Patch Bars

SUMMER PICNIC

Bethune Fruit Salad

Alabama Barbecued Fish

Harvest Vegetable Medley

Classic Potato Salad

Oatmeal Raisin Cookies

FAMILY REUNION

Crunchy Cabbage Apple Slaw

Lite 'N Lean Oven Fried
Chicken Breast

Creamed Green Beans & Potatoes

Fancy Walnut Glazed Brownies

Pineapple Rice Pudding

ABOUT THE NUTRITIONAL ANALYSIS

Nutritional values were obtained from a computer software program. For those ingredients not available in the program, values were provided from product labels, manufacturers or trade organizations.

The nutrient figures and calculations given for each recipe are based on the following:

1. Calories from fat, % calories from fat, and % calories from saturated fat are rounded off to nearest whole number. The other figures are rounded off either to the nearest gram (total fat, saturated fat, carbohydrate, protein) or nearest "5" (cholesterol, total calories, sodium).

2. In those recipes which call for either Crisco Shortening or Crisco Oil, the nutritional values are shown for Crisco Oil. Crisco Shortening values generally decrease total fat calories (<1-3%) because Crisco is less dense than Crisco Oil, and increase saturated fat values (1-3%) because Crisco has a slightly higher saturated fat level than Crisco Oil. In all cases, saturated fat levels for Crisco Shortening recipes is 10% of calories or less.

3. If a recipe calls for a marinade, only the amount absorbed and/or used in making a sauce is included in the nutritional values.

4. Fat, carbohydrate and protein figures are expressed in grams (g). There are 28 grams in one ounce. A teaspoon generally weighs about 4-5 grams, but depends on the material being measured and the size of "teaspoon". Cholesterol and sodium are expressed in milligrams or one-thousandth of a gram.

CHOOSING THE FOODS YOU EAT

The Balancing Act...Menu Planning

The best diets are nutritious, tasteful and satisfying. They include contrasting food groups, colors, textures, shapes and flavors. Herein lies the key to successful menu planning: Balance, Variety and Moderation.

Balance the basic food groups, **Vary** the foods and **Moderate** fat, calories, sugar and sodium. The easiest way to plan a nutritionally balanced meal is to include only one serving from the meat, poultry and fish group, two or more fruits or vegetables and two starchy foods which include potatoes, pasta, corn and breads.

Menu planning can give you a chance to enjoy more indulgent favorites. Plans for a big celebration dinner means having only a light breakfast and lunch time snack so that you can enjoy the meal and stay within daily recommended guidelines.

What's Up With Fat?

Just as soul food became a strengthening bond for African-Americans, the connection about food and health has strengthened over the years. Of all the messages about diet and disease, eating less fat is undoubtedly the most frequently heard. Numerous government agencies relate excess fat to major health problems including obesity, heart disease and cancer. Americans consume more fat than people living in many other countries.

Discounting The Myths

These days, most of us know we should cut down on the amount of fat we eat. but the question is: How does "knowing" translate into "doing"? There's no doubt about. A lot of people are very confused.

The Goods On Fat

Fat is actually a nutrient which has very important roles in food and diet. Your body needs some fat to stay healthy. The right amount of fat is necessary for good health. Fat is also essential for proper child development.

There are some vital aspects of fat. The vitamins A, D, E, and K rely on fat to take effect. Fat cushions internal organs from shock or injury and helps you to stay warm. There is a part of fat which is essential to life that your body cannot make. A concentrated source of energy, fat supplies twice as many calories compared to carbohydrates or proteins.

Highly preferred because it makes food taste good, fats give a feeling of satisfaction and fullness because they stay with you longer after you eat. You are less likely to get hungry again quickly. Rich, smooth, creamy sensations in food are due to fat. Flavors are carried and blended together by fat in foods. Tender flaky pie crusts, light fluffy frostings and moist chewy cookies owe their succulent baking qualities to fat. Fat also conducts high heat for frying.

The Low Down on Fat

There is a lot of evidence that most Americans eat too much fat. Unfortunately, the qualities of fat are easily compromised by health risks from excessive amounts. Too much fat, which has 9 calories per gram compared to 4 per gram for protein or carbohydrate — combined with eating too much and too little

exercise can result in obesity which increases the risk for heart disease and diabetes.

Unused fat is stored as fat, and as the body's second choice for fuel, fat from food becomes body fat when it is not used as energy. Weight control is more successful when fat is limited regardless of total calories. Controlling dietary fat is therefore more important than limiting total calories, although we should watch how much we eat.

A poor balance of fats can also raise cholesterol, a fat like substance that is found only in animal foods. Cholesterol can block blood vessels leading to heart attack and stroke. There are two kinds of cholesterol: dietary cholesterol — which we acquire "ready made" from foods we eat, like animal and dairy products; and serum cholesterol — the cholesterol in our blood that comes from both dietary cholesterol and the cholesterol our body produces itself.

Most fat in American diets comes from just three groups of foods — meat, dairy, and oils. They appear in your diet in two ways: "visible fats" are spreads, salad and cooking oils; and "invisible fats" are a natural part of such foods as dairy and meat products.

Fat can be either mainly *saturated* or *unsaturated*. If unsaturated, fat can be either primarily *polyunsaturated* or *monounsaturated*. It's easier to just remember that fats which are highly saturated are generally solid at room temperature. Fats of animal origin, like meat, bacon, poultry drippings or lard and dairy foods like cream and butter, are also highly saturated. There are also a few liquid oils like coconut oil, cocoa butter, palm oil and palm kernel oil which are also highly saturated and solid at room temperature. Saturated fats are believed to raise serum cholesterol in the body.

Generally fats which are high in unsaturated fats, such as vegetable oils, margarine, or vegetable shortening, are liquid or very soft at room temperature, and are linked to lowering body cholesterol.

It is a national goal for all Americans to reduce their total dietary fat from 37% to 30% of total calories. To achieve this, polyunsaturated, monounsaturated and saturated fats should be balanced with the greatest restriction on saturated fats, which should be 10% or less of calories. Some health groups believe cholesterol should be limited to less than 300 mg. daily, but by lowering total fat and saturated fat consumption in particular, cholesterol will generally decrease also.

All these long chemical sounding names boil down to a few basic reminders: control the amount of all added fat and limit meat and dairy foods to no more than two servings per day. To calculate your total daily fat consumption target, simply divide your optimum weight in half. That number is the most fat, in grams, that you need in a day. To make it easy, think of one ounce of fat

equalling 28 grams. Saturated fat should be no more than 10% of your total fat intake.

It is challenging to build a diet based on the dietary guidelines. The key is to balance and recognize that some foods will be higher in fat content, others will be lower. This allows you to enjoy a variety of foods. On any particular day, if you happen to exceed your target for fat consumption, simply cut down a bit on fat the next day. The more varied your diet, the better.

Fat Choices For Slim Living

There are numerous choices for selecting foods lower in fat which can be tastefully enjoyed in healthful recipes and meals. The marketplace is making great strides in providing consumers with the lower-fat products they want. Food manufacturers have produced thousands of new reduced-fat and low-fat products.

Public organizations and private industry are working harder to make the food supply healthier, provide better nutrition information on products and provide more choices. Many of the recipes in this book call for some of the reduced and nonfat products now available. In addition, when cooking or baking fat or oil is suggested, they are recommended because they are low in saturated fats yet provide great tasting foods.

Nonfat and reduced fat foods fall into two categories; traditional foods which have had the fat removed such as nonfat yogurt, milk and cottage cheese; and fat replacers, ingredients that are similar to fat with much fewer or no calories or cholesterol. Fat replacers are currently used in foods like nonfat frozen desserts.

The meat industry also responded to concerns over dietary fat by reducing the fat content of beef and pork, resulting in much leaner products. The pork industry responded by breeding leaner animals. There is also better fat trimming of retail cuts in the markets.

The Challenge of Choices

Although many more meals are eaten away from the home today, Americans are still spending more than half of their food dollar in the grocery story. Home cooked meals preserve the loving family togetherness African-Americans have always cherished. A kitchen warmed with the appetizing aroma of a tempting meal can put love and feeling back into a hurried lifestyle — one often filled with the fast pace of livelihood, obligations and duties shuffling simple pleasures and precious moments aside.

The value of home cooked meals includes the healthful nourishment of loved ones. Just as favorite recipes are handed down to the next generation, nutritious meals should be passed on to children. This is yet another way to influence the continued improvement of the quality of life for African-Americans.

Homecooked meals begin with food selection, and African-Americans have come a long way from having no choice but to accept pig parts and corn meal. With choice comes responsibility, yet food shopping can be a challenging and confusing experience when combining health, taste, price, convenience and wholesomeness.

Organization is the key to a well spent grocery store trip. Plan weekly menus to determine what's needed, check which foods are on hand, then prepare a list. Look for savings and specials in weekly grocery story circulars and manufacturer's coupons. Shop after a meal. An empty stomach is easily tempted.

Living By Labeling

When selecting foods, read product labels as a tool for building a healthful diet. Although labeling, particularly for claims, can be complex, the government is moving toward new rules so you can keep better track of the various nutrients you get from all the foods you eat.

While shopping, it's best to select perishable and frozen items last for food safety. Shelf stable items should be first, then fresh and refrigerated foods with the frozen food aisle the last before checkout. Always check package freshness dates.

Finally, fresh produce is an extremely important part of healthful diets, but it's value is only as good as the quality. Although fresh tastes better, canned and frozen are just as good when fresh is unavailable or in limited supply. Spring and summer are good times to take advantage of nature's bounty and the wide variety of produce available.

Tips for Health Conscious Cooking & Eating

These are the basic fundamentals for healthful eating:

• Cook and bake with liquid vegetable oil or margarine instead of lard.

• Avoid deep-fat frying, cooking vegetables with animal fat, baking with lard or butter and seasoning with salt or prepared seasonings containing salt or sodium.

• Cook and bake with liquid vegetable oil, vegetable shortening or margarine

instead of lard, butter or other animal fat.

- Avoid deep-fat frying. Instead roast, bake, broil, grill, or stir fry.

- Avoid heavy seasoning with salt or prepared seasonings containing salt.

- Cook and season green vegetables with smoked turkey, turkey bacon, or lean ham hocks instead of fatback or bacon.

- Season food with black and red pepper, garlic and onion powder and lemon and vinegar instead of salt.

- Select lean cuts of pork and beef and bake, broil, roast or grill meat, poultry and fish. Cut off excess visible fat.

- Remove the skin, which is mostly fat, from chicken and turkey before cooking or eating.

- Switch to low fat dairy products such as skim or two percent milk, low fat yogurt, low fat cottage cheese, low fat or no-fat sour cream, low fat or no-fat cheese or evaporated skimmed milk.

- Include more fiber rich foods such as beans, whole grain products, fruits and vegetables. Eat more pasta, rice and potatoes.

- Use lean ground beef or ground turkey in place of hamburger.

- Limit high fat, heritage dishes such as chittlings, organ meats, or fried foods to special occasions.

- Snack on fresh fruits, vegetables, plain popcorn, and pretzels instead of potato chips, ice cream and cookies.

- Avoid foods high in cholesterol or saturated fats such as eggs, ice cream, shellfish, shrimp or lobster, organ meats, or heavy fatted red meat.

- Limit fat in your diet so the total is no more than thirty percent per day. Also make sure your saturated fat level is no more than ten percent.

- Use low cholesterol or no-fat mayonnaise in salad dressings.

- Skim fat off meat juice before making gravy.

NUTRITION GLOSSARY

Calories: A measure of body energy or heat obtained from fat, carbohydrate and protein.

Fats: A concentrated source of energy, one of the three main classes of nutrients found in food and essential to the body. Fat has more than twice the energy of protein and carbohydrate per unit of weight. Total fat is the sum of three different kinds of fats: Saturated, polyunsaturated, and monounsaturated fats.

Cholesterol: A fat-like substance present in the body and found in foods of animal origin. There are two kinds… dietary, which we acquire from ready made foods we eat and serum… the cholesterol in our blood that comes from both dietary cholesterol and the cholesterol our body produces itself.

Saturated Fat: Fat which tends to be solid at room temperature. Contained primarily in animal foods like meat and dairy products, it is linked to elevated levels of cholesterol in the blood.

Polyunsaturated Fat: Fat which tends to be liquid at room temperature. This category includes most vegetable oils and is linked to decreased levels of blood cholesterol.

Monounsaturated Fats: This type of fat is found in canola, olive, and certain nut oils like peanut and is linked to a decrease of blood cholesterol.

Carbohydrate: One of the three main classes of nutrients found in foods and essential to the body for calories; primarily from plant sources. Carbohydrate can be *simple*, like table sugar or *complex*, like flour, pasta, beans, or vegetables.

Protein: One of the three main classes of nutrients found in foods. Essential to the body to build living cells. Meats, poultry, egg whites, fish, dairy products, grains and beans are food sources of protein.

Vitamins: Organic material required in small amounts that allows the body to use energy and carry out other vital processes. Vitamins are present in natural food stuffs (as vitamin C) or made by the body from "provitamins in food (as vitamin D).

Minerals: Required nutrients in small amounts which cannot be made by the body and which regulate body processes.

Fiber: The part of plant foods which cannot be completely digested and which aids in cleansing the body.

Sodium: A mineral which helps maintain the proper bodily fluid balance. The primary source is table salt and added salt in prepared foods.

Dietary Guidelines: The Federal Government's principal statement on nutritional advice.

NATIONAL COUNCIL OF NEGRO WOMEN, INC.

In 1935, Mary McLeod Bethune, the legendary educator and humanitarian, founded the National Council of Negro Women (NCNW) a national organization of national organizations centered around the concerns of African-American women. Mrs. Bethune said that from her vantage point as Special Advisor to President Franklin Delano Roosevelt, she had come to know the value of collective power.

Today, NCNW is comprised of 33 affiliated constituency based national organizations and 250 chartered community based NCNW Sections, with a combined outreach to 4,000,000 women. The NCNW operates in 42 states with vital programs addressing women's special concerns including: education and career advancement, leadership training, family life, economic opportunity, motor vehicle occupant protection, preventive and service programs in teenage pregnancy, drug abuse, juvenile delinquency, health protection, hunger and malnutrition, child care, and on-the-job training.

The NCNW carried a major role in the Civil Rights Movement. It was the initiator of Turnkey III, a home ownership program for low-income families. It conducted a campaign against hunger and malnutrition. To enhance opportunities for women to find employment, it founded the Women's Center for Education and Development in New York, the Raspberry Child Development Center in Okolone, Mississippi, the Fannie Lou Hamer Child Care Center in Rulesville, Mississippi. In 1974, in cooperation with the National Park Service, NCNW placed in Lincoln Park the first memorial to an African-American woman or to a woman of any race to be erected in a public park in the nation's capital—the Bethune Memorial.

In 1986, in response to the negative projection of the Black family, NCNW launched the Black Family Reunion Celebrations as positive educational and cultural experience lifting up the values, traditions and historic strengths of the African-American family.

NCNW's International Division conducts development activities throughout Africa in an effort to improve the economic status of women through agriculture and food production, community development and income-generating projects.

The Bethune Museum and Archives on Black women's history located in the Bethune Council House in Washington, DC was established to document and preserve the organizational history.

The National Council of Negro Women is a member agency of the National Council of Women of the United States, International Council of Women/ National Assembly for Social Policy & Development and the N/USA combined Federal Campaign. NCNW maintains non-governmental organizational status with the United Nations.

Index